THE POPE'S LAST CRUSADE

THE POPE'S
LAST CRUSADE

How an American Jesuit Helped
Pope Pius XI's Campaign to Stop Hitler

PETER EISNER

wm

WILLIAM MORROW
An Imprint of HarperCollins*Publishers*

THE POPE'S LAST CRUSADE. Copyright © 2013 by Peter Eisner. All rights reserved. Printed in the United States of America. No part of this book may be used or reproduced in any manner whatsoever without written permission except in the case of brief quotations embodied in critical articles and reviews. For information address HarperCollins Publishers, 10 East 53rd Street, New York, NY 10022.

HarperCollins books may be purchased for educational, business, or sales promotional use. For information please e-mail the Special Markets Department at SPsales@harpercollins.com.

A hardcover edition of this book was published in 2013 by William Morrow, an imprint of HarperCollins Publishers.

FIRST WILLIAM MORROW PAPERBACK EDITION PUBLISHED 2014.

Library of Congress Cataloging-in-Publication Data has been applied for.

ISBN 978-0-06-204915-5

14 15 16 17 18 OV/RRD 10 9 8 7 6 5 4 3 2 1

To my parents

It is on the whole more convenient to keep history and theology apart.

H. G. *Wells*, A Short History of the World

CONTENTS

THE POPE'S LAST CRUSADE

PROLOGUE

A Settling of Accounts

New York City, May 20, 1963

THE REVEREND JOHN LaFarge was fully aware of his place and moment in life. He had dedicated himself to kindness and goodness, to peace and principles. Now in his final years, at age eighty-three, he recognized that his life was coming full circle.

"If by chance death comes suddenly and unannounced—and who can be sure that it won't," he had said, "it will come as a friend. Our own terminal Amen will ring true as the response to the Creator's primal Amen which sent us into this world."

He had accomplished a great deal, though there was still a lot left to do. High among the priorities these days was his support for Martin Luther King's upcoming march on Washington. LaFarge had spoken out strongly and frequently about civil rights as fundamental to the promise of America. He was frequently in touch with King and others planning the march, especially his longtime friend, Roy Wilkins, the executive director of the NAACP. For half a century, LaFarge had been one of the Catholic Church's clearest voices calling for racial justice.

LaFarge had been a young Jesuit priest working, praying, and living with poor blacks in rural Maryland and defended their chance to obtain equal education and equal rights. He marveled at their resilience; they were downtrodden yet they still possessed "that great flame of faith . . . for three centuries had glorified the lives of Maryland's black folk."

He knew, however, that "without adequate schools, the Faith would perish, and the folk themselves would be defrauded of their legitimate development." LaFarge had long wanted the Catholic Church to be a leader in fighting discrimination. Before World War II, LaFarge was a lonely voice among white clergy when he called for an immediate end to racism. In 1936, he had written an influential book, *Interracial Justice*, which called on churches to lead the fight against racism. "Once the light of science is turned upon the theory of 'race,'" he wrote, "it falls to pieces and is seen to be nothing but a myth." The obliteration of racial injustice and intolerance would continue to be his life's work.

He still felt the fire of justice and saw reasons for optimism. Dr. King had been leading a protest movement in Birmingham, Alabama, where eleven hundred African American students had been arrested for civil disobedience against segregation—bravely seeking the simple right to sit at a luncheon counter, to drink from a water fountain, or to read a book in a library. The civil rights movement was maturing. Great leaders had emerged; white men and black men walked together, demanding justice. The end of legalized racism was in sight.

The younger Jesuits around LaFarge adored him and noticed with dismay that Uncle John was ailing, haggard at times and hiding his discomfort as he ambled about the Jesuit community residence at *America* magazine on West 108th Street. Sometimes he appeared to be in so much pain that he could hardly take a step at all.

Not that LaFarge had pulled back on his schedule. He never complained about physical ailments and always maintained his good humor. He had lived and worked with his Jesuit brethren at the *America* magazine headquarters since 1926, rising from associate to the editor of the magazine, and now writing a frequent column. Even today, he came and went, prayed, shared meals, and discussed current events with the others around him.

And yet Uncle John was a distant, mysterious figure. He seemed to carry secrets with him. Perhaps, in these final days, LaFarge's determined silence was wavering, and he was ready to unburden himself. Every evening after supper, the Jesuits gathered in the downstairs recreation room, where they chatted and sipped after-dinner drinks. One night, LaFarge began talking about something he had never mentioned. He began by asking if he had ever told them the story of his trip to Europe, the summer before World War II. He knew he hadn't and all other conversation stopped.

Exactly twenty-five years earlier, in May 1938, LaFarge had been sent to Europe on a reporting assignment; his goal was to study the church's welfare under siege, while at the same time taking the pulse of the continent. LaFarge described his trip, in part, as a fact-finding mission. He had heard very clearly what was being said about Europe and Hitler and the threat of war, but he wanted evidence, wanted to understand and to describe life under Hitler and the prospects of war. It was his first trip to Europe in decades and his first as a foreign correspondent. There was an aspect of nostalgia to the trip—recalling the time as a young man when he had set out on his first life adventure at the turn of the century, steeped in old-world literature, devoted to his faith.

But everything was different in Europe—and he wasn't sure what he would find. He did not trust the reports in the New York newspapers and the dispatches from news agencies. Was Europe on the brink of an inferno? Would a new world war engulf Europe?

Or was it all an exaggeration? He wanted to listen, to ask questions of people he could trust, of common folk, and of politicians. Being a correspondent had given him a privileged status to meet with opinion makers, other journalists, key politicians, and friends in the clergy. LaFarge was able to observe the final throes of freedom.

By the spring of 1938, Hitler's Greater Germany extended into Austria; the priest had expected to be followed, monitored, and spied upon.

Then came the part of the story never told. Midjourney the nature of LaFarge's mission changed. After two months traveling across Europe, he arrived in Rome, where he had expected to stay for a two-week pilgrimage before returning home. For reasons not clear, Pope Pius XI found out the American priest was in the city and summoned him to a private meeting. He told LaFarge that *Interracial Justice* was a groundbreaking book, and he agreed with LaFarge that Nazi Germany was employing the same racist ideology as a means of conquest, violence, and murder. The pope had become the world's leading voice in opposition to Nazism and Fascism and laws threatening the lives of European Jews. Adolf Hitler saw the pope—a man whose army was nothing more than the scriptures—as a threat to his drive toward world domination. Closer to the Vatican, Benito Mussolini shared Hitler's hatred of this troublesome eighty-year-old pope. Mussolini saw Pius XI as a rival for the affections of the Italian people.

The pope had drawn LaFarge into his effort to awaken world leaders to the imminent menace that Hitler was marching to world war. Pius XI had few allies at the Vatican. Most of the cardinals and bishops around the pope preferred the status quo. Many were appeasers and anti-Semites and some even secretly sided with Hitler and Mussolini. For that reason, the pope had reached beyond the Vatican, had identified and singled out a progressive American priest. LaFarge had intended to return to New York in July, but he changed his plans and remained in Europe for the summer of 1938. Now, in 1963, he was a bit older than the old pope had been that summer. He was going to tell the story of what he had done and what had happened during five fateful months on a continent and in a world collapsing into war. The other Jesuits' faces were reflected in Uncle John's spectacles as he gazed off, focused on a distant time, far away.

CHAPTER ONE

Nostalgia Confronts Reality

SS Volendam, *North Atlantic, May 1938*

THE NORTH ATLANTIC was pleasant in the spring of 1938 with weather good enough at midday to face the chilly wind at the rail and look for signs of life—seabirds, an occasional whale—or the trace of another vessel on the horizon. In the evenings, John LaFarge could gaze up to an eternity of stars against the blackness. He occasionally saw meteorites streaking downward, celestial light, and the waning moon could be seen weakly over the twin smokestacks above the SS *Volendam*'s decks as it cut through the sea.

The isolation he felt gazing upward matched the emptiness on board. There were so few other passengers, it was almost as if LaFarge was traveling alone on the ten-day trip to Plymouth, then onward to Rotterdam. Not many private citizens had the means or interest in going to Europe. The *New York Times* acknowledged how uncommon international travel was with a regular feature tracking the incoming and outgoing ships in New York harbor and the names of prominent travelers. On April 23, 1938, it reported "The Rev. John LaFarge" as one of the passengers leaving that day on the *Volendam*, from the Fifth Street Pier, Hoboken, New Jersey, 11:00 A.M.

Ships left New York comparatively empty and returned fully booked with passengers who managed to find passage to New York or any other destination away from Europe. LaFarge, however, was not a tourist; he was a journalist. His editor at the Jesuit magazine, *America*, had sent him to report on the Thirty-Fourth International Eucharistic Congress in Budapest, a sexennial meeting that would draw Catholic clergy and laypeople from thirty-seven countries. At the same time, the trip would also give LaFarge the chance to visit London, Paris, Rome, and other capitals to examine church-state issues and report on the prospects for war.

LAFARGE CELEBRATED Mass each day of the crossing for a congregation that included nine nuns and anyone else of faith. The rest of the time, he read or took notes for a possible second edition of *Interracial Justice*, which would update issues concerning repression and discrimination against blacks in America. More and more, newspapers were reporting the rise of anti-Semitism in Germany and Hitler's persecution of Jews and increasingly of Catholics. LaFarge saw clear parallels between racial discrimination in the United States and what was happening in Europe. He had been working closely with the National Conference of Jews and Christians and just before leaving New York, he had signed onto a joint document that focused on Hitler's recent occupation of Austria, which had been accompanied by new attacks on religious figures and especially on Jews.

The document said: "Although there are differences between Catholics, Protestants and Jews . . . they stand together on common ground in defending human rights and liberties. We therefore join in expressing our profound abhorrence of the course of oppression and incitation, the denial of the rights of minorities, the restriction on freedom of conscience and the arbitrary suppression of political and civic equality already instituted in Germany and now extended into Austria."

THE TRANSATLANTIC shipping lines transmitted daily news summaries by wireless and posted the information on the ships' bulletin boards. News agencies reported that the Gestapo had begun expelling Jews and seizing their property in Austria. And frantic Jews lined up for visas at U.S., British, and Australian consulates, among others, where they were not always welcome.

LaFarge took these days at sea as a respite and a time to read, gather notes, write, sleep, and eat. In his letters home to his family, he described the trip as uneventful. His few companions saw him as a serious, introspective, sardonic, middle-aged, bespectacled priest with twinkling brown eyes and a cowlick dangling over his forehead. He was a fifty-eight-year-old Jesuit and had been a priest since his ordination at age twenty-five.

LaFarge, the only member of his patrician family to join the priesthood, was proud to wear the collar. As a Jesuit and a priest, he had taken a vow of poverty. St. Ignatius of Loyola, the founder of the Jesuits, described the Jesuit ideal as striving to be "an ordinary person." LaFarge interpreted this as a directive to strip himself of pride and ostentation and to live a simple, humble life. Yet he was many other things and often fretted about being prejudged as being a closed-minded cleric. He was a student of history and a lover of art and music, and he played the piano quite well. He was passionately interested in the politics of the day and was committed to education and social development.

LaFarge was born in 1880 and was named after his father, whose father was a Frenchman from Brittany named Jean Frédéric de LaFarge. He had fled captivity after serving under Napoleon. The senior John LaFarge was a prominent artist and stained-glass designer. The story was told that Frédéric-Auguste Bartholdi worked out his design for the Statue of Liberty while visiting the elder LaFarge's art studio in Newport, Rhode Island. Mrs. LaFarge, Margaret Mason Perry, was a descendant of Thomas Pence, an early settler at Plymouth, Massachusetts; she was also the granddaughter of Commodore Oliver Hazard Perry, and most notably, a great-great-granddaughter of Benjamin Franklin.

When young John LaFarge was seventeen years old in 1897, he took the advice of a family friend, Theodore Roosevelt, to study the classics at Harvard College. At the time, Roosevelt was the police commissioner of New York City, but he had big plans for himself and enjoyed promoting the plans of others. LaFarge breezed through Harvard, and then finally told his father he wanted to join the priesthood. His parents, despite their own varied connections with the church—his mother was far more devout and practicing than his father—were disappointed by this news. LaFarge said he had dreamed of being a priest since he was twelve years old.

He turned once more to Roosevelt, who by then was the vice president of the United States. "The boy has a vocation," Roosevelt argued with LaFarge's father. "God has sent him certain lights and certain graces and it would be folly not to let him follow them."

LaFarge entered seminary in Innsbruck, Austria, in the summer of 1901 and was ordained a priest on July 26, 1905. He worked at various temporary assignments and continued studying languages, which he had started while at Harvard. He learned French and German and practiced Italian and the Danish and Slavic languages enough to gain some fluency.

His first full-time assignment as a young priest came in 1911 when he was sent to St. Mary's County, Maryland, one of the poorest precincts of the nation. He worked there for fifteen years, attempting to provide vocation and other education for blacks. LaFarge also worked on the creation of regional Catholic interracial councils that were precursors to the National Catholic Conference on International Justice, which has been cited as a moral force behind the landmark *Brown versus Board of Education* desegregation case.

In 1926, LaFarge was assigned to work in New York City as a staff member of the influential Jesuit weekly, *America*, which the Jesuits founded in 1909. It was the only national Catholic weekly magazine in the United States. In 1937, his book *Interracial Justice* was published. Based on his experience working with blacks in Maryland, this audacious, groundbreaking book was primarily a call for Catholics to promote equality in their teachings. But he was also speaking out in support of civil rights. Interracial justice, he wrote, supposes the same rights to life, liberty, and the pursuit of happiness for all, including African Americans.

In 1938, when LaFarge left on this, his first foreign assignment, he had already spent twelve years as an associate editor at the magazine.

THE *VOLENDAM* dropped anchor at Plymouth Harbor on the afternoon of May 2, 1938, and LaFarge and nineteen other passengers transferred to a launch that took them the short distance to the port near the mouth of the rivers Plym and Tamar. It was about 5:30 P.M. when he gathered his bags and portable typewriter and stood before a smiling customs official.

To his horror, LaFarge could not make out a word the Englishman was saying, due to the man's clipped accent. This was not LaFarge's first trip to England, but he had never before had this problem. His only recourse was to provide answers to what he thought were the plausible questions for the circumstance. His destination that evening, he said, was Bristol where cousins awaited him; he had less than forty-five minutes to make the train. The merry old official said something else and again LaFarge was stumped. But according to LaFarge, "the customs officer merely waved a card at my nose, bade me welcome to old England and pushed me into a thoroughly British taxi with a sullen, bearded driver and right-hand drive."

A quick cab ride took him to the train for Bristol with time to spare. To prepare for the two-and-a-half-hour journey, he reached from the train window down to the platform where a vendor obliged him with a newspaper and a cup of English tea.

As the train pulled away from the Plymouth station, LaFarge opened his newspaper and read a front-page report on preparations for Hitler's visit to Rome for talks with Mussolini. About the same time LaFarge reached Europe, Hitler had boarded a custom railroad car at Berlin's Anhalter station southbound for Rome. Tens of thousands lined the train route to the German border, down through Nazi-occupied Austria and into Italy. Each time the train slowed, Hitler greeted the masses with an open palm salute and toothless smile.

The Nazi propaganda machine was touting the trip as an extension of the German Reich's first great victory six weeks earlier in Austria. The Wehrmacht had plowed south across the Austrian border on March 12, and within hours, Austria belonged to Hitler. Britain was rearming and hoping for peace and did nothing; nor did France, which was more concerned about the German-contested Alsace and the rest of its 290-mile border with the Reich.

When Hitler triumphantly followed his troops into Austria in an open armored car, he had declared that Germany's victory was the first step toward the thousand-year Reich. And when he reached

Vienna, church bells rang, and the Catholic Church heralded his arrival. The archbishop of Vienna, Cardinal Theodor Innitzer, immediately signaled his support for the führer. "Catholics in the Vienna diocese are asked on Sunday to offer thanks to the Lord God for the bloodless course of the great political change," he declared. "Heil Hitler."

Hitler was pleased at the unexpected endorsement from the Catholic Church, but at the Vatican, Pope Pius XI was appalled. The pope thought Innitzer was a weak man and a coward. After Innitzer's declaration, members of the Austrian Catholic Church who disagreed with the cardinal and opposed the Nazis were arrested and beaten.

The pope angrily summoned Innitzer to Rome and berated him for two hours during a private meeting. The Vatican secretary of state, Cardinal Eugenio Pacelli, who always argued for moderation, had counseled Pius not to demand Innitzer's resignation. The pope relented, but was adamant on making a public display. He forced Innitzer to publish a retraction of his praise for Hitler.

None of this mattered to Hitler, though he did note that Pope Pius XI was still the troublesome enemy that he and the Catholic Church had always been. Hitler's minions clamped down on Austrian freedoms and sent tens of thousands of opponents, Jews and Catholics, democrats and Communists to concentration camps. With freedom of the press one of the first casualties, Innitzer's retraction was never published or broadcast in Germany or Austria.

Hitler's trip on May 2 was his first venture beyond Germany and Austria and was meant to cement the Axis alliance. The *Times* of London reported that "Herr Hitler's visit . . . seems destined to become legendary, for the preparations which have been made for it are stupendous. The cost is estimated at between three million and four million pounds [$200 to $300 million in 2012 U.S. dollars]. A new railway station and a new road [the *Viale* Adolf Hitler] have been built for the Führer's arrival in Rome. . . . Grandiose effects of decoration and illumination have been devised, not only in Rome but in Florence and Naples as well."

World attention focused on Hitler's journey to Rome, especially in the United States, where officials monitored the cultish reception. A few hours before Hitler's arrival, Ambassador William Phillips, accompanied by his wife, Caroline Drayton Phillips, had traveled on a regularly scheduled passenger train on the main line from northern Italy down to Rome after a weekend stay in the north. "Every station up till half an hour of Rome was bedecked with German and Italian flags and for long distances every house, villa and hut close to the railway were [*sic*] displaying the two flags," Phillips remembered. The ambassador noted that the flags and the decorations served to cover over the poverty and slums of the countryside. "I only hope the poor wretches who live in these hovels will be allowed to keep these flags which have been furnished them. They could be turned into much needed clothing," he also wrote.

The newspaper LaFarge read on the train to Bristol carried detailed coverage of Hitler's tour. Mussolini had converted Rome into a glowing extravaganza, determined to outdo the grand reception he had received from Hitler the previous year. The führer was greeted by a city radiant with torches and monuments bathed in light. The *Times* of London described the event as "one of the most elaborate and magnificent receptions of which there is record even in the annals of the Eternal City."

There were two news items of special note concerning Hitler's trip to Rome. First, thousands of police would guard Hitler and Mussolini, and ominously, newspapers reported, German Jews in Rome, Naples, and Florence were being detained throughout Hitler's eight-day visit.

LaFarge's newspaper also reported that Pope Pius XI had decided to leave Rome three days before Hitler's arrival. The *Times* of London linked the pope's departure to Hitler's arrival and reported, "the tendency has been shown in some quarters to attribute a political significance to the Pope's decision."

AS LAFARGE GLANCED up from the newspaper, he could see little of the English countryside because it was already shrouded in early-evening darkness. From the train, he could not see even the contours of the villages along the way. This was not unusual, because these areas of England rarely had any kind of lighting at night, but as he thought back years later, the scene mixed in memory with the blackouts that would occur across Britain and all Europe when the Germans began their bombing campaigns. As the train moved toward its destination, LaFarge increasingly sensed that he was experiencing an England that was calm but waiting for terror to strike.

LaFarge put aside the newspaper and prepared to visit with his cousins in Bath. He alighted at the Bristol Temple Meads Station, the oldest major train station in the world. For a hundred years, the Temple Meads cathedral-like central clock tower dominated the center of the city with its Tudor spires, spectacular stained glass, and detailed stone and woodwork. He switched quickly to the local train to Bath, where his cousin, Hope Warren and her husband, Robert Wilberforce, received him. "What a curious sensation," LaFarge recalled, "riding near midnight in that autorail in a totally unknown country, only a few hours off the steamer."

LaFarge awoke refreshed on the morning of May 3. Quickly reaccommodating to land, he went with his cousins on a tour of the countryside he had known as a young man. He made a point of revisiting the timeless magnificence of England: a visit to the eighth-century Saxon Church at Bradford on Avon and to the Glastonbury Tor, the hill occupied by settlers since the Neolithic period. There he said a prayer to Joseph of Arimathea, who appears in legends about the Holy Grail. All in the rain, no surprise for England.

He then visited the Bath Abbey, first founded in the eighth century and rebuilt in the 1500s. He walked on the slab that entombed Lieutenant General Henry Shrapnel, who gave his name to exploding cannon shells. Contrary to LaFarge's assumption—"I suppose he exploded!"—Shrapnel died of natural causes in 1842 at the age of eighty, supported all the while by a comfortable government stipend for his invention.

LaFarge's first impressions produced the desired result, a marked contrast with America's preoccupation about politics and war. "Just as I had anticipated," he wrote to his sister Margaret a day after arrival, "people over here seem much less excited over the political situation than at home. I am more and more impressed by the complete isolation, outside of a few superficial contacts, that exists between here and there. It is a different world."

After a few more days in Europe, however, LaFarge found it impossible to sustain this notion any longer. One could not ignore the sense of impending war. He was haunted by memories of the Europe of his youth in 1905 that represented a lost world "quite as if I had never before set foot beyond the ocean . . . as if one had visited Paris or London or Rome in a previous existence."

ON MAY 4, after two days with his relatives, LaFarge traveled to London to conduct meetings and interviews. He would be visiting Czechoslovakia during the trip so he scheduled a luncheon conversation with Jan Masaryk, the Czech ambassador to Britain, a man consumed by and despairing over his country's future.

Masaryk was the son of Czechoslovakia's founding father, Tomáš Garrigue Masaryk. The younger Masaryk was U.S. educated, and his mother was American.

Masaryk had just returned from 10 Downing Street, where he met with British prime minister Neville Chamberlain and the foreign secretary, Lord Halifax. They had discussed the ongoing negotiations with Britain over Hitler's charge that the Czechs were oppressing Germans living in Sudetenland, a scythe-shaped strip of territory wrapped around Czechoslovakia on its German border. Most of the country's three million ethnic Germans lived in Sudetenland, which had been ceded to the newly formed Czechoslovakian state in 1918 through the Treaty of Versailles at the end of the Great War. Hitler warned that while Germany was a peaceful nation, it would fight to redress the indignities it had suffered ever since the end of the war.

Chamberlain wanted Czechoslovakia to appease Hitler and give in to his demands. The *New York Times* declared: "Britain has written off Czechoslovakia as an independent state."

Masaryk told LaFarge that Chamberlain and his foreign secretary would not give him a clear answer on whether there was room for further negotiations: "If Great Britain is not going to support us," he told LaFarge, "then I shall simply pack my valise, take a trip to Berlin and lay all the cards on the table before Hitler. The game will be up, and I shall simply accept what Hitler chooses to leave us." But the scraps would be nothing. Secretly, Hitler already had drawn up his plan for the conquest of Czechoslovakia.

Masaryk also predicted that Hitler and Stalin would eventually join forces. As bad as Hitler and Nazism might be, Communism was seen as considerably worse by LaFarge, his fellow churchmen, and the Vatican. This was at the heart of the Catholic Church's slow, cautious response to the dangers of Hitler and Mussolini.

Roman Catholics had reasons for thinking that Communism

was the great enemy of Christianity. In the aftermath of the Russian Revolution, Catholics were attacked and churches had been shuttered; in Spain, priests and nuns had been massacred. If Nazism and Communism joined forces, many Catholics reasoned, the threat to Catholicism and to the world was multiplied.

LaFarge did not forget Masaryk's despondency, his anger at the British, or his predictions. The meeting with the Czech ambassador brought LaFarge his first experience close to the center of politics and intrigue. He sensed spying eyes all around and worried that Nazi agents might be intercepting his communications. Before he left America, he had devised a rudimentary code system of prayerful phrases just in case security concerns arose. He told his editor, Francis X. Talbot: "If I send a card from Germany or Austria, following will be meaning of greetings at end:

> *"**Oremus pro invicem** [Let us pray for one another]—things are very bad, worse than you imagine.*
> *"**Pray for me**—About as we heard in the U.S.*
> *"**Say a prayer for me on my travels**—Not so bad, fair show of resistance, etc.*
> *"**Greetings and prayers**—Situation complex and difficult to analyze."*

LaFarge expected to be followed, spied upon, spat upon, even shunned by those "anti-religionists" and Communists, but he still needed to see the impact of Hitler and the Nazis for himself. Events and his travels were about to take him much closer to the heart of the story than he imagined, where a Jesuit might indeed have some impact.

CHAPTER TWO

A "Crooked Cross"

Castel Gandolfo, May 4, 1938

POPE PIUS XI had retreated a week earlier than expected to his summer palace at Castel Gandolfo, about twenty miles southeast of the Vatican. He knew his move would be taken for what it was—a pointed snub. The pope wanted no part of the triumphal celebration in Rome of the growing friendship between Germany and Mussolini's Fascist state.

On May 4, he commented on the presence of the Nazis in Rome for the first time in public. "Sad things appear, very sad things, both from far and near," he told a general audience. "And among the sad things is this: that it is not found to be out of place or untimely to fly an insignia of another cross that is not the Cross of Christ."

His words echoed throughout Rome, Italy, and the world. But this wasn't the first time the pope issued condemnations of Nazism and Hitler. The pope had a considerable arsenal of rhetorical weapons to use against Hitler and Mussolini. Even from

Castel Gandolfo, he could reach beyond the Vatican as few others might, by radio and the international press. Impulsive by nature, the pope could not be contained.

He convened a meeting of church leaders a few hours before leaving the Vatican. The Great War, as World War I was known, "was to be the last war," he said in that April 30 meeting. "Men said it was to be the beginning of a reign of peace. Instead of which, behold, it has been the herald and forerunner of an inferno of confusion and contradiction." If the Vatican language was not direct, the message was clear; Nazi policies were leading to a new world war.

Just after 5 P.M. on April 30, servants had shuttered the windows of the papal residence at the Vatican and the pope took the elevator to the ground floor. He was dressed in the simple black vestments of a priest so he wouldn't attract attention. The piazza was relatively empty, but a few people gathered and cheered when they saw him emerge at one end of St. Peter's Square. Among his entourage were his private secretary, Monsignor Carlo Confalonieri, several members of the Swiss Guard, and one of his official physicians. He left behind orders that the Vatican museums were to remain closed to visitors from May 3 to May 10, the duration of Hitler's tour of Italy. The Vatican explained publicly that the facilities needed to be "reorganized." He had also sent a letter to churchmen that reiterated his rejection of Hitler and Mussolini, referring to their totalitarian goals as anathema to religion and declaring that they promoted racism through fake science. He warned members of the curia to avoid all official functions, dinners, or celebrations or receptions honoring Hitler. In addition, the official newspaper, *Osservatore Romano*, the only publication left in Italy that was free of Fascist censorship, was not to report Hitler's visit.

The newspaper reported facetiously that "the Holy Father was not going to Castel Gandolfo 'for petty diplomatic reasons, but simply because the air at Castel Gandolfo made him feel good, while this air made him ill.' "

Word spread quickly that the pope was on his way to Castel Gandolfo. People began to line the Appian Way as soon as the pope's four-car motorcade left the outskirts of Rome. By the time the procession reached the village of Albano, hundreds had gathered in the main piazza, waving and cheering as the pope rode past. Thousands had gathered in the central piazza of Castel Gandolfo, where an orchestra serenaded him as the motorcade arrived at the front gates of the palace.

The wooden doors opened and Pius XI was shepherded into the inner courtyard. He rode the small elevator to his rooms on the third floor and soon stepped onto the balcony of the palace and gave his blessing. The small crowd cheered and waved flags: the Italian *tri-colore*, green, white, and red, intermingled with the yellow-and-white banner of the Vatican fluttering in the wind. The band played the Italian royal march, the papal hymn, and then, much less pleasing to the pontiff's ears, the Fascist marching song. Such were the times.

The pope waved once more, then turned and retired to his private chapel and quarters on the opposite side of the building from the piazza. From here, the pope could look out toward the Mediterranean in the distance or turn outside to the balcony adjacent to the Vatican Observatory. He also had a commanding view of Lake Albano, a perfectly serene perch from which to contemplate the world beyond. Castel Gandolfo was always a relief from the closed quarters of St. Peter's. From this cloistered place, he could strategize and regroup.

The pope had a remarkable ability to gather the world's attention. He was the leader of about 350 million Catholics, about 16 percent of the world population, and no other religious or moral figure was comparable. His words were translated into dozens of languages, read and displayed on the front pages of newspapers everywhere. He had issued thirty-two encyclicals in his sixteen years on the throne of St. Peter, and each of them carried weight beyond the Catholic faithful. With the dawn of the telegraph and the radio, he had a worldwide audience for his pronouncements on morality and the human condition. This was his weapon against tyranny.

He spoke daily through *Osservatore Romano* and Vatican Radio, both of which issued regular political commentaries about European affairs. He would need to make use of this power judiciously in the coming months. The world was facing the abyss, drawn there by Adolf Hitler. The pope was not alone in thinking that the German führer was insane.

THE WEEKS PRIOR to the pope's retreat to Castel Gandolfo had been intense. Two weeks earlier, on April 17, Easter Sunday, the pope had delivered his annual *Urbi et Orbi* benediction "to the City of Rome and to the World" before an overflow crowd of one hundred thousand people in St. Peter's Square.

Since Pius was recovering from a variety of illnesses, including angina and perhaps a heart attack, he was confined to waving and issuing his blessing to the crowd from a chair. He also used a wooden contraption that supported him from the back when he felt too weak to stand, similar to Franklin Roosevelt being propped up and made to seem as if he was standing. Those looking up to the pope, the setting framed by Bernini's seventeenth-century sculptures of the Apostles, saw him appearing cheerful and surprisingly well. A *New York Times* reporter said the pope "was rather pale and he had lost considerable weight, but his eyes sparkled behind the thick lenses of his spectacles with the old vivacity, and his gestures as he raised his right hand in blessing had regained their energy."

That was the image the pope sought and maintained. Pius XI indeed had regained considerable strength since a heart attack late in 1936. Many around him had thought he might not live through that Christmas. But the holiday came and the illness receded. Inevitably, the press speculated about his health and physical appearance. News agencies maintained a constant pope watch, vying to be the first to report the news of his death. It was a macabre business.

A second Christmas had come, and he was still well enough. "Despite his eighty years and his recent grave illness," the *New York Times* had reported, "the Pope stood the strain of the five-hour ceremony in his heavy pontifical robes very well although at the end he was visibly tired and he went to bed immediately afterward for a long rest."

Pius XI ruled the Holy See with an imperial style and a withering gaze. He had also been obstinate in resisting the best arguments of those around him. They regularly bothered him with comments about his health. He was irritated and snapped at them when they mentioned his infirmities.

Cardinal Carlo Salotti told him one day, "You have been an example for all men to follow. No man works harder than Your Holiness for God and His Church. But hard labor has need to rest in its time. . . . Why not take a long rest?"

The pope had no time for this. He was annoyed with Salotti for even raising the issue. "The Lord has endowed you with many good qualities, Salotti. But he denied you a clinical eye," Pius XI said.

Finally, the cardinals convinced the pope to see someone who did have a clinical eye, the chief of the Vatican health service, Doctor Aminta Milani. The pope confessed to Milani that he had been feeling ill. His legs were painful, he had trouble breathing at times, and sleep was difficult. After an examination, Milani said the pope was suffering from circulatory problems and dangerously high blood pressure. Doctors at the time could generally identify cardiac disease and recognized that heart failure was a major cause of death among people over fifty years old. They could also measure high blood pressure and understood the consequences, but they had few remedies. Milani, a respected physician trained in medical pathology at the Royal University of Rome at the turn of the century, prescribed bed rest, occasional injections of stimulants, and bloodletting.

The pope said, however, he had no intention of going to bed and with good reason rejected bloodletting, a process that had progressed little since the Middle Ages. Bloodletting had been questioned in the last hundred years and had been determined as useless by doctors in the United States and much of Europe.

The cardinals warned the pope, however, to follow Milani's treatment or face grave consequences. Pius relented, but he said he would submit to the treatment only under certain conditions. The procedure would be done while he worked in the papal offices, not in bed, and he would not take time from his schedule.

The pope's American personal biographer, Thomas B. Morgan of the United Press, described the operation. On the appointed day, the doctor came to the pope's office and made a small "puncture behind the ear." It "was performed in his library chair and he withstood it with the fortitude of a martyr," Morgan wrote later. "When it was over and a pad of gauze placed upon the wound, the Holy Father told the physician that that was enough." The blood draining basin was removed and the pope ordered the physician to withdraw as well. He then followed through with his schedule of meetings and audiences for the rest of the day. All those who approached the pontiff noticed that he was holding his handkerchief to his ear in obvious discomfort. "He asked no sympathy," Morgan said, and "resented it when given." The pope survived the treatment.

A "CROOKED CROSS" 25

Sometime later, the pope asked Milani and the other doctors attending him to tell him plainly and accurately how much longer he would live. They told him that he would survive, but no one could say for how long.

Pope Pius XI realized he had a serious heart ailment that might lead to his death, but he wanted to survive, and as he said, "we cannot look upon youth without a very sincere love, without a certain envy." He seized whatever time he had to launch the most important campaign of his papacy.

While his criticism of Hitler was long standing, Pius stepped up his opposition because he recognized the dangers of Nazism and the crazed violence that threatened not only Jews, but all humanity. He distanced himself from others at the Vatican who remained more alarmed by the Bolshevist Revolution in Russia and Karl Marx's famous banner: religion is the opiate of the people. This Vatican faction agreed with Hitler's pledge to obliterate Communism and believed on those grounds he could not be all bad.

The pope had clashed with the führer even before Hitler had maneuvered himself to the chancellorship of Germany in 1933. Hitler had sent his deputy Hermann Göring to Rome in 1931, two years earlier, but the pope refused to meet with him. The Vatican had signed a diplomatic accord known as a "concordat" with Germany soon after Hitler took office in 1933. But the pope began challenging Nazi violence immediately. Vatican commentaries, including a report that said that National Socialism might be better named "national terrorism," censured Nazi regulations and methods.

In the spring of 1937, the pope began a new series of attacks. Less than four months after having been given the Last Rites of the church and having been considered near death, he issued a startling encyclical that amounted to an indictment of Hitler and the Nazis. The encyclical, *Mit Brennender Sorge (With Deep Anxiety)*, had been written in secret. The pope ordered the text to be smuggled clandestinely into Germany, where it was then read from the pulpit on Palm Sunday, March 21, 1937. The encyclical criticized the Nazi government for having submitted Catholics to "oppression and prohibition" of their faith. No longer, the pope said, would he remain silent before such abuse. He prayed "for those who because of their faith have been persecuted and made to suffer, even to the extent of being put in prisons and concentration camps." Those faithful, though not specified, easily might have referred to Jews as well as Catholics who faced the wrath of the Nazis. He also passed judgment directly on Hitler's idea of the master race: "None but superficial minds could stumble into concepts of a national God, of a national religion; or attempt to lock within the frontiers of a single people, within the narrow limits of a single race, God, the Creator of the Universe."

Hitler took the speech as a declaration of war. He vowed retaliation, saying he would "open such a campaign against them in press, radio and cinema so that they won't know what hit them." But he did it carefully in his own way—Hitler understood the importance of maintaining good relations with the Catholic Church, because the pope had considerable moral sway. "Let us have no martyrs among the Catholic priests," he said, "it is more practical to show they are criminals." The following day, the Gestapo fanned out across the country and seized all available copies of the pope's message.

In June 1937, two months after the encyclical, the pope convened a meeting of bishops to criticize the growing harassment of Catholics in Germany with the implicit warning that the Vatican could break diplomatic ties with Berlin. He demanded an end to arrests and mistreatment of priests, bishops, and students. "Our brothers were carrying out their duties as churchmen. They have not interfered in the political sphere and they have not committed a breach of the law . . . As long as such measures are not nullified there can be no assurances of freedom in the church or of free election."

The pope planned to broaden his complaints against the Nazi regime and knew he could be a bulwark against the madness if he could survive a while longer. Perhaps he could rally world leaders to action before it was too late. He wanted to live.

BEFORE HE WAS a bishop of the church, Pius had been Monsignor Achille Ratti, possibly best known as a pioneering mountaineer, a daring, world-class Alpine climber. These days his life as pope was reminiscent of tackling a seemingly unassailable peak, yet now he was attempting to awaken the world to Hitler's march to war.

Mountain climbing involved physical challenge and courage; dealing with church politics and world affairs also involved guile and specialized skills: "While with the hard fatigue of climbing, where the air is rarefied and purer, our physical strength gains vigor, it comes about, too, that by facing difficulties of every kind, we grow stronger for meeting the arduous duties of our lives," Pius wrote in 1922.

He was using that strength of spirit now to battle a foe on moral terms. In a rare moment of self-reflection, the pope urged Thomas Morgan, the American reporter who befriended him, to delve into his background and draw his own conclusions.

"Divine Providence has called us to work and the Alpine climbing is over," he told Morgan. "You too will have plenty to do. But you can see the mountains. Go to them . . . where the air is pure and where one is really re-created and refreshed both in body and soul."

Ambrogio Damiano Achille Ratti was born in the northern region of Lombardy on May 31, 1857. His home village, Desio, was ten miles from Milan in the foothills of the Alps, a region controlled by the Austrian Empire on and off for 150 years. It was a time of shifting political boundaries—the Italian army attacked Lombardy in 1859, swept north, then drove out the Austrians in a series of battles and annexed Lombardy to the new Italian state.

Poor farmers and workers had been drawn to Desio in the mid-1800s with the promise of work in the silk manufacturing mills in the area. Among them, Ratti's father, Francesco, was industrious and became successful enough to be promoted from worker to machine operator and then to be named manager of a silk mill. It was unusual at the time to find a case of such upward mobility from near serfdom to an emerging working class; Francesco later became the owner of his own textile mill. With increasing fortunes, the family had moved up economically and lived fairly well.

Morgan visited the silk mills of Desio and imagined what life had been like in the mid-1800s. Exploring the countryside, he met an old gentleman, Battista Cittario, who remembered the young Achille Ratti running and jumping and fighting, "the most sure-footed of all the boys. He was good in everything," Cittario said. "He often went to church with his mother for she was a very devout woman." Morgan also visited the public elementary school a few miles from the pope's home village, where he had been sent to study when he was ten years old. A report card on file from 1867 showed the boy received perfect tens in all subjects. With the intercession of a favorite uncle, Don Damien Ratti, the parish priest of nearby Asso, Achille Ratti was sent to study at a seminary school. The young man was bound, preordained it seemed to Morgan, to become a priest and to be an unusual one.

His uncle introduced him to the religious life, but this uncle also took the young Ratti on excursions, Morgan wrote, "to the precipitous heights of the Alpine ranges . . . He was thrilled with the extent of the plain, the beauty in the ruggedness and steepness of the hillside reaching down into what seemed the unfathomable depth of the blue waters [of Lake Como]. And when he faced the north, the Alps, standing like giant sentinels challenging the courage of man, frowned upon the earth and dominated it."

After his ordination in 1879, Ratti served for years as a teacher, a scholar with three doctorates, as a librarian first at the Ambrosian Library in Milan, founded in the seventeenth century and famed for its Greek and Middle Eastern manuscripts, and finally as head of the Vatican Library in Rome. Along the way, he studied Hebrew with a rabbinical scholar who became his lifelong friend. All the while he could have been mistaken for a bookish man alone were it not for his mountain-climbing conquests.

Over the years he took on increasingly new and dangerous challenges. "It is no exaggeration to say that in his own chosen sport, the name of Achille Ratti goes down in the records of the Italian Alpine Club as does the name of . . . Babe Ruth in baseball . . ." Morgan wrote.

Ratti continued climbing until 1913 when he was fifty-six years old. By then, he had mastered many peaks rarely attempted, including Monte Rosa, a climb designated by the British Alpine Association as "dangerous and foolhardy."

Morgan wrote detailed accounts of some of the more daring climbs with color and such descriptiveness that it appeared that the pope had worked with him, even dictated portions himself. His assault on Monte Rosa at 15,203 feet—about 580 feet lower than Mont Blanc, the highest peak in the Alps—came in 1889, the first ascent of its kind in history. "The hours were interminable," wrote Morgan. Ratti shared the ordeal with his fellow priest, Monsignor Luigi Grasselli.

"Night was falling," Morgan continued. "They held their breath as they watched the threat of inexorable gloom enveloping them and none had a place where he could stand without clinging to the face of the rock. They were like prisoners spread-eagled in some medieval torture. They could not endure such torment in the increasing cold of the night. The release of a hold meant disaster."

The next year they climbed successfully Mont Blanc and eventually the easier-to-tackle but more dangerous Mount Vesuvius. The pope told Morgan that the volcano "received us with a deep roar, followed by an explosion which, illuminating the bottom, or rather the entire basin of the crater, amazed us with the terrifying grandeur of the spectacle taking place before our eyes. . . . Flames leapt up from the base to the mouth of the monster, because from the lava-jetting cone deep down, as from a well of living fire, there gushed forth an elegant—I must call it that—spray of incandescent material. This gigantic fountain issued forth . . . like a fairy rain on the steep slopes of the cone."

ACHILLE RATTI had heard from his family about authoritarian rule when he was a child in the final years of the Austrian Empire's long occupation of northern Italy. Italians had little love for their German-speaking occupiers, perhaps a lesson Ratti applied years later to the regime of the Nazis under Adolf Hitler, who was an Austrian. Papa Ratti, as Italians called him, did have international experience. In 1918, Pope Benedict XV had named him the Vatican's ambassador to Poland, which had been restored to independence after the end of the Great War. His career as a librarian ended with the Polish appointment.

Ratti was at his post in Warsaw in 1920 when the Polish army repulsed the invading Soviet army. The experience contributed significantly to then Bishop Ratti's view of the world—as had lessons of Austrian rule in his home region of Lombardy. The church was also under attack after the fall of Czar Nicholas II in the Russian Revolution. Lenin's Bolsheviks destroyed churches and imprisoned priests throughout Russia. Nevertheless, as pope in the 1920s, Ratti sought a gesture that might make life easier for Catholics still in Russia. He sent food aid to the new Marxist-Leninist state, but the gesture did not result in improved relations with Moscow. The birth of the Soviet Union brought into vogue with Catholic churchmen the phrase "Godless Communism." The church confronted the question of whether Hitler was a worthy ally against Communism, whether "the enemy of my enemy" was a friend, or one more enemy?

This was a central issue at the Vatican when Pope Benedict XV died of pneumonia in 1922, and when Achille Ratti, who was then sixty-four years old, became the compromise choice to replace him. He was elected pope by the College of Cardinals on the fourteenth ballot after one other prelate had turned down the job. Ratti's opponents said he was not worldly enough to govern and that he had lived his entire life in a world of books. Though he had been a librarian for a long while, the criticism was unwarranted. In terms of daring and adventurousness, there has been no other priest—or any other pope before or since—who traversed mountain passes that now bear his name and none other who had the stamina to climb unattainable peaks. Somewhere at the heart of his increasingly passionate drive against Hitler and Mussolini was the drive to break the mold and to do what others would not or could not do. These were not the aspirations of a bookish, retiring man.

AS HE RECOVERED after 1936 from his ailments, the pope would carry on with a normal schedule—he had much left to be accomplished. Central was his intention to continue, even accelerate, the pace of his attacks on Hitler and Mussolini, to reject anti-Semitism, and to seek new ways to warn the world about the growing threat of war in Europe. Hitler and Mussolini were mightily concerned by the pope's recent actions and declarations. Such was a measure of the moral power of the papacy. Pius XI knew well that his speeches and the resulting worldwide headlines enraged Hitler. He criticized the Nazis and their anti-Semitic tirades with increasing vigor in the hope this would spur international action before it was too late.

Along with his speech about Hitler's presence in Rome on May 4, the pope authorized a similar statement by his American aide and interpreter, Monsignor Joseph Hurley. This new statement again emphasized the images of two crosses, the Christian cross and the crooked cross of Nazism. The pope had banned coverage of Hitler's trip, but there would be strong language, both on Vatican Radio and in the Vatican newspaper, *Osservatore Romano*.

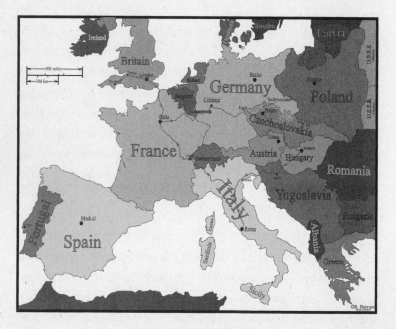

John LaFarge's European trip, May–October 1938.

"There are two crosses now side by side in Rome . . . the cross of Christianity and the crooked cross of neo-paganism," it said, without crediting Hurley as the author. Hurley's anonymous words were translated and read on Vatican Radio in Italian, English, German, and French and published in *Osservatore Romano*. The "crooked cross" became the image of Vatican-Nazi relations. The statement sent Hitler into a fury, and Mussolini ordered the seizure and destruction of any copies of the Vatican newspaper circulating outside the Vatican walls.

Cardinals at the Vatican reacted with fear, worried about reprisals against Catholics in Germany, Austria, and Italy. Britain and the United States were also surprised by the strength of Pius's words. Once he been considered a conservative pope who embraced authoritarians and enthusiastically sought and endorsed landmark diplomatic agreements with Mussolini and Hitler. He had authorized the accords with both countries so that the church could perform its basic missions of education and preaching to the faithful; in return, the church agreed not to interfere in German or Italian politics.

Mussolini and Hitler, both Roman Catholics, claimed some moral legitimacy as a result of the agreements with the Vatican, which they cast as tacit endorsements from the pope. That impression was proven wrong, and the pope found ways to leverage the agreements in his dealings with both totalitarian regimes. Pius XI criticized both governments for imposing harsh limits on civil society and for building up dictatorships that tried to replace religion with a brand of idol worship—the führer and Il Duce. To counter this, the pope increasingly challenged the Nazi's outrages; and Hitler, who was waging his own public opinion campaign, got the point.

After the pope's outburst against Nazis and their swastika, the Vatican ignored the rest of Hitler's visit to Italy. Other news media, of course, did report on the visit.

Officially, Hitler's trip was a resounding success, except for the glaring absence of Pope Pius XI. His view of Hitler was commented on everywhere. The pope, after all, was vicar of Rome, and his decision to avoid such a celebration was more than a slight. The world would know, said the pope's secretary, Monsignor Carlo Confalonieri, that "at least one person who would not bend: it was an old octogenarian of a Pontiff." The pope's silence was a statement itself, nevertheless, to the Italian people and to the world.

Paris, May 12, 1938

From England, LaFarge took the ferry across the channel and spent a week in Paris with the Jesuit community there. In Paris and all along his journey, he was surprised that people knew who he was. Months earlier he had written an article for the Catholic Student's Mission Crusade bulletin, which called for Catholic missionaries to become more involved helping impoverished American blacks. The article was translated into a number of European languages. People would approach him: "You must be Father LaFarge. We saw your picture in the SMC Bulletin for June." His opinion was so sought after in Paris that he gave a prominently advertised speech on May 17 to several hundred people, discussing "American Democracy: Its Successes and Its Problems."

"What is President Roosevelt likely to do?" "How will he protect France and Britain against Hitler?" "Will the Americans fight?" people asked him. The questions LaFarge heard were unanswerable that spring of 1938, as Hitler traveled southward to Italy and the crowds bowed down before him as he prepared to supplant the shadow of Imperial Rome and the church itself.

LaFarge compared his impressions with an article written by the prominent *New York Times* columnist Anne O'Hare

McCormick. He wrote to his friends in New York, loath though
he was to have his mail intercepted, and recommended they read
her commentary about Hitler and his trip to Rome.

McCormick wrote: "It is hard to explain why the spectacle
of Hitler riding in triumph down the Imperial Way in Rome
is more suggestive than his appearance in the *Ringstrasse* as the
conqueror of Vienna." Perhaps, she said, because he had his own
imperial designs.

"He believes he is the ordained leader of the German race. In
his own eyes he is a savior, the prophet of a new national religion
which will unify all Germans and make them prevail . . .

"Meantime, the best brains of the world are not getting very far
in anticipating or stopping the march of today's Little Corporal.
Either that untrained and nebulous intellect works well or else we
see in Hitler the true figure of the crazy time in which we live."

CHAPTER THREE

The Imposition of the Reich

May 19, 1938, French/German Border

*B*LEIBEN SIE HIER, *bitte*," a Nazi border guard told John LaFarge. "Please wait here."

The suspicious Nazi official seemed to think that LaFarge could be a Roman Catholic agent because he was dressed as a priest, was an American, and had maps of Italy and Czechoslovakia. LaFarge was led to an empty room where he waited as told.

He had boarded the late-afternoon train from Paris for the five- or six-hour journey to the German border. LaFarge was apprehensive along the way and unable to focus on reading. Central Europe had been experiencing a drought, so the rain that fell may have been an irritation for a sole traveler with more than he could carry by himself, but the foul weather was a godsend for the parched fields. He spent much of the trip in the dining car, where the international cuisine was served with care, and LaFarge relished the unlimited supply of french fries. The train was full when it left Paris, but more and more passengers left the train at each local stop. By the time they reached the German border, only two passengers remained, LaFarge and a sad-eyed Polish lady in a black dress who said she was transiting Germany to return home.

LaFarge could not avoid the boldly proclaimed glory of the new Germany as the train had pulled into the German border station. "One glance out the window was enough," LaFarge wrote in his notes on the trip. "EIN VOLK, EIN REICH, EIN FÜHRER [One People, One Reich, One Führer] greeted you in enormous letters. The Latin alphabet changed abruptly to German Gothic. Swastikas and Heils blossomed out as if by magic. We were in Hitler land. I was in Hitler land, along with 60 million Germans."

A fat, old Prussian customs officer called for him after a while and apparently had decided he needed backup. Two menacing plainclothes agents inspected LaFarge's books and reading material, concerned that he was carrying an Italian grammar phrasebook. What was this man up to?

"So," said one of the agents, "you have been in Rome."

"No, I am going to Rome," LaFarge replied.

"You were in Rome when Hitler was there?"

"No, I have not been in Rome," LaFarge told the official. "I am going to Rome after I go to Koblenz and Budapest."

One of the officials then asked why LaFarge was going to Koblenz.

He replied that he was visiting an old friend there.

The agents continued to question him until they were satisfied if not convinced that LaFarge posed no imminent threat. They could see that his passport did not have an Italian stamp. Unless he had entered and left clandestinely, that was proof he hadn't been there yet. Passing on to another subject, the Germans furrowed their brows and conferred once more when they pulled out a book about Spain he had received as a gift.

"Does the gentleman realize that this might be a forbidden book?" one asked him with an air of triumph.

No, LaFarge answered, he hadn't even opened the book, pointing out that the pages where still bound together.

The inspectors sullenly examined every document, letter, note, article of clothing, clean or dirty, before deciding the "forbidden book" would be confiscated, perhaps mailed to him later.

Finally, LaFarge was free to wait for the next train to Koblenz; the old Prussian border guard, freed of the two inspectors, became suddenly friendly, almost making up for the way he had treated LaFarge. He even helped the priest board the train when it arrived.

As it pulled out of the station, LaFarge felt nervous but relieved and foolish for not having thought about what he packed nor having taken care for what he said. The guards had not addressed him in the proper manner as *hochwerden*, the German equivalent of "father" or "reverend." They referred to him as "sir." They might have thought he wasn't really a priest, even though he was dressed as one. He spoke excellent German and they thought he had been to Rome; they said that he was also carrying a controversial book, although the book wasn't controversial at all.

They might have concluded that he was an American spy. In his own heightened state of paranoia, one thing had been fortunate. The inspectors hadn't found his map of Poland—the last thing a spy would want to be found carrying in Hitler's Germany. The tension of being in Germany would never leave him, even if he knew he was simply an agent of the Lord.

The rain was spattering hard against the windows when the train pulled into Koblenz Station. A taxi took him to the parish house of the venerable old Liebfrauenkirche—Church of Our Lady—where he was greeted by his old friend, the Reverend Heinrich Chardon, pastor of the twelfth-century church. LaFarge and Chardon had studied together at seminary in Innsbruck thirty-five years earlier. The parish priest quickly produced a dusty old bottle of Rhine wine. "On the label were a pilgrim's scrip and staff, and the image of the Apostle Saint James, patron of pilgrims," Chardon said. "Twenty years old and reserved for this visit."

They stayed up talking until 2 A.M., and LaFarge had many questions. "I soon found the Hitler atmosphere was nothing imaginary, but thick enough to cut with a knife." Censorship was total, informants were everywhere, and there was no news. "You could not write. Obviously you could not telephone, and it was dangerous to send messages. As for the papers, they were devoid of information."

Chardon told LaFarge that he and his staff were required to report their whereabouts at all times. Beyond the lovely fields and farmhouses and beautiful old buildings, Germany was being transformed into a soiled, isolated land where all who set foot were required to pay attention or pay the price.

LaFarge slept well that night and woke up to see a glorious sky and no remnants of the rain. He soon met with church parishioners who had as many questions as the border guards. As they gathered around the foreigner—a rare American visitor—one parishioner asked where LaFarge had been traveling. He told them he'd just been to London and Paris.

"But how fortunate . . . to escape," said another. "We understand that in Paris the streets are running with blood; there is a terrible revolution and people are being murdered by the Jews and Bolsheviks."

Few would accept his assurances that France was not experiencing any danger or violence. He also told them he was not escaping; he was on a brief trip and would book passage on a ship back home to the United States.

"America!" another lady declared. "And you are going back to America? You are safe here and America is so terrible. In New

York, I understand, the people are hung from every lamppost; it is filled with gangsters and lynchers and your life is in danger every moment."

Hitler's propaganda machine had consumed and twisted the German populace. It was time for LaFarge to use his prearranged code to send a message to his editor Francis Talbot. *Oremus pro invecem*, he wrote—"Let us pray for one another." The meaning was simply this: "Things are very bad, worse than you can imagine." Propaganda, isolation, and frenzy were transforming the continent. The people of Koblenz were believing crazed rumors with no chance to hear from the outside world.

Later that day, LaFarge looked down on the city from the heights of Ehrenbreitstein, where he could view the series of fortresses that had guarded the Rhine region for a millennium. Koblenz, the two-thousand-year-old city at the confluence of the Rhine and Moselle rivers, was a focal point of Hitler's hatred of the Western powers after the European armistice of 1918. The city had been headquarters for the Inter-Allied Rhineland High Commission, created by the victorious Allies after the Great War. Germany, as the vanquished nation, had been monitored for more than a decade from the headquarters offices here.

LaFarge saw marches of the Hitler youth, SS soldiers on guard at every corner. He saw that the effects of Nazism summed up Chardon's fatalistic lament—"We are all going to be in Dachau sooner or later, so what's the use of bothering?" Dachau was the first German concentration camp and had served as a detention center for mostly political prisoners since 1933.

Chardon shared the same fear felt in Rome and throughout Europe; he and other clerics in Germany faced intensifying attacks and were being driven underground. LaFarge wondered whether Catholicism could even survive the onslaught of Nazism. Chardon, who could hardly leave his church, asked LaFarge to celebrate a clandestine Mass at the chapel of the Franciscan Brothers of the Sick in Koblenz. The Franciscans had been targeted the previous year in an extension of Nazi persecution of the Catholic Church that stepped up after the pope issued his anti-Nazi encyclical the year before.

One hundred seventy members of the order had been arrested on trumped-up charges of "corrupting young people." The government had already shuttered the chapel, and the diocese was largely doing its work in secret, whether it was running a recreation program in a ramshackle building too dingy for the Nazis to bother appropriating, or at the chapel itself. That Saturday, Chardon gave LaFarge "the massive key with which I was to let myself in the back door." LaFarge said, "I was to speak to nobody, merely celebrate Mass and depart. They came to Mass, he said, in order to pray for liberation from Hitler. The following morning, therefore, I unlocked the sacristy door, found the altar boy waiting, went out on the altar and found the chapel filled with a silent congregation. Not a sound was uttered except the murmured responses of the server. I never felt so close to any congregation in my life."

Everyone present received Communion. When the Mass was completed, LaFarge left silently, went through the back onto the street, and locked the door. He returned to the parish house, said good-bye to Chardon and headed back to the train station where he purchased a ticket for his next destination, Prague. He would discover over the weekend that Czechoslovakia and Germany were on the brink of war.

Koblenz to the Czech Border, May 21, 1938

LaFarge saw something was wrong when the conductors on the night train from Koblenz to Prague dropped the curtains in the dining car. When he returned to his seat in the coach, he noticed that they had also dimmed the lighting, allowing only low-level, blue light in the corridors. None of the crew told LaFarge what was happening, not wanting to alarm the passengers. People were panicked about the possibility that Germany would attack Czechoslovakia and the train crew didn't want the train to be seen from the air and then become a potential bombing target. At that moment Germany was moving troops close to the Czech border, very close to the route the Prague night train was taking. Czechoslovakia had summoned hundreds of thousands of reserves to duty and sent them to the disputed Sudetenland border. War appeared imminent.

Just as World War I was sparked by the assassination of Archduke Franz Ferdinand of Austria, Europeans knew that provocations, real or imagined, could move Hitler's Wehrmacht into Czechoslovakia. They were also aware that provocation could be manufactured, as it appears to have been.

Before dawn that Saturday morning, two Czechs of German heritage on a motorcycle attempted to run a roadblock at the Czech entry crossing at Eger. They evaded one guard and then drove straight toward a second policeman, who said he had tried to shoot out their tires but ended up wounding both men as they escaped uphill. Czech Sudeten police were familiar with the men, George Hoffman Fonsau and Nicholas Boehm Oberlohna, pro-Nazi provocateurs who had previous run-ins with authorities and had served time in prison. Fonsau and Oberlohna died at the local police barracks.

News of the incident spread quickly, and the German army marched to within miles of the border. Czech president Edvard Beneš swiftly deployed four hundred thousand army reservists to the Sudetenland border zone. Beneš broadcast an appeal for calm, but the fact he had gone on national radio to do that produced the opposite effect; his words intensified the fear of an impending war. "We are living through the gravest moment since the end of [World War I]," he said. "This calls for calmness [and] cool nerves . . . It means that we must know no fear in the days that are coming. That we must in fact banish fear and stand for everything."

When Sir Neville Henderson, the British ambassador to Germany, asked German foreign minister Joachim von Ribbentrop about the troop movements, he was told "to mind his own business . . . that Germany did not want to make trouble, but could not stand by while German blood was shed in Czechoslovakia."

All this was going on during LaFarge's long train ride. Since there was no radio on the train and the train conductors said nothing, he had no idea of what was happening. All he could do was sense the strained, tense atmosphere all the way to the Czech border. Worse still, the border post was Eger, exactly where the two men had been killed hours earlier. The train reached the border midevening; customs inspection on both sides was unusually quick and perfunctory, silent and tense. On the Czech side, people finally told him about what was happening. There was "general fear of an immediate German invasion," and Czechoslovakia was preparing to defend itself against an anticipated Nazi attack.

The train traveled on into Czech territory for another three hours eastward to Prague. The train lights didn't come on until after they had arrived at Prague's main station. On the platform, people shouted for porters in a cacophony of German and Czech and French among other languages. A porter half dragged and carried LaFarge's cases outside to search for a taxi in the driving rain; the weather added to the gloom and desperation.

But the porter abruptly abandoned LaFarge when an imposing German military officer demanded service first. "Half paralyzed with fear, the porter dropped my things on the sidewalk and lugged the big valises inside under an ever-pointing finger," LaFarge remembered. It felt like an allegory for what was happening between the two countries. "Behind that threatening voice was the voice of Hitler, and that voice spoke not Czech but imperious German."

LaFarge found a taxi but by then was soaked by the rain. He tried to make his way swiftly to the Jesuit seminary house where he was staying for the night. The roads and highways were clogged with military vehicles and soldiers heading west toward Sudetenland. Saturday had been a workday, and President Beneš's call to battle was so pressing that men were reporting to their military posts without even going home first. The atmosphere was turbulent.

The Jesuit center was overcrowded and chaotic like everywhere else in Prague that night. LaFarge's host, Father Jaroslav Ovecka, set up a makeshift bed for him in the seminary's geography museum. LaFarge "slept amid maps, globes and charts. Czechoslovakia was still upon the map that night."

The rain stopped on Sunday, and though news reports said there was less danger of an attack, the constant drone of military traffic suggested otherwise. Appeals came in from Britain, from France, and from around the world for calm and restraint. But the Nazi newspaper *Angriff* kept the propaganda machine running by proclaiming that the Czechs would be held responsible for any violence against "members of the Greater German nation . . . The German Reich, which as the only big power in Central Europe bears the supreme responsibility for peace in this part of the world."

The German claims were of course twisting the truth. Hitler and the Nazis were responsible for peace because the führer was the one who would decide whether to start the war. With Czechoslovakia, he was waiting even though the incident at the

Czech border had been a promising opportunity. His generals told him the Wehrmacht had not completed preparations yet. All in good time. It was not the moment to launch an invasion, especially when Czechoslovakia was mobilized and waiting. The Nazi army would go in when Czechoslovakia was least ready and least able to defend itself. As Joseph Goebbels pushed the propaganda campaign, he noted the fact in his diary. "The Führer . . . knows what he wants. So far he has always hit upon the right moment to act."

When LaFarge met with Jan Masaryk two weeks earlier, he had only a distant understanding of the Czechoslovakian problem. Now he understood Masaryk's fatalistic view; war appeared depressingly inevitable. He also remembered how the Czech ambassador almost begged him to meet with Beneš when he arrived in Prague. Somehow a Jesuit journalist was supposed to listen, understand, and then move mountains with logic and words of peace. LaFarge heard that Masaryk had traveled from London and was now in Prague, but he decided not to meet with the Czech leaders.

"In all this excitement I did not have the heart to visit either Mr. Beneš or Mr. Masaryk." He feared that such a meeting would have been irrelevant, and that he would come across as "a clerical bore." "I could not see what I could do about it all."

As he walked the city's streets, and later in Bratislava on the road to the Budapest Eucharistic Congress, he could sense that these were the last days of Czechoslovakia's freedom from tyranny.

Budapest, May 27, 1938

LaFarge's colleagues in New York had to piece together the snippets of words he was cabling back to them. His telegrams were missing articles and participles because each word cost five dollars or more, and he was on a priest's budget. The messages, complete with errors typed in by non-English-speaking cable operators, were spare. His cable from Budapest read:

IMPOSSIBLE EXAGGERATE IMPLACABILITY
ENEMY TRAGEDY ALLEN SITUATION . . . WORLD
DRAMA ENACTIVA

It was meant to say, "It would be impossible to exaggerate the implacability of the enemy we face and the tragedy of the alien situation. I am the witness to a world drama being enacted before me."

The disaster was growing. Jews had been dispossessed and stripped of their rights in Austria, and they were wandering in search of an elusive safe haven. Aliens in their own lands, they were being cast out of Austria by the Gestapo, denied entry into Czechoslovakia, expelled once more and hunted down yet again by officials in Hungary, who rejected their presence as well. The Jesuits at America House read the reports too. A reporter for the *New York Times* watched uniformed Nazi thugs on the rampage terrorizing Jews:

> *It has been a common practice for squads of Storm Troopers to make the rounds of cafes in Vienna, order all Jews to stand up, and then march them out to kneel in the gutter and scrub off the pavements . . . Lye or hydrochloric acid was put in the water. The weather—and it was normally cold and rainy during this time—made no difference in the sport. The hands and knees of the victims were soon rubbed raw.*

People whose families had lived in the same country for centuries were now discarded and set to the winds and whims of crude indecency. Jews in Germany, Austria, Yugoslavia, Romania, and now Hungary were without hope. LaFarge had already seen them fleeing the savagery. To the dismay of LaFarge and others, Catholic leaders themselves were divided between pro- and anti-Semites.

Such was the mood in Hungary, the next stop on LaFarge's European tour. On May 27, he took another train, this time bound for Budapest among thousands of religious pilgrims. Attending the Eucharistic Congress in Budapest had been the central purpose of LaFarge's trip. It was meant to be a great joyous celebration of the faith. But the conference was weighed down by the fall of Austria, the crumbling of Czechoslovakia, and the sense that more was to come.

Scarcely two weeks after Pope Pius XI had snubbed Hitler in Rome, the Nazi leader followed through on a long-standing threat: any Germans—and now newly conquered Austrians—who wished to attend the congress would need to obtain a travel visa. The visa application implicitly obliged would-be travelers to declare they were active in the Catholic Church, a declaration that would certainly place them on a list for potential Nazi harassment and reprisals. No one, not even German or Austrian cardinals, had dared seek permission to travel—and none of the twenty-five thousand Germans and thirty thousand Austrians who had planned to attend did so.

Never before had such a congress taken on so much political significance. The newly formed Hungarian government had passed new anti-Semitic laws that curtailed the ability of Jews to participate in politics and society. It was the first such anti-Semitic legislation outside German jurisdiction.

The pope's personal representative at the Eucharistic Congress was Cardinal Eugenio Pacelli, the elegant, austere Vatican secretary of state. Pacelli arrived in Budapest just as the anti-Semitic laws were announced. Guest of the Hungarian regent, Admiral

Nicholas Horthy at the Royal Castle, Pacelli delivered the main speech of the event and avoided criticism of Hungarian anti-Semitism or the Nazis. On the contrary, some of his remarks sounded instead like a veiled attack on the Jews. Jesus, he said, "who so often was the recipient of the rage of his enemies, he who suffered the persecutions of those of whom he was one, he shall be triumphant in the future." At the same time that Jews were being disenfranchised in Hungary, Pacelli appeared to refer to the old church prejudice that Jews (of whom Jesus "was one") had killed him. It was doubtful that LaFarge or many of the attendees could parse out the cardinal's words that night. LaFarge saw Pacelli at a distance but did not meet him. Like Pacelli, he was housed among the nobility, at the villa of old friends, the Baron and Baroness de Hedry. The baroness's sister had been a supporter of LaFarge's mission work in rural Maryland.

LaFarge forced himself to be lifted up by the exuberant mood in Budapest. The Eucharistic Congress was an ornate celebration. Children gave flowers to LaFarge and other visiting pilgrims as they arrived at the city. The papal yellow-and-white flag flew all about. The central spectacle was a mystically beautiful ceremony along the Danube, which divides the old city of Buda and much newer Pest on the east bank of the river. The water shimmered with the light of thousands of candles held by worshippers close to shore. The medieval citadel at Gellért Hill and Fisherman's Bastion—the restored stone bulwark where Hungarians could not repel the Turkish siege and invasion five centuries earlier—were alternatively set in relief by five searchlights that swept across the countryside.

Pacelli knelt at the bow of a steamer on the Danube before a three-foot-tall Eucharist altar inset with jewels and silver. An army of Catholic clergy, monsignors, priests, and nuns surrounded him, all holding candles. The candlelight shimmered all along the river as the procession started at dusk.

One thousand choir boys sang as Catholic youth held torches aloft; hundreds of thousands of people knelt along the banks of the river; most also carried a flickering candle. All the heat and light seemed by the force of spirit and numbers to symbolize much more than a religious procession, to burn away, to wash away the reality of impending war.

"A city and a nation, and delegates from many lands, poured out their hearts in solemn adoration to the Eucharistic King, with all the dignity and splendor they could muster," LaFarge wrote in his memoir.

LaFarge was among them, watching as Cardinal Pacelli "carried the Sacred Host in a spot-lighted glass chamber at the prow of a steamer swiftly moving down the dark Danube, and symbolically limned against the huge mass of Buda's mighty rock." But LaFarge could not shake the feeling of terror and doom: "One sensed the gathering background of totalitarian hate during the mysterious night procession."

Afterward, Pope Pius XI's voice could be heard on loudspeakers broadcast via shortwave from Vatican Radio. He prayed for peace and that God might "quell the darkness and perturbation of souls by which we are so troubled." The pope said that perhaps there was "hope of better times, dissipating the clouds which seem to threaten fresh storms, and illuminating that darkness and claiming that unrest of souls."

Pius was seated in a broadcast room at Castel Gandolfo about five hundred miles away. As he spoke those words, a thunderstorm broke over Budapest and rain drenched the final ceremony of the Eucharistic Congress. As LaFarge and the other participants scattered for shelter, they could not have helped to notice the irony and some might have considered the storm an ill omen.

CHAPTER FOUR

The Pope's Battle Plan

"The story isn't yet told. The answer to the riddle is to be revealed by history."

ANNE O'HARE MCCORMICK

Castel Gandolfo, June 23, 1938

TWO DAYS AFTER the Eucharistic Congress, the pope celebrated his eighty-first birthday. He had recovered so well from his illness a year and a half earlier that the Vatican doctors had suspended their full-time attendance at the pope's rooms in Castel Gandolfo. Pius awoke daily at around dawn, had breakfast, and then conducted a range of meetings, reestablishing full control of church administration. As the weather warmed in late spring, he also resumed his daily walks behind the summer palace, in the sculpted hedgerows interspersed with Roman statuary, copses where one could stop to meditate, and a balustrade from which one could look down on the Albano valley.

He was a most solitary figure on those walks and did not take counsel easily, not even from Pacelli, who came for meetings at least four times a week. Hitler's anti-Semitic campaign had become the pope's great preoccupation. The issue before him was not just the matter of protecting Catholics, but also the question of protecting humanity. This was the church's moral responsibility.

AS THE NAZIS increased their threats against the Jews, the pope realized that today it was the Jews, but then it would be the Catholics and finally the world. He could see in the day's news that the Nazis would stop at nothing less than world domination.

Pius envisioned a gesture that would go beyond daily condemnations of each atrocity uttered by the Nazis. He sought a verbal offensive with a major statement that would attack the underpinnings of the Nazi machine. Pius appeared to have found the vehicle; he had received a copy of a book, *Interracial Justice*, written by an American Jesuit named John LaFarge. The book portrayed the lives of American blacks who lived in the poorest strata of society. It said the church had to establish itself as a moral force in combating racism in the United States. The pope did not know LaFarge was in Europe and en route to Rome.

The similarities between the descriptions of racism in America and the threats of anti-Semitism in Europe were easy to see. LaFarge's book was about the plight of blacks in the United States, but the concept applies, he wrote, "to all races and conditions of men . . . all tribes and races, Jew and Gentile alike. . . ." Pius saw that LaFarge's writings could be applied to a new Vatican declaration that would attract international attention, a statement that would sound the alarm and warn world leaders about the Nazis and the Fascists in uncompromising terms.

This was the moment to strike. In March 1937, the pope had last issued an encyclical—the highest statement the head of the Vatican can make—condemning Nazism. But he felt compelled to do so again, this time with the words of an American Jesuit who understood the insanity of race. This time his encyclical would be broadcast throughout the globe, and it would answer the maniacal quest for conquest with basic truths.

Rome, June 24, 1938

The parched days of spring had been broken by occasional early summer rains, but nothing could dampen the spirit of Father John LaFarge on his first visit to Rome since 1905, when he was a young seminary student.

LaFarge was staying in a room at the Gregorian University, the four-hundred-year-old Jesuit college not far from the Spanish Steps. It was a privileged location, central to politics and the eternal nature of Western culture and the heart of Catholicism. As he strolled to the residence, he skirted the Quirinale Palace, several blocks at another level in the other direction, where just a month and a half earlier Hitler had been greeted triumphantly by Mussolini and by the titular monarch, Victor Emmanuel III. The recently completed monument to the king's grandfather, Victor Emmanuel II, was downhill opposite the Piazza Venezia. It was a garish assemblage of columns that Romans jokingly referred to as the wedding cake.

LaFarge had arrived in Rome on June 5 via Yugoslavia, crossed the border at Trieste, and then traveled south from Venice. Immediately he saw Il Duce's jaw-jutting image everywhere: Mussolini, the great leader, supporting the Italian army; Il Duce standing with the people; a joint profile of Hitler and Mussolini in their uniforms and Hitler's swastika prominent on his shoulder. *Viva, viva Mussolini!* was plastered on the walls. LaFarge noted in his diary that, "Magnificent slogans exhorted the people to morality, industry, loyalty, and other virtues, signed in each case with the mysterious letter M. Asking an Italian friend what the M stood for—it might stand for morality or Machiavelli or something else—I received only a shocked glance as a reply."

One morning, a fellow American Jesuit at the Gregorian University arranged a VIP tour for LaFarge with a high-ranking member of the Fascist City Council. The official arrived late for the tour and said that he had been delayed in a meeting with Mussolini.

"You know, we were having the Council meeting and I told Mussolini that I had an appointment at eleven o'clock with Father LaFarge," the official said. "But Il Duce said, let Father LaFarge wait. The affairs of state are more important."

LaFarge was as susceptible to flattery as anyone, but he doubted the story. The official took LaFarge on an extensive tour of Mussolini's signature welfare projects, including a rural reconstruction program, newly established towns built on drained and recovered swampland.

"Nothing that I had seen in the United States, even in the far West, was as new as these extraordinary constructions," LaFarge said. The buildings were "splendidly built, all Italian style," he said, "with broad streets, immense squares, imposing municipal buildings and elaborate churches, one of which, in good medieval spirit, included Mussolini as a toiling harvest-worker in the mosaic representing the Assumption of the Blessed Virgin."

When Mussolini visited his urbanization projects, he would recognize nothing short of perfection. Il Duce was reimagining Italy. On one occasion, touring one of the towns he had built on marshes, Mussolini demanded why the buildings had screens on the windows. When told they were a precaution against mosquitoes, he replied, "Mosquitoes have been abolished." Workers immediately removed the screens.

Mussolini's construction projects were theoretically intended to relocate people from crowded urban working-class conditions to lower-density housing with good sanitation and social services. The projects sometimes fell below projections, forcing the transferred workers to travel long distances to their jobs. And not all the housing projects were completed as well as the model LaFarge was shown. LaFarge had already gone out on his own and peered beyond these Potemkin Village undertakings for the stage set they were and had seen Romans on the periphery who were living in misery. One shantytown, nicknamed Shanghai, was worse than the worst slums he had seen in the American South. Another hovel housed forlorn Italian Army veterans of the recent Fascist conquest of Ethiopia. All were quarantined in squalid boxcars, waiting for further orders if they survived the pestilence some had brought back with them.

At the same time, LaFarge loved the Eternal City of Rome, the ancient objects of the empire, the relics, and the churches. The dome of St. Peter's, which was visible from many points of the city, reminded him of his faith and gave him solace and warmth. The Roman Forum was most prominent and the Coliseum was a bit farther down from the university. He was moved and inspired by the opportunity to say Mass at a chapel in the Santa Brigida Church on the Piazza Farnese. On tours around Rome, he delighted in the food, fresh meats, *bel paese* cheese, and fine wines.

On Wednesday, June 22, LaFarge was capping off his visit to Italy by attending a general audience with Pope Pius XI at Castel Gandolfo. It was not easy to obtain entrance for such group audiences, but Vincent McCormick, the Jesuit rector of Gregoriana University, had made this happen. McCormick had asked the pope's chief of staff the day before if the pope might have time "to say a word in commendation of my work at the general audience," LaFarge wrote in a diary note. The chief of staff met them on their arrival at Castel Gandolfo and said the request had come too late. "The only thing to do was to have a private audience," the official said, but such meetings were usually arranged weeks ahead of time. LaFarge was to leave Rome by June 29, and the official held out little hope.

McCormick and LaFarge entered the pope's summer quarters in time for the general audience and stood with a group of clergy while others teemed forward to wait for the pontiff. Four staff-bearing Swiss Guard Halberdier troops stood guard, dressed in their singular uniforms, traditional stripes in the colors of the Medici family, blue, yellow, and red, a metal morion helmet adorned with red ostrich feathers on their heads. Pius XI finally entered the room, smiling and apparently hardy and in good spirits, despite reports he had been weakened by illness.

The audience was rather brief and impersonal and was over quickly. The pontiff spoke about marriage and family and the work of missionaries and blessed those assembled. When the crowd dispersed, LaFarge and McCormick went to the fourth floor in the apostolic palace to visit the papal astronomer, Father Johan Stein, a fellow Jesuit. The Dutch scientist-priest showed them around proudly and advised his guests to step gingerly; the pope's private quarters were directly below them.

LaFarge and McCormick then returned to Rome. LaFarge was content with the day, thinking no more of the event than adding one more pope to the tally sheet—he had now seen three popes, all from a distance.

Then two days later, on Friday, June 24, LaFarge was making preparations to wind up his European tour—he would make a quick trip to Spain where Francisco Franco was consolidating power, then double back through Paris en route to Rotterdam and home—when a messenger arrived with a sealed yellow-and-white envelope that bore the unmistakable mark of the Vatican. Only one person used this stationery with the seal of a crown and the crossed keys of St. Peter. This was a letter from the pope, more properly a summons from him. The Reverend John LaFarge,

Society of Jesus, was requested to attend a private audience on Saturday, June 25, at 11:45 A.M.

LaFarge was overwhelmed and humbled. How could it be? "I was mystified," he wrote in his diary. The summons brought "a sense of wonder which nothing else in the world could give." How could a little-known American priest with neither pulpit nor station receive direct communication from the Holy Father?

The invitation was cause for analysis and a sleepless night. Pope Pius XI, now eighty-one years old, was said to be frail despite his healthy appearance the other day and was decreasing the frequency and duration of such private meetings.

LaFarge took advice from Father McCormick, who recommended that he jot down notes about his life and highlights of his missionary work that he could recite when asked, along with reminders that would serve to answer any possible question the pope might direct his way. It had been made clear that LaFarge was to come alone. He did not know what to expect.

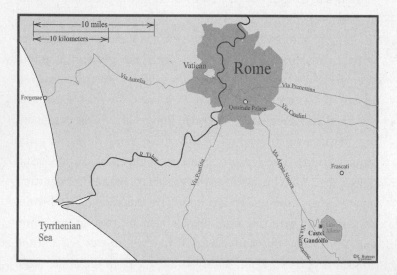

Rome and its environs.

John LaFarge could be excused for not sleeping well that Friday night. On the morning of the visit, he had coffee and breakfast and then at midmorning borrowed a car from the university motor pool for the drive down the new Appian Way. Hot summer weather had settled in across Italy and all Europe with temperatures exceeding 90 degrees. Open windows offered some respite. The winding road paralleled the route of the famous original Roman road of the same name that was still in existence, rutted and hardly passable for cars.

Leaving Rome to the southeast, he drove past Roman ruins and ancient churches, and then along a sloping portion in the Alban Hills shaded by stands of olive trees, and finally over the bridge named for Pope Pius IX. During an unusually long thirty-one-year pontificate in the 1800s, Pius IX had decreed papal infallibility and rejected any move to accommodating to modern times in the Roman Catholic Church.

LaFarge was in an altered state of mind. He had expected nothing vaguely approaching a meeting of such import, and he was memorizing the little speech he would recite to the pope about his ministry and his writing. The Jesuit knew well that Pius was a man of letters. He also knew the folklore—the pope as mountaineer—and that Pius was the first pope to even set foot beyond the confines of the Vatican in more than half a century, the first pope to ride in a motorcar, and the first to have his voice transmitted by radio.

The pope had a reputation for being a tough, headstrong, withering presence. That was true—policy was directed by the pope not his subordinates, whatever their real opinions about church doctrine, and their politics, might have been. Not even the pope's closest advisers, such as Cardinal Pacelli, the secretary of state who was said to shudder at merely considering contradicting the pope even on a minor matter, dared challenge Pius to his face.

LaFarge was surprised by the ease with which he could approach the papal residence, drive by well-known cardinals strolling on the cobblestone piazza, and then park unimpeded under olive trees that provided some respite from the blazing heat. Once inside the summer palace, he was directed across the central courtyard to a small elevator that led to the papal rooms. He was there well ahead of the appointed time and a monsignor told him the pope's meetings were running behind. Three cardinals were ahead of him and he would have to wait for at least forty-five minutes.

The elevator door opened; perhaps the most prominent member of the College of Cardinals emerged—Cardinal Pacelli. The cardinal glared, barely acknowledged the priest's presence, and walked off. Shortly afterward, Cardinal Eugene Tisserant, a close ally of the pope and one of the pontiff's best friends, crossed the patio. The two cardinals were a study in contrasts. Pacelli was a gangly, pale, even ghostly presence; Tisserant, a Frenchman, was a burly man who sported a long bushy black beard flecked with gray. He did not seem to notice LaFarge.

After a while, an attendant ushered LaFarge into an anteroom, where he watched as various clergy and laypeople entered and left the pope's study, which had a sign over the entry door, PIUS XI *PONTIFEX MAXIMUS*. Finally it was LaFarge's turn to enter; the pope must have used some silent buzzer to signal the secretaries that he was ready. This was to be a private meeting with the pope. LaFarge stood up nervously. "I was shown into the pope's study by myself entirely," LaFarge wrote. "No one [was] there with me, and [the] door shut."

LaFarge stood for a moment before Pope Pius XI, the 258th successor to St. Peter, and then bent to the carpet to kiss the pope's shoe. Pius motioned him to rise and take a seat before his desk. LaFarge looked around the room. A walking stick was leaning against a table near the pope's desk, the pope's white skullcap rested on the table. LaFarge had the impression that the pope had recently been strolling outdoors. He could see the sumptuous gardens and tree-lined paths beyond the balcony ahead of him and a distant view of the Mediterranean beyond.

The pope made small talk to put him at ease and spoke informally. The first hurdle was to choose the language in which they would speak. Pius understood English, but spoke only haltingly; LaFarge's Italian was not conversant. The pope was amused by LaFarge's confusion. They alternated briefly between German and French and then settled on French. LaFarge was struck by the pope's vigor, "a natural vigor which few who reach that age enjoy."

Finally, the pope told LaFarge he literally could not sleep when he thought about the rise of Nazism. "He grieved over the present divided state of the world, over the growth of racism, condemned by reason, science and faith," LaFarge remembered.

Pius told the younger man he had read *Interracial Justice* and considered it a triumph. LaFarge saw a copy of the book prominent on the pope's credenza. Americans, the pope said, had a greater understanding of these issues in part because they had access to LaFarge's book. But he had come to the conclusion that LaFarge's book also helped explain the deteriorating situation in Europe, that "racialism and nationalism were fundamentally the same . . . the most burning issue at the present time."

LaFarge was surprised the pope had even heard of his book, which was written in English, distributed mostly in the United States, and published very recently. *Interracial Justice* was an exhortation for the Catholic Church in the United States to accept and dedicate itself to the letter of the Declaration of Independence, that all men are created equal, that African Americans could not and should not be treated differently or deprecated or denied basic human and civil rights.

LaFarge went further in the book, taking quite an absolute

progressive stance, writing that "modern anthropological and ethnological science overwhelmingly rejects the theory that even purely physical traits are permanently or fixedly inherited by any large determinable group of human beings. It is an analogy falsely transferred from an animal race: an analogy not unlikely when human beings are treated as animals."

The pope asked about LaFarge's views on race in America and discussed the relationship with the case of the Jews in Germany. Pius said he had been searching for just the right person to work with him on his next foray into politics and the most pressing, dangerous matter of the moment. And now, providentially, LaFarge has come to Rome. "We will issue an encyclical on these matters, one which you must prepare," Pius told LaFarge.

LaFarge was to write an encyclical that would use the same reasoning he employed when discussing racism in the United States. He needed to convey that Hitler's increasing assault on the Jews was based on a myth. The myth and the barbarity and inhumanity being unleashed in Europe must be challenged. He was to write a papal declaration such as never had been seen before, one that firmly and categorically represented the church's vision of the conflagration facing Europe. This would be the church's strongest statement ever, an encyclical that rejected anti-Semitism and the Nazi doctrine that espoused it. So doing, LaFarge would articulate church policy, and his thoughts and words about race and humanity would be inscribed in Catholic doctrine and would be parsed for guidance worldwide. This was overwhelming, a step that a humble Jesuit from Newport could hardly dream of. LaFarge was dumbfounded and flooded with doubts.

How, he asked Pope Pius, could he do such a thing? The pope smiled and gave him free rein. He said: "*Dites tout simplement, ce que vous direz si vous etiez Pape, vous-meme,*" LaFarge wrote, recalling the pope's exact words. "Say simply, just what you would say if you yourself were pope." LaFarge said he felt unable and unworthy to carry out such a project. The pope would hear none of it. "I could have chosen someone else to write this, more senior, better known writers within the Church," the pope told the Jesuit. He told LaFarge he certainly was capable of writing what needed to be said. And it was an assignment that might amount to the greatest opportunity the pope had to rally world opposition to the Nazis. "I decided you are the right person for the job," he told LaFarge. "God has sent you to me to do this. You are heaven-sent."

The pope expected the statement to be as strong and unyieldingly direct as he thought LaFarge's words were about racism in the United States. Pius made it clear that no one in the curia knew about his decision to issue the encyclical, likely not even Pacelli, and certainly not Wlodimir Ledóchowski, the leader of the Jesuit order and therefore LaFarge's superior. "Properly, I should have first taken this up with Father Ledóchowski before speaking to you," the pope said. But he had not. "I imagine it will be all right . . . after all a pope is a pope."

The pope told LaFarge that he expected him to complete the job in secret and directly for him. "It is said that a secret of the pope in Rome is Punch's secret," a secret that everyone knows but no one admits they know. "But it should not be like that. And in this case, this is a true secret that we are sharing with you," the pope said. The pontiff told him he would await the final document.

AS LAFARGE drove back to Rome that afternoon, the same words kept coming back to him: "I am mystified" by what has happened. LaFarge was now in the service of the pope. The time was short, and he was to begin work immediately. He was surrounded by a web of shadows and shrouded schemes, and he still could not even fathom how he had come to the pope's attention. Now, the Vatican was directly asking him to act on a dangerous world stage. "Frankly, I am stunned," LaFarge told friends in confidence. The task was great and there was little time. "The Rock of Peter has fallen on my head."

POPES HAD BEEN called "Prisoner of the Vatican" for more than half a century. Locked into ritual and an image and surrounded by acolytes, many popes had dreamed of walking again among the people. The Catholic Church and its popes had governed Rome, the environs, and a broad swath of territory—the Vatican Free States—across central Italy for centuries. After decades of strife—the Napoleonic wars, the Franco-Prussian War—King Victor Emmanuel II consolidated modern Italy and seized Rome in 1870, relegating the remaining papal territory to the confines of the Vatican. For fifty-nine years the popes ranged no farther than the outer circle of the walls around St. Peter's. Pius had made the strategic decision to conclude a historic treaty with the Italian state that would create guarantees for the Vatican and ultimately provide a new era of political importance and financial stability for the church. The successful negotiations culminated in 1929 with the Lateran Accords. The Lateran Accords designated the Vatican as a city-state and returned the 135-acre territory of Castel Gandolfo to the Holy See. As a result, the Vatican became a nation like any other country in the world. Now the pope was in search of global reach.

Castel Gandolfo, its name of uncertain origin, had been a Roman retreat for almost two millennia as well as a refuge for Renaissance-era nobility. The site had first been used as a papal residence in the late sixteenth century, though by the 1900s it had fallen into disrepair. With the 1929 Lateran agreement, Pius XI authorized a major renovation. The new construction and land-scaping linked three-hundred-year-old villas with lands where Roman emperor Domitian built a palace in the first century A.D., subsequently expanded by his successors. Pius XI envisioned Castel Gandolfo as not only the summer home of the Vatican, but also as a modern working farm and self-sustaining community—dairy, stables, chickens and ducks, an olive grove, and a garden with housing for several dozen farm workers and other employees. A reporter touring the grounds as the renovations were under way in the early 1930s said that Castel Gandolfo would be "a spot of rare beauty . . . one of the loveliest spots on earth."

The pope moved into his renovated sanctuary in 1934, visited each year afterward, and spent six full months there in 1937. He expected to do the same this year, 1938. Key advisers from Rome spent the day, and some moved in for the season so he was able to conduct regular Vatican business all the while. But at break time, as often as his age and illnesses permitted him, the pope would take up his walking stick and stroll along the miles of cool shaded pathways.

The atmosphere at Castel Gandolfo was indeed an important stimulus for the pope, better than being shuttered at St. Peter's. The crisp air and rolling green cliffs surrounding Lake Albano were good for the soul. Open spaces, the countryside, and mountains had been part of his life before he took the throne of St. Peter.

His first actions when he had taken office in 1922 signaled his expanded view of the role of the Vatican and the papacy. He emerged on the outer balcony overlooking St. Peter's Square and delivered the *Urbi et Orbi* blessing—to the city and the world—which hadn't been done since 1870. His decision to step beyond the inner sanctum of the Vatican presaged a significant new role for his office and his stature beyond the Catholic Church. It was after this that he retook Castel Gandolfo.

As he had once climbed peaks never scaled, he now sought other new heights. While some had criticized the 1929 Lateran Accords with Mussolini as an accommodation to the Fascist state, Pius XI used the new role of the church to spur a new era.

But much more than that, the pope promoted and embraced modern science beyond the interests of any predecessor and won a rare distinction. In November 1931, the American magazine *Popular Mechanics* profiled the pope and his use of technology. "Always the twentieth century wins out, always the old gives way to the new," the article said. "The Vatican City stands today the symbol and embodiment of science and religion in complete harmony." Among the innovations, *Popular Mechanics* wrote about the Vatican Observatory, which had just been transferred to Castel Gandolfo that year from St. Peter's, including its forty-centimeter German-made Zeiss refractor telescope. The observatory was becoming an international gathering point for astronomers. The pope also established a new fleet of automobiles, which eliminated centuries-old horse-drawn carriages, ordered installation of a modernized set of elevators at the Vatican, an automatic phone system, and a new printing plant, and he considered buying a fleet of helicopters to shuttle around Rome.

THE POPE MARKED his ninth anniversary on the throne of St. Peter on February 12, 1931, with a ceremony that would have profound reverberations. Heralded by a six-man honor guard playing silver trumpets, he swept into an office filled with wires and vacuum tubes to greet Guglielmo Marconi, Italy's favorite son, the father of radio and now a member of the Italian Senate. These were the newly created offices of Vatican Radio. At Marconi's instruction, the pontiff turned dials and yanked levers—Marconi spoke for a moment as the pontiff, dressed in white, sat before the microphone and announced: "This is the first time in history that the living voice of the Pope will have been heard simultaneously in all parts of the globe."

The pope spoke first in Latin, then in Italian. The pope's first words were a passage from Isaiah: "'Listen and hear, O Peoples of distant lands.'

"We speak first to all things and to all men, speaking to them here and as follows with the words themselves of Holy Scripture: Hear, oh heavens, that which I shall say, and listen, on earth, to the words of my mouth.

"Listen all people; lend your ear all you who inhabit the globe, united toward the same end. Both the rich and the poor. Hear, oh islands, and listen, oh distant peoples."

When he was done, Monsignor Francis Spellman interpreted the pope's words in English. In the course of his speech, the pope praised Marconi "for this new invention," the wireless, which the pope described as "the last word in technicality and science." Marconi, he said, "had promised us one of the most modern of inventions. This promise he has fulfilled so magnificently that he may ask what yet remains to constitute the latest development in radio."

Care in transmitting the pope's words was unprecedented. The sounds were modulated and converted into a series of radio waves. Engineers around the world received and amplified the shortwave signal, then transmitted via a network of global relay stations. At each step, operators adjusted the signal and bounced it along the way. Locally, the signal was transferred to the AM radio bands for direct transmission.

"Listeners in the United States reported hearing a 'waxing and waning howl' intermingled at times with the Pope's words," the *New York Times* reported. "Otherwise the program was remarkably clear and free from fading."

Radio operators in London found it easier to grab the signal back from a station in the United States, but that didn't work. The static was too great to understand the Italian-accented Latin or Spellman's translation. Nevertheless, this was a giant step for the Vatican.

Broadcast by wireless, which people in some countries were also referring to as radio, had existed already for a generation, but the novelty was such that the pope was almost redefining the meaning and use of radio: his voice gave new power to radio broadcasting. The occasion of the pope's inaugural speech on Vatican Radio was declared a miracle itself as a redefinition of what humankind might accomplish. The pope could not only preach to the faithful, but could also counsel the faithless and provide instant order and a unified front among his legions of priests around the world. There would be no doubt or delay in interpreting what the Holy See might think or might judge of the world—here was the supreme leader of the Roman Catholic Church speaking with all immediacy.

He began to do so with regularity, with general declarations and focused commentaries. He often ranged increasingly into the realm of politics and pleas for peace. "Few events in the history of the world can compare with the profound impact the Head of the Holy Roman See had during his address direct to the entire planet," said an editorial in the *New York Herald*. "Such a thing could not have been foreseen by any preceding pope. This is a miracle of science, and no less a miracle of faith," the editorial said.

Perhaps it was a triumph of science if not a miracle, but Vatican Radio served to provide Pius XI a world audience. Now, seven years later, in 1938, the pope's voice and the translation of his word would extend beyond the faithful; he could now exert an editorial, political, even moral force in these years of challenging the Nazis, and increasingly stood alone. Vatican Radio now broadcast in Italian, English, German, and French, an alternative and a moral compass in Europe and beyond. There was no other comparable voice worldwide that could generate impact and controversy and sway emotions like the pope, using his electronic pulpit and his Vatican printing press that produced the *Osservatore Romano*.

The pope knew the radio provided a moral leader with an opportunity to reach beyond the confines of space in real time. The power of technology was an obvious new opportunity. All other media, radio, and newspapers in Italy were controlled by Mussolini's Fascists, who lashed out against the pope for "peevish" silence on Hitler's visit to Rome.

During Hitler's visit to Rome, the *Times* of London reported criticism by an Italian Fascist newspaper, representing Mussolini's point of view, blasting the pope and the Vatican for being "the only newspaper in the world which has ignored the Führer's presence in Rome. It is certainly far from edifying to see an old, austere journal like that of the Vatican City lose its reason and sense of proportion."

CHAPTER FIVE

The Flying Cardinal

Hyde Park, New York, June 1938

PRESIDENT ROOSEVELT WAS keenly interested in developments in Rome during the spring and summer of 1938 and received frequent personal and direct reports from the U.S. ambassador to Italy, William Phillips. Roosevelt had chosen Phillips for the post in 1936, an interesting and important choice. He graduated from Harvard University in 1900, three years ahead of Roosevelt and a year before LaFarge. Phillips stayed on at Cambridge for three more years attending Harvard Law School. There was no indication that LaFarge and Phillips knew each other. If Phillips and Roosevelt weren't friends at Harvard, they became close in 1910 when Phillips married Roosevelt's second cousin, Caroline Astor Drayton, an heir to the Astor fortune. Phillips and his wife were close to Franklin and Eleanor Roosevelt (she was of course also a relative of Caroline and the two had played together as children) and recalled spending private evenings at the White House whenever schedules permitted. Phillips was a Republican, but the difference of parties was no barrier. Aside from his kinship with the president, Roosevelt thought Phillips would be a good intermediary with Mussolini—as a member of the Republican opposition, the Italians might see Phillips as being independent minded and approachable. Phillips's immediate previous assignment as undersecretary of state, second ranking at the State Department to Cordell Hull, also had been arranged by Roosevelt. Like so many others at the State Department in the 1930s, Phillips had been slow to recognize the danger presented by Hitler and the Nazi Party. Diplomats in Germany, notably the U.S. ambassador to Berlin, William E. Dodd, warned early on about Hitler's arms buildup and the treatment of Jews, but the State Department paid little attention. Orders were to deal with Germany, as always, in accord with the niceties of bland diplomacy.

In two years in Italy, Phillips had realized quickly that Dodd's warning from Germany had been accurate. Roosevelt had now charged him with a general task—to develop good relations with the Italian government and to use every possible means to dissuade Mussolini from tightening his alliance with Hitler. Roosevelt had encouraged Phillips to bypass protocol and, in addition to routine mission reports back to the State Department, he expected his ambassador-relative-friend to send frequent personal updates on the state of affairs. When he faltered, Roosevelt chided him to keep up the correspondence.

Thanks to Ambassador Phillips's letters, the president was not surprised to hear that Pope Pius XI was being so confrontational with Hitler. Pius was clearly opposed to the Nazis, even though his top aides didn't appear to be in full agreement with him. In 1936, Roosevelt had met with Cardinal Eugenio Pacelli, the highest-ranking Roman Catholic leader ever to visit the United States. The president was rightly ebullient, having just won reelection with a surprising landslide. Two days later, he was relaxed, even amused when Pacelli arrived at Hyde Park for a luncheon chat.

News media had been calling Pacelli "The Flying Cardinal," because of his unprecedented, weeklong, coast-to-coast U.S. airplane tour. People bowed before him when he laid a wreath at George Washington's home in Mount Vernon, visited the Empire State Building, gazed at the Boulder Dam and the Grand Canyon, and blessed Niagara Falls and the Golden Gate Bridge. His public pronouncements had been mild statements in favor of peace and calls for adherence to Christian teachings.

Some speculated that the visit was an attempt to establish diplomatic relations between the United States and the Holy See, which had been broken off following the dissolution of the Papal States in 1867. Officials in the United States and Britain, secular governments with majority Protestant populations, questioned the value of securing this relationship with the Vatican, but Roosevelt recognized the political advantage it could give him with Catholic constituencies in key states. The pope may have wanted to link the Vatican's worldview with that of the United States—total opposition to Nazism.

Joseph P. Kennedy, FDR's wealthy backer and chairman of the U.S. Maritime Commission, was accompanying the Vatican emissary. So was the Most Reverend Francis Spellman, who had been sent home from the Vatican and was now the auxiliary bishop of Boston. Spellman and Kennedy were important American Catholics, both destined for bigger things.

The cardinal and his entourage had taken a morning train from New York City, riding in a private car. Bright autumn sun shimmered off the majestic Hudson River as the train wove out of the city, past Sing Sing Prison, and close to the riverbank, where seagulls and ducks were feeding in the Tappan Zee and where residents feared a proposed bridge would damage the wetlands. The Vatican mission arrived at Poughkeepsie, a few miles south of Hyde Park just after noon.

Pacelli had declined a change of clothes offered by Spellman, who like the other accompanying Catholic clergy was dressed in a simple black suit and Roman collar. Pacelli stood out, regaled in his cape, crimson-appointed robes, and large metal crucifix. Roosevelt had sent a White House reception party to the station to pick them up.

The White House reported that the president and the cardinal "discussed American social affairs and their mutual observations of trends in the United States." But in fact, the conversation was far more specific and would have ended badly had Roosevelt not maintained his good humor. He discovered quickly that Pacelli was fixated on Communism.

The president recalled the meeting during a dinner conversation six years later. He described the encounter as a "mental sparring contest," according to Florence Kerr, an administration official who was one of the dinner guests. FDR said he and Pacelli "chewed on that for three days. He [Pacelli] went back to Rome saying that the great danger in America is that it will go communist. I told him it wouldn't . . . I said, I think they are just as apt to go Fascist as they are to go communist." The back-and-forth continued: the president scoffed and the cardinal insisted.

> "The greatest danger in America is that it will go Communist," Pacelli repeated more than once.
> "The great danger in America is that it will go Fascist," FDR replied.
> "No."
> "Yes."
> "No!" Pacelli repeated more forcefully. "Mr. President, you simply do not understand the terrible importance of the Communist movement."
> "You just don't understand the American people," the president replied.

The conversation ended at an impasse, apparently civilly so. By midafternoon, the cardinal was on his train car headed back to New York.

Two days later, after being greeted by thousands of Catholic schoolchildren outside St. Patrick's Cathedral, Pacelli rode to Pier 59 and boarded the Italian liner *Conte di Savoia* for his return trip to Italy.

IN 1937, Pope Pius released *With Deep Anxiety*, his first great assault on Nazism, a papal encyclical that confronted Hitler and his Gestapo. The American and British governments took note. Suddenly, Pope Pius XI appeared to be on the same wavelength as Roosevelt. Officials in Washington and London thought the pope could be engaged in the fight against Hitler, and in particular against Hitler's growing courtship of Mussolini. Even if "the Pope could not push Hitler," one British analyst said, "he could certainly push at Mussolini. He might even be able to push Mussolini away from Hitler."

By 1937, onetime critics, including diplomats and Jewish leaders, praised Pius XI as a leading voice for peace and liberty. The Nazis tried to spread rumors that the pope, born into a traditional Italian family in northern Italy, was actually a Communist and secretly Jewish; they spouted similar nonsense about Roosevelt.

The pope's growing criticism of Hitler may have sparked interest in Washington, but it produced great anxiety in the Vatican, particularly for Cardinal Pacelli. Beyond being considered second to the throne, Pacelli had been groomed all his life to be *papabile*—a future candidate to be pope.

Eugenio was born in 1876, one of four children. His father, Fillippo, a prominent canonical lawyer, eventually became dean of the Vatican Sacra Rota Romana, the Holy See's high court of appeals. His mother, Virginia, had twelve brothers and sisters; two had entered the priesthood and two were nuns. Pacelli clung to his mother, who made sure his upbringing was centered around the church. He spent his childhood in several well-off but modest apartments in central Rome, never more than half an hour's walk from the Vatican. He had served as an altar boy and sometimes put on clerical robes to play-act the role of a priest celebrating Mass. He was sent to Catholic elementary schools and then to a public nonreligious school, where he was an excellent student. He was also a music lover who enjoyed the classics; he played violin and piano in accompaniment of his two sisters.

When he was thirteen, he wrote a straightforward, light-hearted autobiographical profile that described his appearance: "I am of average height. My figure is slender, my face rather pale, my hair chestnut and soft, my eyes black, my nose rather aquiline. I will not say much of my chest, which to be honest, is not robust. Finally, I have a pair of legs that are long and thin, with feet that are hardly small."

He began his religious studies at the Gregorian University, close to the family house, but left the university after a few months for undefined health reasons. His sister later said the ailment involved problems with eating seminary food. After he recovered, he received extraordinary permission to study for the priesthood at home without ever having lived in a seminary. His ordination in 1899 was attended by bishops and even cardinals. It was unusual for a novice to draw such attention, but it shows that even at age twenty-three, he was already on track as a potential *papabile*.

He rose quickly, working his way up from a lower-ranking job at the Vatican Secretariat of State to subsecretary and then secretary of ecclesiastical affairs. He was immediately thrust into diplomat affairs when he was sent to England in 1901 to deliver Pope Leo XIII's condolences for the death of Queen Victoria. He met Winston Churchill on a second trip to London in 1908. At the time, Pacelli was thirty-two, and Churchill, who was thirty-four, had already been a Member of Parliament for eight years.

Pacelli was appointed the pope's official representative to Bavaria in 1917 and then for all of Germany. He remained as the apostolic delegate to Germany until 1929 when Pius XI recalled him to Rome, elevated him to cardinal, and eventually named him secretary of state. Pacelli's time away had given him a passion for all things German. He loved German automobiles, and according to Monsignor Joseph Hurley, who worked for him, "was a devotee of [Richard] Wagner's music—the sturdy, triumphal, surging kind . . . not the softer compositions." He spent summer vacations in Switzerland where he could keep up his fluency in the language. He also had a rather bossy and controversial German housekeeper, Sister Pasqualina Lehnert, who served him for forty years.

Pius and Pacelli had strikingly different backgrounds. The pope came from the north, Pacelli was Roman; Pacelli was tall and gangly, the pope was short and stocky; perhaps most important, the pope was taken to making rash emotional decisions, while Pacelli, the deliberative diplomat, was slow and methodical in his decision-making process.

Pacelli was careful to submit humbly to the pope's wishes, yet he did not always follow those orders exactly. There had been times when he delayed or altered the pope's orders or public statements. Other times, he argued gently and directly with the pope to tone down some of his outbursts against Hitler and Mussolini. He thought it was prudent to not incite retaliation by Hitler or by Mussolini for rash statements.

Despite their contrasting personalities, Pius and Pacelli worked together well. Many at the Vatican said Pius himself realized he was a rash and impetuous leader, and he wanted a cerebral, cautious diplomat at his side, even if he might not heed the advice. The pope did not take much counsel from others, but Pacelli managed to inject his point of view, which most often tried to temper the rough edges of policy, all for what he saw as the good of the Vatican. Many in the church believed the relationship between Pacelli and the pope was based on mutual dependence—the pope recognized that he needed that form of counterbalance to his fiery approach.

Castel Gandolfo, June 26, 1938

At the time when Hitler was taking over Austria and Czechoslovakia and forming his alliance with Mussolini, Pope Pius found himself with few allies among the highest-ranking men surrounding him. His subordinates, especially Cardinal Pacelli, who happened to be a good friend of Ledóchowski, were constantly begging him to temper his anger. The pope's previous encyclical against Nazism in 1937, *With Deep Anxiety*, had provoked attacks on Catholic priests in Germany and almost caused a rupture in relations between the Vatican and the Nazis, much to the dismay of Pacelli and others around him. Every time the church spoke out, it faced a wave of reprisals.

Now Pius intended to go much further with this new encyclical. John LaFarge was to produce a strong statement that would make international headlines. Not only would he fervently reject anti-Semitism, he would challenge other Catholic leaders to speak out and pressure Hitler and Mussolini to curtail their measures against the Jews. Although the pope knew such a statement could bring on new, even stronger attacks against Catholics, which most church leaders feared were too risky, he was willing to go forward and fight Hitler on moral grounds.

As always, the pope was hemmed in by bureaucracy. He wanted LaFarge to work in secrecy, and he might even have placed him in seclusion if he had had the infrastructure to do so on his own. To use LaFarge, Pius was obliged to call in Wlodimir Ledóchowski, who, like Pacelli and most others at the Vatican, had no interest in inciting Hitler.

Pius had always withstood the pressures from the rest of the curia, but now his flagging health made it uncertain that he would have the time and the strength to control those around him. He had summoned LaFarge on his own without Pacelli's involvement even though the secretary of state was at Castel Gandolfo when LaFarge arrived. The pope had avoided telling Ledóchowski ahead of time because he knew how the Jesuit leader would react.

But on Sunday morning, June 26, Pius summoned Ledóchowski to Castel Gandolfo. Pius, who never conducted business on the telephone, was following up on what he promised LaFarge the day before by briefing the Jesuit superior general on the new encyclical. The pope most likely asked Ledóchowski to keep this a secret, even though he knew such a prospect was unlikely considering what a seedbed of gossip the Vatican was.

If Pacelli was the second-most-important person at the Vatican, Ledóchowski ran a close third. As leader of the worldwide Jesuit order—he was known as "the Black Pope," or the superior general, or more commonly, the general—he was by no means a rival to the pontiff, but he was an all-powerful, forceful man in the lives of the Jesuits and all Catholics. Ledóchowski was not a cardinal, and no Jesuit had ever been elevated to the pontificate. He had been superior general since 1915 and had been in Rome almost without break since then, giving him more seniority at the Holy See, in terms of physical presence at least, than even Pope Pius XI.

Pacelli and Ledóchowski were confidants in constant contact with long tenures in the curia, and they were among the most proficient political operators at St. Peter's. While Pacelli was a member of the so-called black nobility of Rome—families that were unofficial courtiers at the Vatican—Ledóchowski was properly a

Polish count. He was born in the Austrian Empire near Vienna in 1866 to Count Anton Ledóchowski, a noble of Polish origin. Count Anton served Emperor Franz Joseph as royal chamberlain, and one of his brothers, Mieczysław, rose to the prominent Vatican rank of cardinal prefect of the Holy Congregation for the Propagation of the Faith.

Ledóchowski's influence on church doctrine was well known. He sometimes sought to change the pontiff's mind on key issues that mattered to him, but his efforts were usually futile. He had asked the pope on several occasions, for example, to be more forceful in condemning Communism when he was criticizing Fascism—as a way of balancing the scales. The pope no longer sought balance; he now believed that Nazism was a greater danger than Communism. This was a major change of perspective not shared by a majority at the Vatican, though it had been recognized for some time by others. As the journalist Dorothy Thompson had said, after being thrown out of Nazi Germany for speaking her mind: "National Socialism is more menacing to Catholicism than Communism. For whereas Communism is atheistic, National Socialism is Satanic."

Ledóchowski had lobbied the pope more than once to link Jews with the spread of Communism. "Perhaps your Holiness would like to make known to the world this terrible danger, one that becomes every day more threatening," he had said to the pope prior to the 1937 publication of the pope's encyclical *Divinis Redemptoris*, "The Promise of a Redeemer," which attacked Communism. The encyclical was the pope's strongest statement opposing Marxism and was issued a few days after the more controversial anti-Nazi tract, *With Deep Anxiety*, which set the stage for future criticism of Nazism as well. The two encyclicals had a certain symmetry in dealing with the world's two totalitarian systems; issuing them so close together perhaps assuaged Vatican dissenters such as Ledóchowski who were more rabidly anti-Communist than concerned about the Nazis. But the pope had no intention of using the anti-Communist encyclical as Ledóchowski intended—as a groundless diatribe against Judaism.

Divinis Redemptoris did criticize Communism on grounds that it "strips man of his liberty, robs human personality of all its dignity, and removes all the moral restraints that check the eruptions of blind impulse." But Ledóchowski insisted on changes once more. Your Holiness, he told the pope, such a strong message on Communism should contain a mention of what he saw as the international conspiracy of Jews, Masons, and Bolsheviks. "Though the atheist propaganda from Moscow becomes ever more intense, nonetheless the world press, in the hands of the Jews, hardly makes a reference, just as it ignores the crimes committed in Russia."

"For not only were all the intellectual fathers of Communism Jewish," Ledóchowski said in his letter to the pope, "but the Communist movement in Russia was staged by Jews, and even now, if one digs deeply one finds that the primary authors of Communist propaganda, though perhaps not always openly, are Jews."

These fraudulent charges had been circulated widely by anti-Semites inside and outside the Catholic Church. The pope challenged these written corrections and in several places penciled in the word "Verify!" Prove it, he was saying. Ledóchowski had no factual responses, and the pope rejected these attempts to change the text.

Similarly, the pope turned down Pacelli's requests that the Vatican be more supportive of Generalissimo Francisco Franco in Spain. Pacelli saw Spain as a clear confrontation between good— the Nazi and Fascist-backed Nationalists—and bad—the Soviet-supported Spanish government. Pius did not see the dispute in such stark terms—he never accepted or trusted Franco and questioned Franco's ties to the Nazis.

The pope even considered a dialogue proposed by the leader of the French Communist Party about creating a united front against the Nazis and Fascists. The pope told a French bishop that it might be a good idea "to take up that invitation, not of course so that we might be drawn toward the Communists, but rather so that we can draw the Communist proffered hand toward us." Not surprisingly, Cardinal Pacelli was against such a dialogue and worked behind the scenes to block it. Conservatives within the Vatican saw Pius's interest in this dialogue as evidence that the pope was losing his grip on reality.

DURING THE June 26 meeting, Pius told Ledóchowski about his meeting with LaFarge and the new encyclical, and Ledóchowski immediately set out to devise a strategy for dealing with LaFarge. He said he would help LaFarge, and even appeared to be doing so, but he was certainly against issuing the document, and his strategy would be to manage the process. Ledóchowski had once told his friend Cardinal Edward Mooney about his methods for manipulating the Jesuits beneath him. "Jesuits obeyed as long as they got few orders; and none against their grain," he told Mooney. A "wise superior can get obedience provided he does not violate a man's love of reasonable independence."

Along the lines of that thinking, LaFarge would think he was acting as an independent agent. Ledóchowski would encourage LaFarge as he prepared the encyclical, but the superior general would eventually control the final product.

LaFarge would not be difficult to manage. All Jesuits had an ingrained sense of obedience, and Ledóchowski had already met LaFarge and lectured him about his responsibilities as a Jesuit journalist. Specifically he had discussed *America* magazine's mission. Ledóchowski directed the magazine's political commentary to focus on traditional church teachings and preaching. As a traditionalist, he expected and demanded adherence to the ancient precepts of the church. *America*, he felt, had the sacred responsibility to explain current events in terms of the church: "People look to us for the interpretation of what is going on," he said, "what religion has to say concerning events." *America* must not be a journal of individual opinion—rather it should express the viewpoint of the Society of Jesus, the Jesuits.

The message was that Jesuits in the United States owed their full fealty to the Jesuit Curia in Rome, to Ledóchowski himself, and thence to the Vatican. LaFarge was evidently cut in the classic Jesuit mold: an obedient, earnest fellow who would do what he was told.

Ledóchowski summoned LaFarge to meet with him the next morning, June 27. LaFarge was unaware of the political maelstroms and intrigues swirling around the Vatican. He was relieved that the pope had told Ledóchowski about the assignment. LaFarge was already starstruck and simply in awe that he was meeting with the Jesuit general. He was also intimidated and fearful. Ledóchowski had a reputation that extended all the way back to New York. Even from afar on West 108th Street in Manhattan, LaFarge had gotten word that the seventy-one-year-old Jesuit superior general could be moody and was not to be trifled with.

"It was fortunately one of his good days, and he was most lively and spoke most entertainingly and he has the wonderful gift of making you feel at ease at once," LaFarge wrote after that first meeting. "Indeed, I had to pinch myself several times to realize I was actually talking to the [leader] himself."

In this second meeting, as with the first, LaFarge was disarmed. Ledóchowski was quite good-humored when he greeted the American and said the pope had spoken with him about the encyclical. Once put at ease, LaFarge told the Jesuit superior that he felt overwhelmed by the assignment from the pope. If he had a hint of something of this magnitude was about to take place,

LaFarge added, "nothing would have persuaded me to go to Rome, much less meet with the pope." Ledóchowski told him not to worry: "nothing to do, but to go through with the whole thing."

That said, LaFarge identified a number of concerns. First, he told the general he wanted to review background materials in the Vatican archives—prior declarations and positions taken by the Vatican on racism and the Nazis. Not a problem, Ledóchowski told him. He made sure LaFarge would have every facility open to him.

Next, LaFarge was worried about the intense heat of the Roman summers. He much preferred working in a mild climate, preferably Paris. A very good idea, Ledóchowski said, and accepted that proposition as well.

Finally, LaFarge said the pope asked him to work quickly. Given the short amount of time, he asked if the superior general could provide him with an assistant to work on the encyclical. Ledóchowski assigned two Jesuits—one would be Gustave Desbuquois, who LaFarge had met in Paris, the leader of the French Jesuit social organization, Action Populaire. The other, Ledóchowski decided, was to be Gustav Gundlach. "The two Guses," as they became known, were discreet and both had prior experience in preparing such documents. Ledóchowski knew both men's work and also knew they could be controlled.

Charming though he might have been, Ledóchowski effectively used his skills to oversee the project. He discussed the need for secrecy and speed. Among other things, if LaFarge's work was ever made public, "every government in Europe would have people in 24 hours at the Vatican, urging the expression of their ideas." All the more reason for LaFarge to go to Paris. He was to leave as soon as possible. Any questions, any doubts should be forwarded back directly to Ledóchowski at the Vatican.

LaFarge mentioned that the Sunday-morning edition of

Osservatore Romano had as usual listed the pope's activities the previous day in a column on the left side of the front page. One could read in small type under audiences: "Giovanni LaFarge, SJ." His meeting with the pope was no secret—only the subject discussed was closely guarded. Ledóchowski suggested that LaFarge use a cover story—he would say he had decided to work on revisions of *Interracial Justice* and would be writing and conducting interviews in Paris.

After the meeting, LaFarge was given access to pertinent documents and diplomatic communications at the Vatican. It was a rather quick review, but long enough to note that political affairs and church relations with Italy and Germany were worse than he expected. Probably out of a sense of excitement or overenthusiasm, he broke almost immediately with the pledge to remain silent. He wrote a letter to Francis Talbot, his editor in New York, that described the situation and discussed his delayed return home, adding that the story must be concealed.

"If people get nosey, you can say I am working on a possible second edition of my book, collecting notes, seeing people. Etc. That is generally true—and telling them that here."

Ledóchowski could consider the meeting with LaFarge as a success. He had followed his precept by making LaFarge think he was getting everything he wanted—full freedom of action. He had established a trusted relationship, and he had employed two known and reliable cowriters who would not stray too far from existing Vatican dogma. And LaFarge's request to work away from Rome was easy to accept. Ledóchowski was probably much happier to have LaFarge at a distance, not able or likely to approach the pope until the work was finished. This would limit the number of people at the Vatican who might find out about the encyclical or with whom LaFarge might be able to communicate. Ledóchowski could interpose himself between Pius XI and his American ghost writer with hopes of toning down the pope's recently increasingly virulent rhetoric.

LaFarge thought he was being given the best possible structure in which to work on one of the most important documents he might ever write. It remained to be seen what the product would be, but LaFarge told a friend that Pius had said: "Remember, you are writing this encyclical for me, not for Ledóchowski." Even so, LaFarge put his faith in the Jesuit leader, not only out of obedience, but also because of the experiences he had in the past with authority figures.

"I had a curious sensation that I was talking to my own father," LaFarge recalled about his conversation with the pope. "His gestures were singularly like those of my father, particularly the characteristic one of the joined index and middle finger raised and waved paternally in the air. Little turns of expression remind me of Father, and there was the same atmosphere, as it were, of conversation." It was easy to understand the comparison between the Holy Father and LaFarge's real father, who now had been dead for more than twenty-seven years. The elder LaFarge had been an inspiring but a somewhat frightening presence in his son's life, and a person LaFarge wanted to please and impress. And now, no one other than the pope was as exalted, awe-inspiring, in John LaFarge's religious life.

But LaFarge did not see Ledóchowski as a father figure, but more as mothering influence. He said the Jesuit superior's "wiry vivacious person reminded me oddly" of Katharine Drexel, a prominent nun and friend in Philadelphia.

LaFarge, nevertheless, left his meeting with the certainty that his Jesuit superior would "facilitate" communications with the pontiff. On June 27, LaFarge packed his bags, bade farewell to McCormick at the Gregorian University, and took a train first to Geneva and then onward to Paris to begin a mission that seemed simple on its face but was to have moral and political repercussions he couldn't imagine.

CHAPTER SIX

A Democratic Response

Paris, July 19, 1938

O N JULY 19, about three weeks after John LaFarge arrived in Paris to begin his secret work on behalf of Pope Pius, he took a break for the arrival of Britain's King George VI.

LaFarge had been invited with several other priests to watch the ceremony from a fifth-floor balcony overlooking the Champs-Elysées. The king rode by in an open black limousine. He wore the blue-gray, full dress uniform of the Royal Air Force and was seated next to French president Albert Lebrun, with Queen Elizabeth and Lebrun's wife trailing behind. Spahi cavalry—French Arab regiments—created a phalanx around them, led by that old hero of the Great War, Marshall Philippe Pétain. Soldiers lined the streets, a military band played, and a dirigible maneuvered overhead close to the Arc de Triomphe.

"We had a splendid view," LaFarge wrote afterward. "It was a wonderful sight, the *Spahis* magnificently mounted, those from Tunis being dressed in red, and those from Morocco in black . . .

The Army was idolized by the people and the crowd was cheerful and in good humor. Periscopes were on sale everywhere."

Reporters compared the event and safety concerns to the spectacle Mussolini had laid out for Hitler in Rome two months earlier. Despite the joyous reaction of the French, tens of thousands of security officers fanned out across Paris. "Two hours before their arrival, troops virtually took over Paris," reported the United Press. "Army tanks rumbled through the boulevards and took up commanding positions in the Place de Concorde and the Champs Elysee, barring all traffic."

LaFarge doubted that the pomp and the show of democracy meant anything in the face of Nazi war preparations.

"I found my French friends in a state of political optimism. As for Hitler, they explained to me, there was really nothing to worry about," LaFarge wrote. "*Nous sommes si calme*," people kept telling him. "But when you have heard people tell you four or five times a day how calm they are, you wonder just how deep is that tranquility?"

Coinciding with the royal visit, the United States had convened an international conference on refugees in Evian-les-Bains, 350 miles southeast of Paris on Lake Geneva. By now, at least 150,000 German Jews had fled Germany, only a fraction of those teeming to leave Europe. President Roosevelt, the prime mover, sent his friend Myron Taylor, a respected businessman, as the U.S. representative. "A forced migration is taking place and the time has come when governments . . . must act promptly and effectively," Taylor said in an ardent appeal to the thirty-two countries attending the conference.

It became clear that Roosevelt, facing anti-Semitism at home, expected others to take in Jewish refugees. No country provided substantive help to the Jews.

Hitler mocked the United States and the other participants

sarcastically for claiming to have "such deep sympathy for these criminals," the Jews being expelled from Germany and Austria. World opinion, he said, was "oozing sympathy for the poor, tormented people, but remaining hard and obdurate when it comes to helping them."

The pope was disturbed by the weak response to the Evian refugee conference. He asked American Catholic leaders to discuss the prospects for resettlement of Jews with U.S. officials in Washington. Meanwhile, he focused on his own campaign. He would not wait for the encyclical before lashing out against anti-Semitism.

LAFARGE WAS WORKING intermittently on the pope's encyclical. Early in July, he had decided to take a series of trips outside Paris to clear his head and to take time to understand what the pope wanted him to do. He visited friends and relatives and traveled to hallowed battlefields of the last war. The United States had been France's great protector when it entered World War I and helped beat back the German army. More than sixteen million soldiers and civilians died on all sides in the Great War; twenty million were wounded. LaFarge visited Reims, which symbolized the war's madness and the carnage. The cathedral at Reims had been rebuilt with the help of the American philanthropist John Rockefeller. "It is not well to be too reflective," he wrote in a letter home. "Not well to let the mind rove still further," LaFarge wrote, "where almost under the spires of the cathedral American boys lie buried by the thousands side by side with German and French lads and many another from other lands, and that freezes the soul still with its silence crying to deaf humanity."

LaFarge saw the rededication of the cathedral as progress overshadowed by a new round of human folly. "Better to thank God that with a thousand reasons for grief and regret, France at least has the one great thing, she has liberty, narrow liberty, if you wish, liberty that limps. But still liberty for the Church to live . . . liberty to build a new France not patterned upon the old. . . ." But for how long?

After visiting Reims and World War I battlefields, he visited relatives on his father's side whom he had met thirty-five years earlier when he was a seminary student. He stayed at the old Manor House where his father had lived for a time as a young man in the village of Ploujean in Brittany. His brother Grant had made the same journey three years earlier, and, LaFarge wrote in his memoir, they both had the same experience of "suddenly finding a hundred reminders of home in such a remote part of the world. They had laid on my table a big box of family papers and documents. In the shimmering summer evening, I read them until long after midnight. I found Father's old sketchbook made in Brittany the year before he came back to the United States and became acquainted with Mother."

John LaFarge the son, the youngest of nine children, remembered his father as a distant presence when he was growing up in New England and New York City at the turn of the twentieth century. "I was never part of my father's early life at home," he recalled, "and had never known him as directly and personally as had my two older brothers, Grant and Bancel. It was Bancel in many ways who took Father's place as a parent, playing the role with me that a young father might assume with his children."

John's brothers taught him about sailing, and his youth was dedicated to plying the cliffs and coves of Narragansett Bay, close to their home in Newport. "The background of my boyhood was the sea," he recalled. "I would stroll down to the western end of the beach to watch the vast heaving waves under the moonlight."

When LaFarge was quite young, his mother told him that his father "does not look properly after us. He means well but nevertheless I am at times forgotten, and there are times when I must turn to Almighty God for help." LaFarge became his mother's friend and partner, he recalled, and shared "her problems, her anxieties and heartaches. I felt manly and protective."

The elder LaFarge was an eccentric bohemian and a prominent man in the arts. He was an influential muralist, designer of church mosaics and stained glass, and was one of the seven charter members of the American Academy of Arts and Letters. LaFarge the artist was a difficult person to know, all the more because he suffered in middle age from lead poisoning that left him chronically ill and often bedridden.

One of young John's earliest memories of his father involved going with his mother down to the harbor at Newport, Rhode Island, in 1891 when he was eleven years old. The elder LaFarge was returning with Henry Adams from an extensive voyage to the South Pacific. "I was glad to know that I really had a father in fact, since my picture of him before that time had been quite indefinite."

By 1938, LaFarge still ached to learn about the man he really didn't know. One of his father's signature works was the mural *The Ascension of Our Lord* above the altar of the Episcopal Church of the Ascension in Greenwich Village, not far from the studio on West Tenth Street where young John had visited him. Visitors to the church were spellbound and came just to gaze at LaFarge's creation. A critical appraisal in the *New York Times* said that LaFarge "has shown that we possess at least one artist [in America who is] the peer, if not the superior of the best workmen . . . Composition, drawing and proportions are masterly."

Henry Adams, in his autobiographical *The Education of Henry Adams*, described John LaFarge as one of his closest confidants and an important and delightful influence in his life and said he was "quite the most interesting person we knew." The book won the Pulitzer Prize in 1919, the year after Adams died and nine years after the elder LaFarge had died. "To LaFarge," Adams wrote, "eccentricity meant convention; a mind really eccentric never betrayed it. True eccentricity was a tone—a shade—a nuance—and the finer the tone, the truer the eccentricity. Of course all artists hold more or less the same point of view in their art, but few carry it into daily life, and often the contrast is excessive between their art and their talk."

As LaFarge read these words, he recalled that the closest he and his father had ever been was during the several months John had spent with him in New York City. Young John retained a much closer relationship with his mother until her death in 1926. But he did carry something of those days with his father. The elder LaFarge's life work focused on arts that touched on the spirit and influenced the spirit of his son. The young LaFarge developed an impressive knowledge of the arts in his own right and had an expert's eye for stained glass, sacred art, and architecture. He was not eccentric by nature, as Henry Adams had described his father, unless he qualified as being the only member of his immediate family to enter the priesthood. And by becoming a Jesuit, he was dedicated to service and, unlike his father, he was following an uncommon, quiet path. As St. Ignatius would have it, the manner of a Jesuit "was ordinary," not eccentric.

Bancel, who was fifteen years older than John, had followed their father's track of producing sacred art. And now, with all the reminiscing about his early life, LaFarge received troubling news from home. Bancel, who had recently completed a stained-glass panel at St. Aidan's Church in New Haven, was ill. The memories washed over LaFarge, and more than once he wished he had never been selected to do the pope's work. He was homesick.

BY JULY 19, LaFarge had established a routine for working on the encyclical, though melancholy and self-doubt pervaded his time in

Paris. His loneliness and thoughts about his family influenced his decisions. He referred frequently to moving quickly and getting home before the end of the summer, but that did not seem likely.

He set up a desk and living quarters on the Left Bank with the Jesuit community he had visited two months earlier, at the magazine *Études*, the French Jesuit equivalent of LaFarge's own magazine, *America*. He had told Father D'Ouince, the head of the *Études* community, what he was doing in general terms, and he was allowed to come and go and work freely.

They worked long days, and often into the night. LaFarge complained of aches and pains and began to look increasingly gaunt and appeared to be losing weight. He needed distractions to alleviate the tension and pressure. Cultural life in Paris was perfect for that—it was more vibrant than ever, a last bastion as countries closed down to the east and Spain remained embroiled in its bloody civil war. French art and especially French magazines were rising in popularity.

LaFarge and his fellow Jesuit writers set up a working arrangement for a hundred-page document, which LaFarge wanted to finish by the end of August. He planned to take it down to the Vatican himself, perhaps make a side trip to Spain, and then to return home.

He and his colleagues got down to work and established ground rules for meeting the pope's expectations. Pius XI had told LaFarge to meld "racism as myth" into an attack on the Nazi racial policies. The pope told LaFarge that his own book, *Interracial Justice*, should be the blueprint for the encyclical. The book proclaimed that the call for justice and human rights is universal, whether for blacks or for Jews. The preface had even quoted the pope: "all the institutions of public and social life must be imbued with the spirit of justice, and this justice must be truly operative. It must build up a juridical and social order able to pervade all economic activity."

LaFarge added that "the Negro-white problem is only one of a multitude of similar interracial problems in this country, and, indeed, throughout the world." There was no question that the pope's argument against anti-Semitism was based on these same principles.

The German Jesuit Gustav Gundlach became LaFarge's chief collaborator. He knew the ins and outs of the Vatican and had worked on earlier encyclicals, including *Quadragesimo Anno*, which was written in 1931 and warned against the dangers of unbridled capitalism and the dangers of Communism. The other man, Gustave Desbuquois, was assigned by Ledóchowski and took a far less active role. Desbuquois served primarily as the translator of the encyclical into French.

LaFarge and Gundlach divided their labors. LaFarge naturally would deal with the heart of the matter—racism and anti-Semitism—while Gundlach would handle the boilerplate, context, and theological setting for the piece. LaFarge would do what the pope intended and be his alter ego in producing the document. But LaFarge concluded that "a certain degree of historical and doctrinal context was necessary" and put Gundlach in charge of bringing that to the document. The clear focus, LaFarge said, was a declaration about "nationalism, racism and the Jewish question" and a practical consideration of the church's role at this moment in history.

Just as LaFarge and Gundlach were settling into Paris, the Vatican newspaper, *Osservatore Romano*, referred to an "unpublished document" that would outline the pope's view on Nazi and Fascist racist policies. This was the pope's way of telegraphing that he was awaiting LaFarge's draft of the encyclical.

LaFarge and Gundlach hammered out the details—exactly how much history was required, how much Catholic dogma. LaFarge was confident about what he had to say on the central matter of racism, but he saw himself a novice compared to his helpers, who were not new to working on major church declarations. He kept his focus on racism and conceded the context to Gundlach, whose most important contribution was to serve as LaFarge's guide in understanding the labyrinths of Vatican power. He had dealt with Ledóchowski and knew the Jesuit leader would try to interpose himself as a gatekeeper to the pope.

Gundlach, who had been a progressive sociology professor and political analyst in Germany during the Weimar Republic, believed the draft should describe the underpinnings of church teachings and how they declared that racism, and therefore anti-Semitism, is based on fakery and myth. LaFarge's American point of view led him to simple language that would echo the Declaration of Independence's pronouncement that "all men are created equal."

Gundlach also understood church doctrine concerning Judaism and anti-Semitism. Though international Jewish leaders celebrated significant progress under Pius XI, the church's history on anti-Semitism was sordid, and Gundlach was not immune to the prejudice. In 1930, Gundlach had identified two types of anti-Semitism, one based on racism, the other on economics and politics. That second form of anti-Semitism boiled down to the idea that Jews were overbearing and overextended their abilities in government, commerce, and culture, thereby damaging Christian society.

Though Gundlach maintained that racist attacks on Judaism were unacceptable and "unchristian," he wrote that "the second type of anti-Semitism is permissible when it combats, by moral and legal means, a truly harmful influence of the Jewish segment of the population in the areas of economy, politics, theater, cinema, the press, science, and art." This was a repulsive concept, but it reflected the times and spoke to the false caricature, held by many Catholics and other Christians in Europe and the United States, that Jews were too "crafty" in business, were morally questionable, and, in the extreme, were to blame for Communism and for killing Jesus Christ.

Nevertheless, three years before Hitler took power, Gundlach had written that "the Church has always protected Jews against anti-Semitic practices proceeding from false jealousy, false Christian zeal or from economic necessity."

The church had promoted anti-Semitism for centuries, but now the pope was taking a major step and expected LaFarge to take the lead. A few weeks into the project, LaFarge thought things were going well. Writing an encyclical meant creating a document with historic dimensions, one that spoke about a specific concern of the church and thereby the pope's concern, but also to create a theological stance for the church that would flow from previous teachings.

LaFarge was sure that he could focus on the substance, but there were always moments of self-doubt. "Every now and then," he wrote, "a chill goes up my spine. But I believe it will work out."

In such a moment of doubt, LaFarge wrote to Talbot and asked how he could presume to speak in the voice of Pope Pius XI. His editor replied in a number of letters over the summer and told LaFarge that he must not consider himself inferior in any way to the scholarly Gundlach. The pope had singled out LaFarge, not Gundlach, to write the encyclical. The pope knew what he was doing and had made the proper choice.

"You are the one best equipped to do this work," Talbot wrote. "You have been preparing for this topic throughout years; you have probably read more on it, thought more on it, analyzed it more, solved it best. You have the supra-national mind. You have worked out already the broad principles, either explicitly or implicitly, in your writing and in your thoughts. You are most familiar with the upheavals of the modern nations, with their ideologies, with their acts, with their aims, and you know the history of the fallen nations."

In the end, LaFarge's growing friendship with Gundlach made the work easier. Gundlach took a liking to the American Jesuit and tried to explain to LaFarge the swirling politics surrounding the Vatican. He told LaFarge that a number of people were against the pope issuing a new, controversial declaration at this time. Gundlach believed that the best way to protect the document from these naysayers was to base it on the most rigorous church teachings and dogma.

Finally LaFarge and Gundlach agreed that the encyclical would have two sections, divided roughly in half. The first would be historic and theoretical and largely written by Gundlach. The second half would be written by LaFarge. Even though the writing group got along amiably, there were still two camps. On one side, Gundlach was verbose and the declared intellectual. Heinrich Bacht, another German Jesuit, was brought in to translate the work into Latin. Bacht appreciated Gundlach's work and believed Gundlach was the most important contributor to the project.

"As I remember it," Bacht recalled in a letter years afterward, "all the work of elaboration fell on Father Gundlach, if only because the good Father LaFarge was absolutely not an 'intellectual' capable of that kind of work."

Bacht's opinion of LaFarge was based in part on a clash of cultures. The European style was ponderous and woven with complex theological syntax. LaFarge tended toward more simple American prose. *Interracial Justice* and his writings in *American* magazine were learned, well-written pieces of work. If being a European "intellectual" meant being obtuse and indecipherable, Gundlach certainly qualified. His writing was based on verbosity; why should a word or two suffice when many more could be used?

"If we go back to the beginnings of the period in which we now live," he wrote in the draft encyclical, "and follow its gradual development up to the present day, when it reaches its culmination, we find that originally there was a spiritual attitude entirely opposite to the one that now prevails. Then, reason felt sure of itself, to the point of believing itself exempt from error; it claimed to have discovered the true principles of every kind of knowledge."

Any good editor could have boiled that down to: "Modern life, especially the advent of the industrial revolution, has brought changes in social organization and in the way people relate to their spiritual lives."

Gundlach also spent pages on such things as, "*Die Mechanistisch-atomistischen Auffassung der menschlichen Gesellschaft*," which was just as ponderous in the English translation, or any language: "The Mechanistic-Atomistic Conception of Human Society." He followed that with the "Mechanistic-*Totalitarian* Conception of Human Society."

LaFarge did not edit Gundlach's prose. He was more focused on keeping everyone working happily and speedily, knowing that his own contribution was the closest to what the pope had asked, especially since none of the others had ever met privately with Pius XI. But this spirit of camaraderie did not stop Gundlach from criticizing LaFarge's writing for being "too pragmatic, not sufficiently principled."

If nothing else, LaFarge's writing was as direct as his journalism usually was; it was neither theoretical nor difficult. Introducing the theme of racism, he said simply this: "Men of good will should do everything they can to put an end to all unmistakably defamatory and discriminatory distinctions in public life, so that relations among social groups may be regulated solely by interracial justice and charity." He was obviously borrowing from his writings about racism in the United States. Although some of the Europeans took LaFarge's style as being far from intellectual, whatever that might have been, LaFarge disregarded the criticism.

At times the disagreements became a bit heated, and Desbuquois, who was spending more time on his own writings and his social-welfare organization in Paris, called in another French Jesuit, Father Barde (no one remembered his full name), to sit in on some of the editorial sessions with LaFarge and Gundlach. But Barde could not take more than two meetings and never returned. One Jesuit recounted afterward that Barde "found Gundlach's philosophical considerations too abstract and unsuited to the theme." Somehow LaFarge managed to keep the relations friendly and balanced, often inviting the others out for social events or breaks to interrupt the monotony.

LEDÓCHOWSKI CAUSED a stir and a delay when he sent LaFarge an urgent letter on July 17 about the need for secrecy. He had gotten word that LaFarge had been speaking about his papal mission with priests other than those he was working with. "You have probably seen that the Holy Father already alluded to the matter [in public]," Ledóchowski wrote, "but that does not prevent us from continuing to be very reserved about it. Follow this rule now and also after the work, with God's help, is finished, otherwise we might have serious problems."

LaFarge had written to two or three priests in New York about the project and several others in Rome. He assumed he could trust all of them, but he was frightened by Ledóchowski's warning. He may not have cautioned the people in New York about spreading the news. LaFarge also suspected that Talbot had confided in the Jesuit provincial superior in New York, Joseph A. Murphy, who might have mentioned it to Ledóchowski. Embarrassed and mortified, LaFarge dipped into his meager funds and sent a cable at six dollars a word to New York on July 21:

TALBOT SEVERE WARNING RECEIVED ON
PADLOCK CANNOT INFORM EVEN MURPHY
IF YOU INFORMED HIM URGE HIM NOT TO
INTIMATE SAME . . .

He signed the cable "Pilgrim," the pseudonym he sometimes used for unsigned columns in *America*. But the message had an air of intrigue and sounded exactly the way he didn't want to sound— like a person using a code name, sending a cryptic message. He feared that it was the kind of message that would likely be read by others.

Ledóchowski, the general, also told LaFarge to stop talking about his work on the telephone; in the future, any communications were to be handled face-to-face. Ledóchowski's American assistant, Zacheus Maher, was on his way to Paris to get a firsthand report on progress.

LaFarge was excited by the cloak-and-dagger aspect to the project. It meant the encyclical was significant, and he was an important player. Gundlach and Desbuquois had dealt with the secrecy surrounding previous encyclicals, especially the case of the pope's *With Deep Anxiety* anti-Nazi message in 1937. That encyclical had caught the Nazi machine by surprise, and the pope had smuggled his message into Germany for dissemination. But even with all the precautions, the Gestapo had known something was up and had been able to interdict some copies before the document was read from the pulpit in several parishes.

The German Foreign Office included the Vatican on its list of diplomatic espionage targets. At least as early as 1936, an organization at the Foreign Ministry known as Pers Z (Z Section of the Personnel and Administrative Branch) was monitoring Vatican transmission and message traffic. It had succeeded in deciphering some codes at the Vatican and other states, including Italy, Britain, and the United States.

Spying was nothing new at the Vatican, and it was sometimes conducted by priests themselves. Any phone line to or from the Vatican could be intercepted. Italy had been tracking church communications all along, an easy task since the Vatican switchboard, post office, trains, and all other means of conveyance passed through Italian hands. The Mussolini government was adept at tapping phones. Regular mail was useless for sending sensitive information to the Vatican. The Vatican regularly sent coded messages, but there was no guarantee they would arrive at their destination. Coded messages sent by wireless were a possibility, but such communications were also vulnerable to being deciphered.

Pius XI had already had other experience with secret operations. He had been using secret communications since the 1920s, when he began clandestine efforts to support church activities in the Soviet Union. He had ordered a French priest to infiltrate Moscow in the 1920s. The priest traveled undercover and established contact with Catholic clergy who were threatened and repressed by the new Soviet government.

The Vatican also had its own encryption apparatus, but its ciphers were eventually penetrated by Germany and Italy. Officials discovered the break and issued new ciphers to church offices around the world in an effort to restore secure communication. The problem was that, over time, both Italy and Germany were able to develop agents among Catholic priests and inserted them in key positions. Italy was successful in using priests inside the Vatican as conduits for information. They apparently were midranking prelates, rather than cardinals and bishops, and their names remained hidden behind code names and anonymous reports.

Hitler's best human intelligence on the Vatican may have come from its agents within the German Catholic Church. The German security branch, SD (Sicherheitsdienst) had been embarrassed by the pope's ability to sneak the 1937 encyclical into the country. By the end of 1938, Nazi security forces had penetrated the German Catholic Church, using agents and electronic surveillance.

Gundlach gave LaFarge the background on all this. But he also explained to LaFarge that Ledóchowski's warning about secrecy was more a way of exerting control. The pope's call for secrecy certainly was about keeping the news about the encyclical away from the Germans and the Italians, but he also wanted to prevent the details from spreading in the Vatican. In this case, the pope had not gone through the usual channels and had summoned LaFarge privately. Even Cardinal Pacelli had been kept uninformed.

LaFarge's decision to work in Paris made it more difficult for outsiders to track the progress, content, even the existence of his new declaration against anti-Semitism. But the pope's own leak also made things difficult. News and anticipation of an upcoming encyclical, on the other hand, would impede any effort by Ledóchowski to delay and suppress it.

Now suddenly, after recommending that LaFarge work swiftly, the Jesuit superior general seemed to be changing tack. Ledóchowski told LaFarge that speed was not always the primary concern. "All these things cannot be achieved within a month," he wrote in a letter. "And anyway, it is not appropriate for you to leave before the work is finished."

LaFarge had told his superior that he might be finished by mid-August and that he hoped to leave for home in early September. Ledóchowski said that was impossible. LaFarge had no intention of leaving before the work was finished, though he was aching to go home. However, in retrospect, he regretted that he had not analyzed Ledóchowski's motivations more carefully.

Did Ledóchowski want to keep the encyclical secret from foreign meddlers, Fascist and Nazi agents, or did he want to prevent it from ever being released? Perhaps Ledóchowski was trying to stall, knowing the pope had a worsening heart ailment.

Gundlach occasionally raised the suspicion that Ledóchowski and Pacelli wanted to temper the church's vehemence toward Nazism and Fascism—they were acting as gatekeepers between the pope and the rest of the world. This had nothing to do with foreign spies—it had to do with Vatican politics.

Gundlach had also received a tip that the Gestapo and other Nazi intelligence agencies had been tracking him since at least April 1, when Gundlach had denounced Hitler in a broadcast on Vatican Radio. The broadcast, authorized by the Vatican, criticized the invasion of Austria and the behavior of the Viennese Church led by Cardinal Innitzer. Gundlach was now persona non grata in Nazi territory and had been warned that he faced arrest if he returned to Germany.

"The whole time we worked on this 'secret project,'" recalled Father Heinrich Bacht, "we were gripped by the fear that the Gestapo would try something, because it had been keeping an eye on Gundlach ever since his famous radio broadcast; in any case people said at the time that there was a quasi-official Gestapo office in Paris."

CHAPTER SEVEN

In the Heat of the Summer

Rome, July 29, 1938

IN MID-JULY, BENITO Mussolini published a study by a group of Fascist Italian scientists that purportedly said that Italians, like Germans, are "Aryans" and must be protected from contamination by other ethnic groups—Jews. Fascist commentators concluded that this meant intermarriage between Jews and non-Jewish Italians would pollute the race and should be banned.

Pope Pius fired back immediately and attacked these Fascist policies, labeling them replications of the institutional anti-Semitism in Germany. The pope denounced Mussolini's so-called scientific study as apostasy—abandonment of religion—and called on all Catholics to reject racism.

"We should ask ourselves why Italy has an unfortunate need to imitate Germany in promulgating laws against Jews," the pope said in a speech in Castel Gandolfo. "We should say that human beings are first of all one grand and sole race, one large and sole generated and generating, living family. In this sense, humanity is one sole, universal Catholic race."

The words could have come out of John LaFarge's book on racism. The pope not only trashed Mussolini's grand plan, but he also implied that the Axis of equals, Italy and Germany marching together, was a fraud. Italy was merely imitating Germany.

The pope's criticism hit home and had pushed Mussolini over the edge, causing him to issue an impromptu rebuttal in every newspaper in Italy and making sure it was printed with blaring headlines. He declared that Fascism was the way of the future, for all of Italy, for all time, and added, "To say that Fascism has imitated anyone or anything is simply absurd."

Mussolini's anger was understandable. He knew these criticisms would be taken seriously because the pope's standing as a moral force elevated him as a significant, natural rival among the Italian people.

Mussolini claimed he had invented his own form of anti-Semitism that had nothing to do with Nazi Germany. After that, Jews were banned from the Fascist Party, and Mussolini became dyspeptic over the "Jewish vermin" around him.

"Enemies . . . reptiles," Mussolini complained to his mistress, Clara Petacci. She recorded in her diary that he said: "I have been a racist since 1921. I don't know why they think I'm imitating Hitler. We must give Italians a sense of race."

Few Italians understood why Mussolini was suddenly lashing out like this. The pope's original criticism appeared only in *Osservatore Romano* and on Vatican Radio. Throughout the summer, the pope continued to berate the Fascists promptly with each outrage he saw. But his words were confined to the Vatican newspaper, which Mussolini had banned outside the walls of St. Peter's. So the pope's complaints reached an increasingly irate audience of one. And Mussolini fumed every time the pope issued a new proclamation.

Cardinal Pacelli, the secretary of state, worried that the rising tension between Mussolini and Pope Pius would lead to a rupture and a scuttling of the 1929 living arrangement between the Vatican and the government. Members of Pacelli's appeasement camp did not want to pick a fight with Mussolini over his anti-Jewish legislation. They had enough power to publish a report in *Osservatore Romano* on August 12 that said the pope had not intended to mock Italian racial laws or to say that Italy was imitating Nazi Germany. The pope, the newspaper implied, would never involve himself in politics.

Pius, however, could not be restrained. Several days later, he launched another salvo and ordered his subordinates to inform Mussolini that "if he wants to kill off the Holy Father, he is using efficient methods. But the Holy Father will first make it known to the world how the Catholic Religion and the Holy Father have been treated in Italy."

U.S. ambassador William Phillips reported back to Washington that the pope had stepped up his attacks on Mussolini and Hitler to a level that did potentially threaten church-state relations. These reports benefited from insights by Monsignor Joseph Hurley, the embassy's insider at the Vatican. Hurley told the ambassador that "the pope would not retract from his position."

Ambassador Phillips sent a report to Washington, saying the pope had declared "in the strongest language which I have known him to use, his denunciation of this racial purification move."

Phillips's ability to report on nuances of Vatican policy always depended on the analysis assistance of Hurley, who was not only the top-ranking American in the Secretariat of State of the Holy See; he was also the highest-ranking American at the Vatican in history. Hurley was the token American at the Vatican Secretariat of State, having replaced Francis Spellman, but at a much higher level of importance. While Spellman had covered ecclesiastical relations, Hurley dealt with policy and diplomacy.

His role at the Vatican extended beyond his official title and was unprecedented and largely hidden from view. The pope, as with several other Americans, had taken a liking to the forty-four-year-old monsignor and had chosen him as his personal interpreter. While the pope had a reading knowledge of English, he could not speak fluently enough in official settings. That gave Hurley a seat alongside Pius at key diplomatic sessions involving Britain, the United States, and other English-speaking emissaries. That also gave Hurley the ability to bypass intermediaries with his direct conduit to the head of the Roman Catholic Church.

Hurley came to use this relationship to the fullest. As a result, Phillips's off-the-record and somewhat clandestine contacts with Hurley allowed the pope and the president to be informed closely by what each other had to say.

Monsignor Hurley was proud to work with the pope so directly. He had already served in the Vatican diplomatic corps in India and Japan, where he sometimes dealt with delicate and inflammatory issues. He had an unusual background for a priest and a diplomat. He grew up in a gritty working-class neighborhood of Cleveland, the son of Irish immigrant parents. On the eve of World War I, Hurley attempted to attend West Point but was rejected because of a local residency requirement. Instead he attended St. Ignatius College, a Jesuit institution where he excelled in his studies, especially debate, but also became known as a fine football player—earning the nickname Breezer Hurley for his speed at dodging defenders on the gridiron—and he also enjoyed boxing.

He remained a forthright, sometimes pugnacious man as a priest, characteristics that conflicted with his superior, Cardinal Pacelli, the secretary of state. But Hurley's temperament was well suited to Pope Pius XI, who also had a humble background and a love for athletics. Hurley's special role allowed him to range beyond the purview of his cautious and disapproving superior, Pacelli, who might otherwise have reined him in. Pacelli sought ways to tone down the bite of papal criticism against Germany, arguing in part that Hitler might act out reprisals against German and Austrian Catholics. Hurley was not interested in such compromise and was able to follow the higher authority of the pope.

Phillips was pleased with his close relationship with Hurley, and the State Department realized the patriotic American monsignor was a worthy intermediary. Contacts with the Vatican were a touchy political subject in the United States. Diplomatic relations were severed three years before the demise of the Papal States in 1870, and resumption of relations was not welcome at the State Department or in Congress. But President Roosevelt was enthusiastic about all possible contacts in Rome toward discouraging and weakening Mussolini's alliance with Hitler. The pope could be an ally in that quest.

Paris, August 13, 1938

Though John LaFarge felt pressure to complete the encyclical and worried about not being home with his ailing elder brother, Bancel, he continued to pursue his other topics, partly because he wanted his secret assignment for the pope to leave time for reporting and writing about current events. His greatest diversion was the Spanish Civil War, which he saw with the narrow perspective of a zealot. Throughout the summer of 1938, LaFarge cheered on the increasingly likely victory of Francisco Franco, whose forces were encircling and suffocating the Republican government.

He was not alone in focusing on Spain. The civil war had divided Roman Catholic opinion. Some like LaFarge thought Franco was waging a necessary war against the forces of Communism. Others saw him as a ruthless tactician ready to seize dictatorial power from a democratic government. These were the seeds of the view of the "red menace" in Western Europe. LaFarge believed fervently that Franco's victory would stop the advance of Communism elsewhere. "If the Reds would carry on as they were doing in the country of Spain," LaFarge wrote, "it was evident that if they had the chance, despite their soothing words, they might be undertaking similar projects in France itself."

Many people, including influential Catholics, disagreed with him. A Communist takeover of Europe was neither evident nor likely, and Communists were not the largest component of the forces fighting Franco. The Spanish Civil War, raging since July 1936, had a major effect on the Catholic Church's response to Nazism in Europe. Many in the church reviled Stalin, who had repressed Catholics in Russia for twenty years. Who was more dangerous? Stalin, who supported the Spanish Republic, or Hitler, who supported Franco and his insurgents? What was the greatest threat facing the world? Spain's Civil War was a bloody debating ground.

LaFarge's notes for an article in *America* describe Franco as a moderate trying to rein in "those in his immediate associates whose record would be favorable to the spread of Nazi ideas." He thought Franco had been forced to deal with unsavory characters because he needed financial support. LaFarge argued that Franco, once victorious, would emerge as a democrat.

The pope had criticized Franco's continued attacks on Spanish civilians; two weeks before his meeting with LaFarge, on June 10, 1938, the pope demanded that Franco stop such carnage. *Osservatore Romano* said: "Useless massacre of the civil population once more has revived the serious and difficult problem of 'humanization' of war, which is itself destructive and inhuman." The Vatican focused on Franco's policies of bombing areas especially in the Basque country, which it said "have no military interest nor are they near military centers or public buildings which affect the war."

LaFarge and his colleagues labored on despite such political distractions and were relieved when the heat wave across Europe subsided in August with cooling rains and milder weather. But on August 13, LaFarge received a telegram that his brother, Bancel, his substitute father and mentor, had died at age seventy-three, at his home near New Haven.

LaFarge grieved that he could not have been at his brother's bedside. Bancel was the central authority figure in his life. "At his death I reproached myself," he wrote, "as I have done before and since, that I never had really expressed, as I should all my indebtedness to Bancel, for if it had not been for him I should never have obtained my education, possibly not at college and certainly not abroad."

A flood of memories came to him: Bancel as a young man teaching this youngest brother to take out their little skiff onto Narragansett Bay and the ocean; Bancel always kind and attentive when the rest of the family was not there. LaFarge recalled that when he attended Harvard, he was often penniless, but Bancel always rescued him with spending money.

Bancel had had a good life, a happy marriage and family with his wife, Mabel, and four children. He was a respected artist and produced beautiful paintings and stained-glass designs, although he neither won the recognition his father had nor had the same satisfaction in his craft. Although they had been apart for years at a time, the brothers felt lasting affection and LaFarge's grief was overwhelming. "I had so hoped to be with Bancel during his last hours," LaFarge said, "it was a bitter disappointment to find myself on the other side of the ocean."

LaFarge's Jesuit brethren did all they could to comfort him. Talbot went to New Haven for Bancel's funeral. "I said Mass for your brother Bancel on the day after I heard the news," Talbot wrote in a letter to LaFarge. "The other members of the Community likewise remembered him in their Masses and Prayers. May God give him eternal rest!"

Talbot also sent word from the parish priest who ministered to Bancel on his deathbed. "Some days before his death, Father Downey was called. He was asked to give the final blessing, for there was imminent danger of death," Talbot wrote. "Father Downey grasped his hand and said a few words. Bancel meanwhile was mumbling, attempting to express himself. Suddenly, as if with a tremendous effort, in a voice that could be heard outside the room, he almost shouted: 'Father, I am very happy that you have come to see me.' The members of the family marveled that Bancel had the strength to speak in such a tone. As far as I know, he did not speak aloud after that."

LaFarge was comforted that Bancel's "last hours were of great peace and really all that was most fitting for such a life. He was laid out in his artist's smock, as befitted one who had given the best of his talents to his chosen profession."

LaFarge struggled with his emotions and found it difficult to focus on his work. Family members had told him that his eldest brother, Grant, five years older than Bancel, was also seriously ill.

The timeline for returning home had been pushed from August to September and now perhaps not even before autumn. He had to concentrate and finish the encyclical. "About other things at home I just cannot think," he wrote to Talbot, thanking him for his support. "If I start thinking, it has no end. All I can do is to pray and hope. After all it is God's business, and not mine."

Rome, September 5, 1938

The Vatican and the Italian government reached a temporary agreement to tone down their hostile rhetoric. But this did not assuage Mussolini's anger at the pope for long and hardly made a difference in the pope's criticism of Fascist policies.

Mussolini told Foreign Minister Galeazzo Ciano, who was also his son-in-law: "Contrary to what people believe, I am a very patient man." But he added, "I will react harshly. . . . No one should make me lose my patience."

The agreement fell apart after only a few weeks. On September 5, 1938, the first day of the school year across Italy, the government announced that Jewish children could no longer attend schools and universities and that all Jewish teachers and professors were fired. It was a great shock that raised greater fears for worse times to come. The school ban signaled clearly that Italy would march with Nazi Germany toward the systematic repression of Jews.

The announcement was accompanied by a virulent anti-Semitic newspaper campaign. The newspaper *Tevere* (Tiber in Italian), long known for its rants, praised the school ban as well as a purge of Jews in the armed forces, judiciary, and politics. "During the Ethiopian War, all the forces that acted against Italy were unleashed by Jews," the newspaper said. "The attempt to strangle Italy was particularly willed and favored by Jewish currents and the Jewish international [conspiracy] with its maneuvers to starve us and stab us in the back."

Another decree effective on September 5 ordered the expulsion from Italy of an estimated ten thousand Jews who had come to the country since the end of World War I. The law even applied to Jews who were naturalized Italian citizens and to those who had converted to Catholicism. As expected, Mussolini's decision to protect "the purity of the Italian race" was hailed by Germany. The measures came less than a year after Mussolini and Ciano had said that there was no Jewish problem in Italy.

Shaking with anger, the pope responded the following day when he spoke to a group of Belgian Catholic pilgrims. He made a declaration that would symbolize the most important months of his papacy. "Anti-Semitism is a hateful movement, with which we as Christians must have nothing to do. . . . No, it is not licit for Christians to take part in manifestations of anti-Semitism . . . anti-Semitism is inadmissible. Spiritually, we are all Semites."

The declaration, spoken by the pope almost in tears, followed no script. These were words from the heart, written by no one, nor vetted by others at the Vatican such as Cardinal Pacelli, who would have counseled caution and moderation. Instead, Pope Pius spoke without ambiguity. It was the clearest statement a leader of the Roman Catholic Church had ever uttered about the shared heritage of Christians and Jews. The pope had essentially said: *We are the same people.*

The pope's heartfelt words were long remembered and repeated. It became a recurring theme that encouraged bishops and cardinals in Germany, Italy, and around the world to speak out. Not all of them did, but those who took Pius's message to heart made their own speeches. The pope's words were grudgingly debated by churchmen who for decades had followed anti-Semitic tracts, listened to unsubstantiated nonsense that Jews started the French and Russian revolutions, and accepted as fact that the Jews killed Jesus of Nazareth.

Mussolini thundered back at the pope in a speech in the northeastern city of Trieste. He was still irritated by the pope's earlier charge that he was imitating Hitler and said that only "half-wits" could think that. This led to a new round of sparring between the dictator and the Vatican. At one point the Vatican had to ask Foreign Minister Ciano if Mussolini had referred to the pope as a half-wit. Nothing of the kind, Ciano replied, unconvincingly.

The Fascist response to the pope soon took a new tack and had something of truth to it. Roberto Farinacci, the journalist and presiding anti-Semite in Mussolini's Fascist movement, advised his Nazi friends that the pope was becoming irrelevant. "The Germans are mistaken in assuming that the Catholic Church agrees with the Pope on each and every issue. We know that on the racial issue the clergy are split into two camps and that the Pope is powerless to do anything about." Farinacci went further, though, and accused the pope of siding with the Communists and atheists.

But as long as the pope felt healthy enough, he had the time and the will to control the dissent to his policies inside the Vatican. He could also still receive LaFarge and his encyclical and force its publication. When would it be finished?

Paris, September 15, 1938

John LaFarge was editing the final touches of the draft encyclical and told Talbot he engaged in "healthy debates" with his Jesuit colleagues Gustave Desbuquois and Gustav Gundlach, "the two Guses." They were often joined by their fellow Jesuit Heinrich Bacht. LaFarge originally feared that these other writers might pressure him to dilute his statements about racism and its connection to the terrorizing of Jews in Europe. He was delighted that Gundlach, who despised Hitler and Nazi Germany, had become his greatest advocate.

The priests knew their words would likely have an impact on politics and history. At breaks from the writing, the men often sipped coffee, ate cake, and, as LaFarge recalled, they debated "the problems of the world."

The crisis between Germany and Czech Sudetenland had been percolating all summer, and the pressure increased toward the end of August when word spread about an imminent German invasion of Czechoslovakia. The number of Jewish refugees was increasing, although no country was opening its doors to these immigrants. LaFarge had included a passage in the encyclical about the forced exodus of the Jews, "this flagrant denial of human rights sends many thousands of helpless persons out over the face of the earth without any resources. Wandering from frontier to frontier, they are a burden to humanity and to themselves."

LaFarge had been hearing how near war was for the entire four months he had been in Europe, and now it was turning to reality. By late summer, it was clear that Hitler was prepared to invade Czechoslovakia. On September 15, British prime minister Neville Chamberlain flew to Hitler's mountain retreat at Berchtesgaden to urge him to seek a road to peace. This began Chamberlain's shuttle between England and Germany, during which he begged Hitler to negotiate a resolution. Britain and France were offering Sudetenland to Germany if Hitler would only take a pledge of peace. Chamberlain would give Czechoslovakia to Hitler, which would result in the disappearance of that country. But Hitler would not stop there.

War was a constant theme in Paris, but LaFarge said that people "managed to put on an appearance of quiet indifference . . . [though] they did appear completely prepared for the worst, as far as defense went. High army officials assure you with what seemed a well-founded satisfaction that every screw was tightened, every man ready to fly to his post; all that was needed was a telephone call, for a 'button to be pushed,' and in twenty minutes the General Staff would see their planes soaring, their artillery rumbling, to the East."

On September 18, LaFarge said the encyclical's final draft copies were being edited and typed. The document would be a timely tool in the pope's arsenal for dealing with the European crisis. LaFarge was satisfied, relieved, and amazed that the job was done. He felt himself to be "exhausted to the very limit of my mind and body," but he thought the final product was a success.

Much of the encyclical was presented in indirect language, especially Gundlach's obscure historical statements and distant references to liturgy. They retained some of the church's rejection of Judaism as a religion; the encyclical did not deny the church's history in that regard. But the Nazi threat led to the conclusion that religious differences should be irrelevant. Even though the entire document would be read widely, only a few pages—those written by LaFarge—would be dissected and published in every newspaper in the world. Those several hundred words would anger the Nazi regime and would be seen as a direct attack on both Hitler and Mussolini. This was what the pope wanted, and in a sense this would be LaFarge's legacy.

The encyclical's title was the first shot to be fired at the monolith of anti-Semitism—*Humanis Generis Unitas—The Unity of the Human Race*. The preamble declared: "The Unity of the Human Race is forgotten, as it were, owing to the extreme disorder found at the present time in the social life of man."

The pope was talking about race, the threat of war, and a fearful future. "In one place a magical remedy is prescribed . . . elsewhere people are roused to enthusiasm by a leader's intoxicating appeal to the Unity of the Race, while in the eastern European sky dawns a promise reddened with terror and blood of a new humanity to be realized in the Unity of the Proletariat.

This statement would declare to the world that the pope sided with neither the Nazis—Hitler and his mania about race—nor with the Soviets.

LaFarge did not want to deal with Communism in this encyclical. He knew the pope had done that before in his 1937 encyclical *Divinis Redemptoris*. Everything had its time and place. Here, the pope would tell the world clearly that there was only one race of humanity, and no other racial divisions existed. The pope had called in LaFarge to make this point. LaFarge, the American

Jesuit, had simplified the question by declaring that racism is a fraud and a myth.

This pope was the first in history to confide in an American Jesuit to take on such a world-changing task. Yet, spurred on and counseled by Gundlach, LaFarge had worked within the system. The draft would have to go through other hands. They needed to build their case, Gundlach said, and pay attention to structure. If for nothing else, the writing had to be circumspect enough both to pass the virtual censorship around the pope and to protect the ideas he had asked LaFarge to provide.

The encyclical's introduction would make a general declaration, pointed directly at Adolf Hitler:

> When we come to the question of race we find most
> completely exemplified the harm that is done by the loose,
> sentimental, almost mystical manner of speaking which has
> been applied to the ideas of nation, people, and State . . . racial
> bond is used, in accordance with present-day scientific parlance,
> to denote the common participation of a group of human
> beings in certain definite, permanent physical qualities, and in
> association with the bodily constitution which is marked by these
> physical qualities are certain constantly observed psychological
> characteristics. But so-called racism . . . contradicts the principle
> that no type of separation can be genuinely human, unless it
> shares in that which forms the common bond of humanity.

The key point emerged deep into the encyclical after a statement of purpose and series of section headings: "Denial of Human Unity; effects of the totalitarian state on human unity; right of association suppressed, manipulation of public opinion, authority derives from God, the waste of war . . ." Then after a methodical development, tracing history and the rights of man, the encyclical came to the essential substance: racism denies humanity; religion can recognize no divisions in race; there is no such thing as an inferior race. More specifically, in dealing with the plight of the Jews, the encyclical stated that Nazis had built a myth about a master race; and that the lies about a master race had devolved into the persecution of Jews; that as a result of racial policies (in Germany and Italy), Jews were under attack and were being deprived of their most basic rights of life and liberty. Racism, LaFarge wrote,

> is not content with denying the validity of the universal moral order as a benefit that unifies the whole human race; it likewise denies the general and equal application of essential values in the field of economic welfare, or art, of science and, above all, of religion. It maintains, for instance, that each race should have its own science, which should have nothing in common with the science of another race, particularly of an inferior race. . . . Respect for reality . . . does not permit the Catholic to remain silent in the presence of racism. [Totalitarianism] destroys the basic structure of humanity as a true unity in true diversity and thereby betrays its own inner falsity and worthlessness.

LaFarge was certain the pope would remember having said: "Say simply what you would say if you were pope." LaFarge had done just that.

LaFarge sent a message to Ledóchowski that the job was done, and the Jesuit General responded that he was pleased and told LaFarge there was no need for him to bring the encyclical to Rome. He could ship it by messenger and return to the United States. Your task is done, the Jesuit leader seemed to be saying:

Now go home. Ledóchowski said he would forward the document
to the pope right away.

LaFarge was tempted by this offer, in part because he hadn't
been feeling well. He was always tired, wasn't eating properly, and
was losing weight. Part of his state of health could be attributed
to sadness about the loss of his brother. Part was also accumu-
lated tension over completing the encyclical, and insomnia. He
had remarked about his health concerns to Talbot and his family,
though he never mentioned any specific ailment. Throughout his
life, LaFarge had been considered sickly, and his family surmised
that he might be having prostate problems. Later in life, he had
several operations that forced months of convalescence, but he
never disclosed details. In Paris, LaFarge had tried to suffer his
ailments in silence, but he had probably made too much of it when
speaking to those around him. Perhaps Ledóchowski's offer might
in part have come in response to those health complaints.

Gundlach warned LaFarge that Ledóchowski's proposal
seemed suspicious and advised him to hand deliver the encyclical
to Rome. Gundlach had once been an ally of Ledóchowski, but
now that he was cluing in LaFarge on the Vatican politics swirling
around him, he was an antagonist. Even so, Gundlach could not
have predicted that Ledóchowski would try to delay publication of
the encyclical indefinitely.

Gundlach warned LaFarge as best he could. Still, he was careful not to go too far. He knew LaFarge's earnestness and devotion
would prevent him from believing that Ledóchowski, the leader of
his order, could have ulterior motives.

LaFarge may not have been thoroughly convinced by
Gundlach's cautions, but he did agree that he should hand carry
the document down to Rome. He sent a message to Ledóchowski
that he "could not accept his offer [to leave for home directly from
Paris], tempting as it was (for I dread the trip). I'm convinced one

must be on the spot to explain the why's and wherefore's and have learned the need of this from various sources." The pope had said he expected to see him again, and LaFarge anticipated questions and requests for revisions.

By September 20, the writing team had finished clean drafts of the encyclical in the required languages. The Jesuits then agreed to split up. Gundlach took a train to Switzerland and would relax there for a few days. At about the same time, LaFarge traveled from Paris down to Rome. They had agreed to reconnoiter in Rome where they would await queries and fine-tuning of the encyclical.

LaFarge checked in this time at the Jesuit community residence on Borgo Spirito Santo, just off St. Peter's Square. Ledóchowski saw him quickly and gave his assurances that everything would work out well. Ledóchowski said he would read the encyclical and then deliver it promptly to the pope.

LaFarge stayed in Rome for a week and met with Ledóchowski a few other times, but never did he press for a meeting with the pope, although it was his right to do so. LaFarge stayed on and waited for further instructions from Ledóchowski or the pope, though none came. It is unlikely the pope was told that LaFarge was in Rome. LaFarge was sandwiched by his duty to the head of the Jesuits—following the chain of command—and by his exhaustion and desire to go home. He was still grieving for Bancel, and he had heard more bad news about Grant's deteriorating health. He felt he needed to be with his family and began to look for passage back home. The possibility of war created a flood of mostly Jewish refugees overwhelming steamship offices with requests for tickets to leave Europe immediately.

By September 23, news came that Chamberlain had hammered out a draft agreement with Hitler that gave Sudetenland to Germany along with the right to occupy the territory by October 10. Essentially the Nazis got Sudetenland without a fight—

and the agreement severed the pact of mutual assistance that Czechoslovakia had maintained with Britain and France.

The Appian Way, September 24, 1938

Cardinal Pacelli drove down to Castel Gandolfo from Rome on Saturday morning, September 24, for a regular audience with the pope, their final meeting before Pacelli was leaving on his extended annual vacation in Switzerland. The tensions in Europe must have dominated their conversation. Even if they did not yet know of the agreement with Hitler, they were aware of Chamberlain's negotiations with the German dictator over the future of Czechoslovakia.

Pacelli told the pope about his meeting the previous day with Diego von Bergen, the German ambassador to the Holy See, and what he'd said about the negotiations with Hitler. There was speculation that the Vatican might become involved directly or as an intermediary toward peace, but the pope merely expressed "optimism because everything is in God's hands." Pius resisted making any statements because he agreed with Chamberlain's critics who said that Hitler could not be stopped by appeasement and peace treaties.

Pacelli left the pope, rode the small elevator down to the courtyard, and returned to his car. His driver was waiting just outside the apostolic palace gates. Soon after they pulled away, they turned onto the road for the ride back to Rome. Rounding one sharp turn on a road riddled with curves and embankments, the driver had to swerve suddenly to avoid a boy riding his bicycle. The driver lost control and sideswiped the boy, who was thrown from his bike. Pacelli was hurled violently forward and smacked his head and cheek on one of the car windows.

The pope heard about the accident quickly, along with a preliminary report that Pacelli was not seriously hurt. The pope sent two members of the household to help in any way they could. They arrived within moments and saw that the cardinal appeared to be well, only suffering some bruises. They sent him back to St. Peter's in a separate car and arranged for the boy to be taken to the hospital in nearby Albano, where doctors treated him for some scrapes and a dislocated shoulder. A Vatican doctor examined the cardinal when he arrived and confirmed that Pacelli had not been seriously hurt. The doctor then drove down to Castel Gandolfo to assure the pontiff that Pacelli was well. It was a disaster averted.

Pacelli felt well enough the next day to leave for Switzerland. The pope was always reluctant to see him go. Despite differences in opinion, the pope had relied heavily on Pacelli in the eight years he had been secretary of state. There was much work to be done.

CHAPTER EIGHT

The Pope's Discontent

U.S. Embassy, Rome, September 1938

WILLIAM PHILLIPS WAS back in Rome in September after escaping the city's August heat. His wife stayed behind in the Italian Alps for a while longer, preferring the daily rains to the sweltering heat that continued. Phillips was scheduled to return to Washington for meetings with President Roosevelt and the secretary of state. But first he needed to focus on his main brief from the president, which involved applying pressure on the Italian government and maintaining communications with the Vatican. He asked for a meeting with Mussolini's foreign minister, Galeazzo Ciano, before he left for America that night. At the foreign ministry, Phillips pushed Ciano to encourage the Germans to be moderate in their handling of Czechoslovakia.

"I reminded Ciano that our relations with Germany were anything but satisfactory," Phillips wrote in his diary. "The Italian Government, on the contrary, was in such intimate relations that it seemed to me of the utmost importance that they should exercise a restraining influence in the event of the occurrence of a real crisis."

Ciano recalled that his response was somewhat distracted and by rote: "I play [sic] the same pro-German and anti-Czech music: all the responsibilities belong to Prague."

Phillips was not having any of that. "So far as I was concerned," he recalled, "I would look to him personally to do everything in his power to restrain the German Government at such a moment."

They went back and forth about relations with Germany and about Hitler and his designs on Czechoslovakia. Ciano did not offer any clear answers and finally changed the pace with a question of his own.

He wanted to know what Phillips thought the United States would do if war broke out in Europe. The ambassador replied by comparing 1938 to the period prior to the U.S. entry in the European war in 1917. There were parallels, and while there certainly was strong antiwar sentiment right now in the United States, things could change.

"A long war might again see the same situation," Phillips said. "When American lives and ships were lost, and if this happened, the emotions of the American people might sweep the country in a briefer space of time."

In such a case, the United States would go to war against Germany. Phillips was resolute and wanted to make sure Ciano heard him clearly. It would be a world war.

Phillips was so troubled by the direction and tenor of this conversation, he decided this was no time to leave his post. He cabled Roosevelt as soon as he returned to the embassy. The president agreed and confirmed Phillips's answer about going to war.

Roosevelt cabled back: "If we get the idea that the future of our form of government is threatened by a coalition of European dictators, we might wade in with everything we have to give. . . . Today I think ninety per cent of our people are definitely anti-

German and anti-Italian in sentiment—and incidentally, I would not propose to ask them to be neutral in thought."

As Phillips monitored events from Rome, he stayed in closer touch with Joseph Hurley, his conduit to the pope. He called the American monsignor to the embassy and placed two items on the agenda. First, he asked Hurley to secure permission to begin publishing President Roosevelt's speeches and other significant statements in *Osservatore Romano*. Italians had no independent information about the United States or about Roosevelt's perspective on tensions in Europe. The newspaper would be doing a great service by providing uncensored news directly from Washington.

Second, Phillips wanted the pope to keep the pressure on Hitler and Mussolini during the crisis over Czechoslovakia. This meant repeated criticism, using the exact same words repeatedly. "I reminded Hurley that in America both the President and the Secretary of State had to keep on saying the same thing over and over again until it was nauseating for them to do so, in order to make an impression on the public."

Throughout the fall, coordination between the United States and the Vatican strengthened, not because Hurley worked for Pacelli, but because Hurley had a direct line to the pope.

Phillips and Hurley won praise from the State Department for breaking through Italian censorship. The Vatican newspaper and radio were regularly publishing and broadcasting key speeches by President Roosevelt and other U.S. officials. The United States was gratified to see "the increasing friendliness to the United States of the Vatican organ," the State Department reported. "Official pronouncements made by the President and the Secretary of State [Cordell Hull] have been given prominent place and sympathetic presentation by this newspaper, which has also from time to time protested against the attacks in certain Italian newspapers on American films."

Hurley ran a considerable risk in making this happen. Quite often he carried U.S. transcripts under his cassock when he returned to the Vatican from visits to the U.S. embassy. Mussolini's agents were watching both the Americans and Vatican officials. Had he been stopped, he could have been expelled, charged with espionage, or worse. President Roosevelt sent him a personal note thanking him for his service to his country.

Berlin, September 26, 1938

Berlin was bathed in glory and cheers. Nazi supporters packed the roads as Hitler waved to them in the semidarkness along Potsdamer Strasse, en route to the Sportpalast, the city's largest indoor arena. The dais was festooned with the German eagle embracing a swastika, and the stage itself was designed in the form of an eagle spreading its wings. Many more swastikas ringed the stage; another banner hung from a second tier in the hall with the familiar refrain, *Ein Volk, Ein Reich, Ein Führer*—"One People, One Reich, One Führer." At the given signal the minister of propaganda, Joseph Goebbels, introduced the führer, who was flanked by other luminaries of the Reich. Goebbels addressed Hitler.

"You can rely on your people, as they rely on you," Goebbels declared. "The people stand behind you as one man. We are aware that no threat and no pressure, from whatever source, can keep you from pursuing your and our inalienable rights."

LaFarge and the other Jesuits had heard that Hitler's speech would be significant, perhaps a matter of war and peace. Ledóchowski invited his Jesuit subordinates to join him for the broadcast after dinner. They gathered around the radio console in the recreation room of the Jesuit headquarters off St. Peter's. LaFarge was seated beside Ledóchowski and felt strange sitting there so close, able to observe the Jesuit leader's demeanor and every gesture. It was a highly dramatic setting that LaFarge would always remember.

"Father Ledóchowski seated himself in his usual alert fashion close to the instrument, while the others grouped around," LaFarge wrote. "The transmission was perfect, as if we were seated in the vast hall itself."

William Shirer, the Berlin correspondent for the Columbia Broadcasting Company, stood on a balcony above the stage, closely guarding his microphone. He looked down upon the assemblage and prepared to interpret the gist of what he was hearing. The world was waiting for Hitler to decide if he was going to declare war over Czechoslovakia. As Shirer prepared for the main portion, Goebbels came to the end of his brief introduction: "We greet you, my Führer, with our old battle cry: Adolf Hitler, *Sieg Heil!*" Shirer's shortwave hookup picked up the delirious cheers of the German people and broadcast them worldwide.

People across Europe and in San Francisco, New York, Washington, and beyond crowded around their radios to hear this. The matter at hand was Hitler's impatience and anger over the delay in ratifying what came to be known as the Munich Agreement on Czechoslovakia.

As Hitler stepped to the podium, the price of gold rose and fell on world markets. He saluted the crowd with his open palm to more furious cheers and shouts, and then he stepped to the microphone.

In Rome, Ambassador Phillips pondered the source of Hitler's oratory skills and emotional power. He found the führer to be a master "at the way in which he worked up his audience to a high degree of emotion." Even without understanding the German, Phillips said, "the mere excitement of the man himself and the effect on his audience caused me acute alarm. . . . He is certainly a remarkable orator—probably there is no one in the world like him. . . ."

LaFarge felt the marvels of radio technology as it brought him directly into the Sportpalast. Hitler had begun in a gentle, dulcet tone, what LaFarge described as "a quiet reasoning voice as if he were taking the great audience into his confidence."

Hitler patiently recounted the recent weeks of negotiations on Czechoslovakia—and trading on the New York Stock Exchange continued to react to every nuance and rumor surrounding his speech. Stocks gained some ground in those first seconds, then fluctuated with Hitler's every vaguely threatening word; the market closed lower. Hitler reminded his global audience that the German Wehrmacht was on the ready, "rearmed to an extent the likes of which the world has never seen."

Hitler's disembodied voice was clear on the wireless, and the echoing cheers and the *sieg heil*s were a crashing ocean of sound behind him.

He rose slowly to a crescendo, threatening the consequences if Czechoslovakia did not bow to his will. The language was fiery, uninterrupted, fiercely enunciated. Shirer repeated the words in a hushed tone to his live English-speaking audience.

"May the world know this," Hitler said in German with Shirer trying to keep up with the English interpretation, "there now marches a people and a different one than that of 1918. . . . In this hour the whole German people will be united to me, my will they shall feel as their will, just as I regard their future and fate as director of my actions."

In his rising fury, Hitler impelled Britain, France, and Czechoslovakia to conclude negotiations and submit. It was an ultimatum for the surrender of Sudetenland to Germany: The Czech president, "Edvard Beneš will have to hand the territory to us on October 1," Hitler said. The alternative was obvious. Beneš, not Hitler, the führer said, "now holds in his hand peace or war."

LaFarge could feel the same hysterical wave of screaming emotion Shirer experienced directly in the Sportpalast nine hundred miles away. Shirer said he had never seen such a performance in all the times he had witnessed Hitler speak to a crowd. "That evening Hitler burned his bridges, or so it seemed to those of us who listened in amazement to his mad outburst."

By midspeech, Shirer said Hitler was frothing and screaming, "shouting and shrieking in the worst paroxysm I had ever seen him in, he venomously hurled personal insults at 'Herr Beneš,' declared that the issue of war or peace was now up to the Czech President and that, in any case, he [Hitler] would have the Sudetenland by October 1 . . ."

Jan Masaryk, the Czech ambassador to Britain, was in London, also listening to the speech. He said it was "so uncultured and shocking that I am proud of my government's decision to take a firm stand against the authors of a mentality which is trying to destroy European culture."

Hitler continued to spout fire. "Beneš the aggressor!" he shouted. "Beneš the tyrant! Beneš the betrayer of civilization. Beneš the enemy of the German people!"

LaFarge listened with distress and fear, yet he also observed Ledóchowski's placid demeanor. "The full import of what I had witnessed in Germany and Czechoslovakia burst upon me," LaFarge said. "Hitler rose rapidly to frantic screams of fanaticism, followed by the terrific rumbling roar from the audience: 'Sieg Heil, Sieg Heil, Sieg Heil!' My own bones quaked at each of these recurrent episodes. Over and over the voice died down and rose again, but Father General's attentive face and eager form remained impassive."

Somehow each time Hitler seemed poised to send in the tanks, he pulled back, making clear this was an ultimatum rather than war itself. He even had kind words for Chamberlain, who acted as an honest broker for the only solution Hitler saw—surrender!

LaFarge looked beyond the radio, beyond the voice to the sound of madness. He heard "the voice of impending war," LaFarge said, "the voice of a blind, dark passion which might erupt anywhere in the world. Echoes of it even appeared in the United States, the voice of the mob, of hate, of hysteria."

Hitler continued: "We will take one common holy resolve. I shall be stronger than any pressure, any peril. And when this will is stronger than peril and pressure, it will break the pressure and peril. We are resolved!"

Shirer said: "For the first time in all the years I've observed him he seemed tonight to have completely lost control of himself." But when Hitler sat down, Shirer recounted the indelible memory of watching Goebbels, who sprang up and shouted into the microphone: "One thing is sure: 1918 will never be repeated!"

Shirer continued: "Hitler leaped to his feet and with a fanatical fire in his eyes that I shall never forget brought his right hand, after a grand sweep, pounding down on the table, and yelling with all the power in his mighty lungs: '*Ja!*' Then, he slumped into his chair exhausted."

LaFarge was frightened beyond words, and none of the Jesuits he was with could bring themselves to break the silence; they didn't move even when the bell rang for evening prayer. Ledóchowski had been transfixed by Hitler's voice from the radio. No Jesuit would break table as long as the Jesuit Superior General remained.

LaFarge watched Ledóchowski throughout the broadcast; no one moved as long as Ledóchowski remained. LaFarge said: "And the bell rang fifteen minutes later for the examination of conscience, customary at the close of a Jesuit's day, but he still remained."

Hitler had seized even the order of prayer among a group of

Jesuits listening to him in Rome, LaFarge said, "making us all stay up and listen to the radio when we would have been quietly saying our prayers. Finally with a last effort the Führer screeched to a finish."

Only then, Ledóchowski stood quickly and turned to the door. LaFarge realized then that Ledóchowski's reaction was quite different from his own. He was calm and appeared to be satisfied with Hitler's speech. Just before he disappeared from sight, the general of the Jesuits turned back to the priests, and said simply: "Don't worry, there will be no war."

"And sure enough there wasn't," LaFarge recalled. "Not then."

Rome, September 30, 1938

The pope thought the Munich accord was a waste of time. He was asked by some diplomats, including French ambassador François Charles-Roux, to provide a statement of support for Chamberlain's initiative with Hitler, but the pontiff refused. His comments were broadcast on Vatican Radio on September 29, the night before Chamberlain, Hitler, French prime minister Édouard Daladier, and Mussolini signed the accord. In indirect terms, the pope let it be known that he doubted the Munich Agreement was worth any more than the paper it was printed on. The headlines the next day bypassed the substance of the pope's remarks and focused on his emotional state. It was said that he broke into sobs repeatedly, and his voice was filled with emotion. He said he recognized that his life was drawing to an end—"Let the Lord of life and of death," the pope said, "take from us the inestimable gift of an already long life" as he prayed he could give his life for peace. Emotional though he was, he was making a point, that he thought Hitler was immoral and could not be trusted. He implied that the

Munich accords were meaningless unless there were "actions corresponding to the reiterated words of peace."

Soon after the formal announcement of the Munich Agreement the following morning, the Vatican newspaper reported that the pope had greeted it with "great joy." But that was not true, and he had said no such thing. The statement was more evidence that the gatekeepers, including Cardinal Pacelli, were attempting to control the message from St. Peter's whenever they could.

Pius was even more specific and emphatic in private on October 14 when he met with Domenico Tardini, the Vatican undersecretary of state, in charge part of the summer and fall while Pacelli vacationed in Switzerland. The pope told Tardini that Hitler could not be stopped by mediation. He said he was disgusted that Mussolini was claiming to be a peacemaker at the last minute in time for the signing of the Munich document.

"Don't you understand?" the pope said in that meeting when Tardini suggested that the Vatican could help rally support to what Chamberlain was trying to do. The pope refused. "This is all warmed-over broth!!" He went on, "Chamberlain provided Hitler with a gold foot-stool! The opposition was right. . . . Chamberlain has given in."

The pope would not use his influence in the world as an intermediary or counsel if Nazi Germany was involved. And neither Hitler nor Mussolini would ever accept the pope as a neutral mediator in a dispute. At the same time, the pope also knew he was being accused of siding with the Communists. Therefore, whether or not he listened to Hitler's ravings at the Berlin Sportpalast, he remained silent on Munich.

Subordinates sought to tone down his confrontational approach on Munich. Piero Tacchi-Venturi, a controversial Jesuit in Rome who had befriended Mussolini early on and often acted as an intermediary with the pope, praised the Munich Agreement nevertheless as Mussolini's "pacifist victory" and "an affirmation of the Catholic and moderate spirit of the regime."

Franklin Roosevelt shared Pius's view of the Munich Agreement. He even told Ambassador Phillips that Chamberlain's peace treaty was no better than "a temporary postponement of what looks to me like an inevitable conflict within the next five years." Roosevelt had listened angrily to Hitler's speech from the Sportpalast, and as the rhetoric heated up, Roosevelt threw his pencil at the wall. He also agreed with Churchill that appeasing Hitler would likely lead to war.

The Czech prime minister, Edvard Beneš, so maligned by Hitler in the Sportpalast speech, remembered and praised Pius, who, among leaders of Europe, steadfastly refused to endorse the Munich accord. "I cannot forget the very sympathetic attitude of His Holiness Pope Pius XI toward Czechoslovakia during the crisis," Beneš recalled in 1943 in a letter he wrote to the Vatican. Critics of the appeasement knew very well—the pope realized that Hitler was the greatest menace facing Europe.

The pope kept up his criticism of the Nazi victory at Munich and the resulting march into Czechoslovakia. *Osservatore Romano* editorialized that Hitler's strategy was to avoid "attacking the Catholic Church until the population had been brought within the Reich, and then proceeding to impose an anti-Catholic program in the region." U.S. ambassador William Phillips, monitoring the Vatican position and informed by his friend Joseph Hurley, said the Vatican wrote the editorial in response to the publication of "an anti-Catholic article in the *Schwarze Korps* [the official newspaper of the Nazi SS]," affirming that "priest politicians" were plotting against the Third Reich. The Nazis considered Pope Pius XI to be the leader of "criminal priests" operating in Nazi territory.

Paris, September 30

A day or two after listening to Hitler's speech with Ledóchowski, John LaFarge had managed to book a steerage class ticket on the *Statendam* for its October 1 departure from France. He gathered up his baggage as soon as he could and left Rome for Paris. He had become increasingly worried about his health and his family. Most likely, he was also scared that war could break out at any moment, leaving him stranded and uncertain when he could travel again.

When he got to Paris on September 29, he wired home to *America* magazine headquarters and informed Talbot of his travel schedule. His brief message read: "SAILING OCTOBER 1 STATENDAM. LAFARGE." He would regret his hasty decision to leave Rome for years afterward and the rest of his life.

On September 30, 1938, his last night in Europe, LaFarge heard the news that the leaders of Britain, France, and Germany had signed the Munich Agreement to cede the Sudetenland to Hitler, with Mussolini in attendance as the guarantor. LaFarge had been gathering impressions about these last historic days on the continent and began mapping out an article about the meaning of the Munich Agreement. He took a month to turn those thoughts into an article for *America*. He could sense both in Rome and now in Paris that there was an undercurrent of "preparations for the worst." He thought this was his value as an analyst, allowing impressions to settle before writing. "War-scares, like hurricanes, are best appreciated when they are over," he finally wrote in an article published on November 5. In both Rome and Paris, people held up a front of normality to stave off panic, he said.

LaFarge wondered what "breathing-space" was afforded by the agreement. He answered his own question: he could see little more in Munich than a time "for re-armament . . . for the liquidation of the Treaty of Versailles . . . for more shame, and wider plans of aggression . . . ," all placing Germany in position to wage war.

"The impression of a foreigner in Paris during those days was that the French were agonized over the prospect of war to an extent that we of the overseas [*sic*] can never appreciate. They knew what war meant and what this war would mean for them . . . they had a right to be alarmed." Similarly, "in Rome, during those two weeks one heard no auto horns; there was much marching and bravado, much more open acknowledgment of unusual times; but there was the same anxious concern. . . . One glance at the grave faces of elder army officers as they huddled with the populace intent over the radio broadcasts in the Via Nazionale; a look at the crowds that prayer for peace in the churches sufficed to show where people's minds, not to speak of their hearts, were directed at that moment."

ON OCTOBER 1, 1938, LaFarge took the three-hour train ride from Paris to the docks at Boulogne-sur-Mer on the English Channel. The *Statendam* was jam-packed with more than eleven hundred passengers, a quite different situation from his eastward crossing from New York four months earlier, when he was joined by only several dozen other passengers.

Also this time it was not a pleasant passage—the steerage cabins were small and located on a middle deck that was not comfortable. Perhaps because of his station as a priest, he managed to obtain an upgraded stateroom for the eight-day voyage.

London, October 1, 1938

Hours after the Munich Agreement, the Wehrmacht marched into Sudetenland in the first phase of the occupation and annexation of the region. German-Czechs hailed them as liberators;

socialists, government opponents, and Jews fled. There were small skirmishes and people died in the Czech military retreat from the region. In the Sudetenland, Austrians who supported the Nazis marauded through newly occupied villages and attacked Jewish businesses and houses. Hitler had succeeded in a gambit he could not have won militarily. At that moment in 1938, the combined forces of Britain, France, Czechoslovakia, and Poland were stronger than the German military. Once again as in Austria, the Western powers stood by idly as Hitler marched on.

The British-sanctioned occupation of western Czechoslovakia was based on Neville Chamberlain's trust of Hitler's goodwill, that this would give Germany the *Lebensraum* it desired to leave in peace. Chamberlain had already been criticized for his fostering of the Munich Agreement.

Chief among his critics was Winston Churchill, who rose to speak from his customary seat in the front row at Parliament and proclaimed: "There can never be friendship between the British democracy and the Nazi power, that power which spurns Christian ethics, which cheers its onward course by a barbarous paganism, which vaunts the spirit of aggression and conquest, which derives strength and perverted pleasure from persecution, and uses, as we have seen, with pitiless brutality the threat of murderous force. . . . We have passed an awful milestone in our history, when the whole equilibrium of Europe has been deranged. . . . And do not suppose that this is the end. This is only the beginning of the reckoning."

Hitler had already confessed in private that he preferred a military invasion and takeover of Czechoslovakia. "That fellow [Chamberlain] has spoiled my entry into Prague," he said. The führer wanted all of Czechoslovakia, Poland, France, and England for that matter. As Churchill and the pope realized, he would stop at nothing.

The Vatican, October 1, 1938

In keeping with his and LaFarge's plan, Gustav Gundlach caught a train southward from Geneva, where he had been resting, and arrived in Rome on Saturday, October 1. He went straight to the Jesuit residence at Gregoriana University, where he was to meet LaFarge and finish up their work on the encyclical. But his American colleague was nowhere to be found.

By that time, LaFarge was waiting to get on the *Statendam* in Boulogne for his trip home. Gundlach tracked down the rector of the university, Vincent McCormick, who confirmed that LaFarge had left in a hurry a few days earlier. His destination was not clear. No one was exactly sure when and why LaFarge had left.

Finally then, on Monday, October 3, Gundlach received a letter LaFarge had sent to him from Paris, confirming the obvious, that he had decided to return to the States. LaFarge had broken their agreement, had not waited to say good-bye, and had not seen the pope. Instead he had relied on Ledóchowski's promise to deliver the encyclical to the pope right away. Gundlach was upset though not particularly surprised. He knew LaFarge had been feeling ill and that he had sick relatives in America. He also knew LaFarge was timid in dealing with Ledóchowski and that LaFarge put a great deal of faith in obedience and trust in his superiors. This was the way of the Jesuits. In this case, Gundlach was certain LaFarge's trust was misplaced.

Gundlach was also aware that Ledóchowski would be happy to have LaFarge out of the picture.

Gundlach sought out Ledóchowski to see what could be done to push along the process. He tried to make an appointment but the Jesuit superior general would not receive him. Gundlach was insulted because he was a trusted Jesuit who customarily had easy access. This affront made him concerned and skeptical, and he continued his efforts to find out what was happening with the encyclical. But he was unable to find out any information, and he had no copy of the encyclical at all. The document seemed to have disappeared. Gundlach was troubled by the atmosphere at the Vatican, particularly when people warned him not to use the telephone or even to write letters.

Instead of panicking, he made off-the-record inquiries with members of the Jesuit general's staff and learned that Ledóchowski had not yet spoken to any of his assistants about the encyclical and nothing had happened. By now, it had been more than a week since LaFarge delivered the document.

Next, he wrote a letter to John Killeen, a fellow Jesuit and one of Ledóchowski's assistants, asking for help. He hoped for a sympathetic response, because Killeen was a colleague of LaFarge's from New York. On Sunday, October 10, Gundlach finally tracked down Killeen, who said that two or three days earlier, Ledóchowski had sent the encyclical and accompanying documents to Father Enrico Rosa at the magazine *Civilta Cattolica*.

A longtime editor and commentator at the Jesuit magazine, Rosa was qualified to provide an opinion about the encyclical, although there was no sign that Ledóchowski was authorized to seek commentary before sending the encyclical directly to the pope. He wasn't supposed to hold on to the encyclical at all. There was no precedent for having members of the Jesuit curia review draft encyclicals en route to the pope, according to a Jesuit archivist, Edmond LaValle, who worked for Ledóchowski.

Ledóchowski and presumably Gundlach also knew that Rosa had authored various anti-Semitic articles and was unlikely to be sympathetic to the encyclical. In a commentary in June 1938, Rosa had agreed with the substance of Mussolini's campaign against the Jews. "The Jews are merely guests of other nations," he had written. "They reside there as foreigners, but although they are foreigners, they conduct themselves so as to usurp the best positions in every field, and not always by legitimate means."

On October 16, two weeks after arriving in Rome, Gundlach decided it was time to write to LaFarge. Just in case the letter would be tampered with, Gundlach used a basic code for his message. The pope was "Mr. Fisher," a lightly veiled reference using the image of the pope as a fisherman—to St. Peter, the first pope, and the fisherman's ring worn by popes after him. Ledóchowski, according to the code, was "our boss," and the encyclical was "our affair." Gundlach had taken a few weeks to gather information and also to calm down. Still, he showed irritation and a bit of sarcasm in the opening of his letter to LaFarge.

"I was here on the first of October, as was arranged," he told LaFarge. "Who could describe my astonishment when I learned upon my visit with the rector that you had departed?"

He then told LaFarge that Ledóchowski had done nothing with the encyclical in the three weeks since LaFarge delivered it. "[John Killeen] told me that our boss had given the text . . . to Signore Rosa of the well-known magazine for inspection," Gundlach said. Killeen promised there would be no changes that were not in keeping with what the authors had written and that he would let Gundlach know if anything happened.

Gundlach chided LaFarge for having been naive and overly earnest:

> *This is the situation; since then I have heard nothing more. Dear Father LaFarge! You see that your intention not to let the document get into other hands was not accomplished. Your loyalty as regards the boss, for which I had shown complete understanding in P[aris], but which even there appeared to me too extreme, has not been rewarded. Yes, the accusation could be made against you that due to that loyalty, the loyalty to Mr.*

Fisher [to the pope] has suffered. If one considers besides that the boss needed fourteen days to give the thing to the so-called "reviewer," and since then has remained himself in silence, one gets odd ideas. An outsider could see in all this the attempt for reasons of tactics and diplomacy to sabotage the task given directly to you by Mr. Fisher through delay.

Gundlach's letter raised the possibility of a conspiracy against the pope. He also accused LaFarge of not having been more alert to what had been happening around them—a plot to block publication of the encyclical. Gundlach believed that there was only one person who could reach out directly to the pope: LaFarge. Gundlach asked LaFarge to do what he thought he should have done originally—contact the pope directly and tell him what had happened. He cast the idea as a suggestion, but with the strong tone of believing this was LaFarge's obligation.

"You—and no one else—received the task at that time," Gundlach wrote. "I suggest that you write (that) you gave the text to our boss to hand on." Now, more than ever, Gundlach continued, LaFarge should tell the pope it was obvious that conditions in Europe were deteriorating and the encyclical meets "actual and urgent needs."

Ledóchowski had gotten what he wanted. All copies of the encyclical had been delivered to him, and LaFarge, the naive American Jesuit, had left for home. He could now decide what to do in his own time. Or perhaps decide nothing at all. He perused the document and decided this was the wrong time for it to be made public. Portions were overly specific and strong—for example, the criticism of Hitler's racial policies. Was this the time to be issuing bellicose statements directed at Germany that might further disintegrate the church's position in Germany—and now in

Austria and Czechoslovakia? Many at the Vatican felt that instead it was a time to be waging peace.

Ledóchowski dealt with the encyclical by ignoring it for a while. He then further delayed the process by sending the encyclical to Enrico Rosa. Rosa was gravely ill and his inability to act helped Ledóchowski—whether or not he knew that Rosa was sick—in his effort to delay the process. Rosa died in late November with the encyclical still on his desk.

Killeen followed Gundlach's letter to LaFarge with one of his own and said that he himself had been ordered by Ledóchowski to send a copy of the encyclical to Enrico Rosa. "Father General [Ledóchowski] sent an accompanying note," Killeen told LaFarge, "but did not advise me of its contents."

Killeen also told LaFarge he was determined to preserve the portion of the text about anti-Semitism—and would do everything possible "in order to safeguard your wishes in the matter, in case Fr. Rosa did think of proposing any changes." However, he added, "I have heard nothing further, and that is where things stand at present." He promised to keep LaFarge posted.

The pope was worsening physically, but he was determined to continue his opposition to totalitarianism. This was becoming increasingly challenging as he kept having problems controlling the chess pieces around him. No one had told him that Rosa had received the encyclical and it was doubtful he would have accepted changes from such a source.

Pius considered the Nazi drive against the Jews such a pervasive issue he planned to make a blanket statement that would redirect the entire view of the Roman Catholic Church. And that was what Ledóchowski was acting to slow down, knowing the pope's days were numbered.

Hoboken, New Jersey, October 9, 1938

'I'hree to four transatlantic passenger vessels carrying thousands of people arrived at New York Harbor every day. Then they quickly made the turnaround back to Europe. LaFarge's eight-day crossing had begun on October 1 with heavy rains that had been inundating the continent from England to Spain for several days. He complained of discomfort and rolling seas, but it could have been much worse. The *Statendam* was steaming westward in a lull between storms. The rain on the continent was the remnant of a hurricane that had raced across the Caribbean and up the Atlantic Coast a week earlier.

LaFarge hadn't heard about the severity of the storms, but he knew his stomach. "The steerage trip back to New York was anything but comfortable," he recalled, "especially as I was not a good sailor." His last-minute ticket was steerage class, but somehow he was listed in first class; his name must have been a late addition. Regardless the class of service, he did not mention ever having left his bunk to officiate at daily Mass. The passenger manifest showed that many people on board were likely fleeing the conflagration: Mr. and Mrs. Emanuel Feuermann and daughter; Dr. and Mrs. Julius Heilbrunn and their two young sons; the Oppenheimer family, the Rosenbaums and the Buchbinders and the Strausses and the Fursts—hundreds of what appeared to be Jewish surnames. There were other less likely names on the manifest, people named Franklin and Grant and Hoskins.

Unknown to LaFarge and most of the other passengers, European governments and banks fearing the outbreak of war had shipped millions of dollars in gold bullion on the *Statendam* for deposit in the United States. The *Statendam* and three other ships delivered $112 million in bullion that weekend—more than $5 billion at the 2012 value of gold.

The weather was clear and mild on Sunday afternoon, October 9, as the *Statendam* passed the Statue of Liberty on the Hudson River. Tugs guided the ship to a berth at the Holland-America Lines' Fifth Street pier with the new Empire State Building visible to the stern, gleaming in the glowing evening light across the harbor.

The scene onshore was bedlam. The dock area swarmed with passengers and longshoremen and motor coaches and taxis. Francis Talbot, John LaFarge's editor and friend, waited for him amid the chaos and, as a surprise, had brought along LaFarge's niece, Frances Childs, to greet her uncle. But when they looked at that same passenger manifest, they did not see the name LaFarge.

"Father Talbot and I met him on the wharf at his arrival," Frances recalled. "Granted the nature of his passage, we were uncertain where to find him, but find him we did, under L in first class, carrying large bundles and looking like the proverbial immigrant!"

Frances saw that her uncle had suffered physically during the five months in Europe. He had lost more than thirty pounds and looked like a pale shadow. LaFarge said little about his trip home, other than complaining about the food, but he was relieved to be away from the constant threat of tyranny.

The next order of business was going to his eldest brother's bedside. Despite his rush to get home, LaFarge had again failed to be present for the death of a close family member, first his father, his brother Bancel, and now Grant. "Alas, just as I was about to leave I received the news of his death and had to content myself with the sad consolation of officiating at his funeral Mass in the Church of St. Joseph in Wickford, Rhode Island," LaFarge wrote. "Generous to a fault, and deeply affectionate, Grant had suffered in silence the stings of disappointment. I could not help begrudging the days and weeks that I might, if not for that summer abroad, have spent near my oldest brother before it was too late."

Adolf Hitler continued to dominate the headlines as LaFarge settled in at *America*'s Jesuit headquarters just off West End Avenue in New York. The Wehrmacht was completing its occupation of Sudetenland and newspaper stories described a Europe that still was advancing toward war. For all practical purposes, events had developed as LaFarge perceived they would when he stood at Prague's Wenceslas Square less than five months earlier and realized he had been witnessing the last days of Czech independence.

When LaFarge came home, the United States was divided into camps—those who agreed with appeasement and those who saw war as inevitable. Some said "save the refugees and fight the Fascists on all fronts"; others praised Hitler for keeping the Communists at bay. LaFarge prayed that somehow peace would be preserved in Europe and that perhaps the Munich accord would achieve it. But he wavered. He had heard Hitler's frightful speech and had seen Ledóchowski's placid reaction. The memory of his meeting with Jan Masaryk resounded and made it more and more clear that one could not choose between Communism and Nazism; they were both authoritarian systems, but Nazism was about to swallow up Europe and beyond.

Meanwhile, he awaited word from Rome, perhaps with questions from the pope or from Ledóchowski, prior to publication of the encyclical.

CHAPTER NINE

Shame and Despair

Rome, October 7, 1938

As soon as Mussolini returned to Rome from presiding over the Munich Agreement in September, he issued a new set of regulations that banned marriage between Jews and Catholics. The pope charged that the measure violated the 1929 Concordat between the Vatican and the Fascist government and demanded urgent negotiations with the government.

Despite his general reluctance to criticize Mussolini publicly, Secretary of State Eugenio Pacelli agreed with the pope in this case, because he felt it was the Roman Catholic Church alone that should decide questions of union in matrimony. For Pacelli, this was a matter that went beyond politics; it cut to the core of Catholic theology. He discussed the resulting crisis openly at a dinner at the Irish embassy, seated next to Caroline Phillips, the U.S. ambassador's wife. It was a rare opportunity for Mrs. Phillips. "The cardinal is one of those fine ascetic-looking priests who are rare and I always feel it a privilege to talk with," she wrote in her diary. "There was much talk of the Fascist laws against the Jews which they believe will prove to be contrary to the Concordat between the Vatican and the Fascist government. We may expect a new controversy."

But while Pacelli made sure his remarks were diplomatic and modest, the pope was responding angrily and emotionally to the anti-Semitic marriage laws. "I am ashamed . . . ashamed to be Italian," the pope told Domenico Tardini, Pacelli's deputy. "And tell that, Father, to Mussolini himself! I am ashamed not as pope but as an Italian! The Italian people have become a herd of stupid sheep. I will speak out, without fear . . . I have no fear!"

Whether or not that particular message was delivered, Foreign Minister Ciano reported in his diary that Il Duce "described the Vatican as a Catholic ghetto. And he said that all the Piuses had brought misfortune to the Church. He described the current Pope as 'the Pontiff who will leave the greatest heap of debris behind him.'"

Vatican prelates visited Mussolini and counseled him to remain patient. Many representatives of the church described the pope as an increasingly solitary voice and implied that he would soon be dead.

A day after Mussolini's marriage decree, on October 9, Hitler stepped up his confrontation with the church when Nazi thugs in Vienna forced their way into the residence of Cardinal Theodor Innitzer, terrorized the cardinal and his staff, burned furniture, and trashed church offices. Innitzer was slightly injured by flying glass. The Nazis said Innitzer had been interfering in politics and had to be stopped. This was a turnaround in the fortunes of Innitzer, the same cardinal who had been considered a darling of the Nazi regime and had met with Hitler and congratulated him after the March occupation of Austria.

The Vatican quickly dispatched Joseph Hurley to Vienna to investigate; Hurley returned to Rome after a few days and filed a report with the Vatican secretary of state's office. Several days after that, on Saturday, October 15, he came to the U.S. embassy to brief Ambassador Phillips. "A mob of 1500 Nazi youths surrounded the palace, some entered the second story, smashed windows, threw into the street holy relics, threw one priest into the street causing both legs to be broken," Hurley told Phillips. "The only police interference during the riot was by one officer who arrested one rioter and the latter was promptly released by his fellow rioters."

The pope called Hitler a renegade and said the attack on Innitzer was sinister. The pope denied the charge against Innitzer. "It is a lie—we repeat, a lie, a lie, a lie" that the Vatican was involved in politics, Pius said, speaking in the third person. "The pope follows only one policy from which no force on earth can separate him: to give something to the common good."

Following these events, Hurley told Phillips he had approval to use the Vatican newspaper and radio to publish and broadcast speeches and statements made by President Roosevelt and the U.S. government. That made the Vatican the only free conduit of information available in Italy, and that information would be broadcast in many languages, including German. The authorization might have come directly from Pope Pius, since Pacelli, as always, would have counseled restraint.

On the morning of October 28, the pope bundled up against the cold and rain for the trip back to Rome from Castel Gandolfo. He bade farewell to the villagers from the balcony during a break in the showers. The rain fell again when he arrived at St. Peter's, but people still stood in the square and cheered. He gave them his blessing and then retired to his private rooms. His energy was flagging. More than four months had passed since he had summoned LaFarge, and still there was no sign of the encyclical that could change history.

At another time, he might have taken strong steps to track down LaFarge and the encyclical, but he didn't. More and more, he was deputizing others to carry some of his burdens. He had even summoned Pacelli from his long vacation in Switzerland to help with the affairs of state back at the Vatican.

New York, October 28, 1938

LaFarge reacted to Gundlach's scolding letter by drafting one of his own to the pope. There had to be a way to tell the pope gently and clearly that the encyclical had been waylaid. Gundlach had cautioned, though, that spies were everywhere. "Nowadays mail often has a curious fate," he wrote. Gundlach suggested that LaFarge go through the apostolic delegate in Washington, Bishop Amleto Giovanni Cicognani, who was a confidant of the pope and who should be able to see that LaFarge's letter reached the pope's desk. But even that was not a certain route.

LaFarge wrote the letter in French in a flowery style and made sure to praise Ledóchowski, the Jesuit superior, in case he read a copy:

> *With the heavy responsibility that Your Holiness deigned to place on my poor shoulders, I am persuaded to recognize my obligation to inform Your Holiness of the . . . circumstances concerning my efforts. Obeying as well as I could the directions that Your Holiness on that occasion had graciously provided me, I worked intensively all summer, helped at the suggestion of our Most Reverend Father General by one of the professors of the Gregorian Pontifical University.*

LaFarge wrote that he had returned "to Rome at the end of September and delivered the document to the hands of [Ledóchowski] who most benevolently had given me every facility in producing it."

LaFarge apologized for not having seen the pope again. "Thank God," he said, that "the physical exhaustion of my energy that affected me in August is now cured. For serious personal reasons, I was forced to leave [Rome] immediately for America. That saddens me deeply because I felt an ardent desire to deliver the document in person."

He added that Ledóchowski had promised to deliver the text quickly. "So I console myself that it surely must already be in the hands of Your Holiness, although I lost the opportunity to present it in person."

Of course, LaFarge knew by now that Ledóchowski had withheld the encyclical and that Gundlach saw Ledóchowski's role as part of a maneuver to block the encyclical.

While LaFarge could not be sure that the pope actually had received the letter after he wrote at the end of October, Gundlach told him that the pope, according to his sources in the Vatican, had made inquiries about the encyclical about two weeks after the letter should have arrived. At the same time, the sources said it might not make a difference. The inner circle told Gundlach the pontiff's heart condition had worsened and he was not expected to survive long. He has "become very frail," Gundlach wrote to LaFarge on November 18. "People around him don't give him much time. It appears that the situation is such that only what other people permit reaching [him] does reach him. But he himself is supposed to be mentally alert but not to bring forth much initiative."

Gundlach's letter was one of the few open acknowledgments of a rift at the Vatican. As the pope weakened and was less able to function, Pacelli gained more power, not only as secretary of state, but also as the *camerlengo*, the man designated to govern the church when the pope is incapacitated—or when he dies. The result was a race for time to locate and publish the encyclical before Pope Pius XI died.

Rome, November 5, 1938

In the fall, the pope and President Roosevelt coordinated a visit to Rome of the church's most controversial leader in the United States, Cardinal George Mundelein. Mundelein, the archbishop of Chicago, would report on the results of a recent Catholic Eucharistic Congress in New Orleans, where Mundelein had been the pope's official representative. There was also the matter of the beatification of Mother Cabrini, the little Italian nun who had worked among the poor of New York and Washington, that would take place on November 13. But those were more excuses than answers about the real reason for the visit.

The mere mention of Mundelein's name was a jab at Hitler and the Nazis. Mundelein, one of the more liberal members of the College of Cardinals, had been more outspoken against the Nazis than almost anyone. In 1936, he had said the Catholic Church in Germany was being "slowly strangled. Religious leaders are in jail. We are being fed propaganda that they are guilty of criminal violations."

And two months after the pope's first anti-Nazi encyclical in 1937, and with the pope's evident blessing, Mundelein had gone much further—he mocked Hitler and those around him. He asked in a speech in Chicago: "How is it that a nation of 60 million people will submit in fear and servitude to an alien, an Austrian paper-hanger, and a poor one at that, I am told, and a few associates like Goebbels and Göring, who dictate every move of the people's lives." Hitler was enraged by Mundelein's speech, which provoked diplomatic protests in Washington and at the Vatican.

Mundelein's trip appeared to be a maneuver conducted by President Roosevelt with the pope's knowledge—perhaps with the help of Mundelein himself. A few days before Mundelein's scheduled arrival, U.S. ambassador William Phillips called Monsignor Joseph Hurley to the U.S. embassy to ask if he knew anything about the visit. Roosevelt wanted Phillips to receive Cardinal Mundelein as a major U.S. dignitary. "This is all most interesting and unusual and of course will cause a great deal of public comment since nothing of this nature has ever happened to an American Cardinal visiting Rome, but the President has good reasons, undoubtedly."

Hurley agreed that the ambassador's official involvement "will be widely noted in the press because previously no visit to Rome by an American Cardinal has called for any notice by the Embassy."

Phillips welcomed Mundelein ostentatiously dockside in Naples on November 5 and took him to lunch on an American warship, the *Omaha*. After the luncheon, Phillips had arranged for a special train to take the American cardinal directly to Rome.

The trip was a demonstration of U.S. solidarity with the pope in opposition to Hitler. The beauty of Mundelein's visit was that while he made no public declaration at all in Rome, the trip managed to anger the Nazis as intended.

Nazi newspapers reviled Mundelein and called him the American "Agitator Priest." Joseph Goebbels's newspaper, *Angriff,* said it was a play by Roosevelt for Catholic votes in midterm elections on November 8 and a diversion from "American reality," which "consists of a hungry farmer family leaving its home, strikers playing cards instead of working, tramping youths who never had jobs, breadlines containing parents with baby carriages, and shanty 'depression homes.'"

The diplomatic offensive against Hitler during Mundelein's

Achille Ratti, the future Pope
Pius XI, circa 1880. Ratti was
from a mountain village in
northern Italy near Milan.
He was ordained a priest at
age twenty-two in 1879. As
he advanced in the Catholic
Church, he also became known
as a world-class mountain
climber. His exploits included
the ascent of 15,203-foot Monte
Rosa, the second highest peak
in the Alps, on a pass never
attempted before.

John LaFarge, at about twenty years
of age. He graduated in 1901 from
Harvard University, where he studied
music theory and played the piano,
while focusing his studies on poetry,
literature, and the classics.

LaFarge in Holland, early
1900s. LaFarge entered a
seminary in Innsbruck, Austria,
in 1901, after Theodore
Roosevelt, a family friend,
helped convince LaFarge's
father to accept the idea that his
son wanted to be a priest.

LaFarge, circa 1915 in St. Mary's County, Maryland. After becoming a Jesuit, he was assigned to work in predominantly African-American parishes in rural Maryland, where he became an advocate of vocational training, education, and equal opportunity.

Achille Ratti, early 1900s. Ratti served as a teacher, as a scholar with three doctorates, as a librarian first at the four-centuries-old Ambrosian Library in Milan, and finally as head of the Vatican Library in Rome.

RIDGE, MARYLAND 1920

LaFarge, circa 1920, St. Mary's County.
LaFarge lived in southern Maryland from
1911 to 1926. He worked on the creation
of regional Catholic interracial councils
and thought such councils should fight for
an end to prejudice. He was transferred to
New York in 1926 as associate editor of the
Jesuit magazine *America*.

Pope Pius XI and his secretary, Monsignor
Carlo Confalonieri, in the Vatican gardens,
1922. Achille Ratti was elected pope in
February 1922. He had been elevated to
the rank of cardinal and archbishop of
Milan less than a year earlier. Previously he
had been Pope Benedict XV's diplomatic
representative in Poland after the end of
World War I.

Monsignor Joseph P. Hurley, right, next to Bishop Edward Mooney in Japan, 1931, with an unidentified cleric. In 1934, the Hurley was appointed to the Vatican Secretariat of State, replacing Francis Spellman as the ranking American at the Vatican. He became the pope's English interpreter and unofficial go-between with the United States.

Cardinal Eugenio Pacelli, the pope's diplomatic representative in Germany, leaving a meeting, circa 1929. Pacelli served the Vatican in Germany for twelve years. Pacelli, later Pope Pius XII, became the Vatican Secretary of State in 1930. Many thought that the pope used Pacelli as a sober counterpoint to his own impetuous style of leadership.

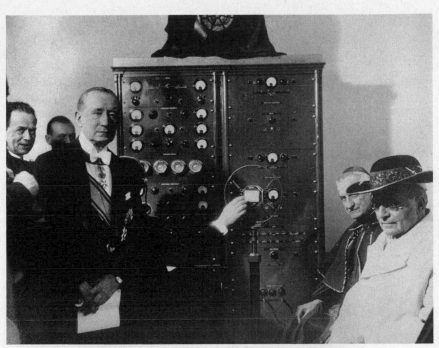

The pope and Italian inventor Guglielmo Marconi, left, inaugurated Vatican Radio on February 12, 1931. Pius used the immediacy of his broadcasts to speak to a world audience for the first time. Marconi said, "This is the first time in history that the living voice of the Pope will have been heard simultaneously in all parts of the globe."

The pope at the microphone in 1932. His frequent
broadcasts ranged increasingly into politics and pleas
for peace. The pope embraced technology, expanded the
Vatican observatory, substituted cars for horse-drawn
carriages, and installed elevators, an automatic phone
system, and a new printing plant at the Vatican.

Ambassador William Phillips and his wife, Caroline Drayton Phillips, in Europe. Friends of President and Mrs. Roosevelt (Mrs. Phillips was a relative), they served in Rome from 1936 to 1941. FDR wanted Phillips to weaken chances of an alliance between Mussolini and Hitler. Caroline Phillips's diary provided frank insights about fascism and anti-Semitism in Italy.

Wlodimir Ledóchowski, the superior general of the Jesuit order from 1915 to 1942. Jesuit leaders are also referred to as "the Black Pope," and Ledóchowski was considered the third most powerful person at the Vatican after the pope and Cardinal Pacelli. Known as a strict force among the Jesuits, he espoused anti-Semitic positions, though he pledged to work with John LaFarge and the pope on the 1938 encyclical.

The pope, 1932; he suffered a heart attack in late 1936 and was not expected to survive. He recovered in early 1937 and began issuing declarations including an encyclical that harshly condemned Hitler and the Nazis. In 1938, Hitler and Mussolini considered him a major opponent and were concerned that his popular appeal would damage their ability to sway public opinion.

Cardinal Eugène Tisserant, the pope's longtime friend and ally, was the only French
cardinal working directly at the Vatican.
Tisserant had served in the French army in
World War I in the field and as an intelligence
officer. He was mentioned as a possible future
pope and was considered a rival of Cardinal
Pacelli.

Mussolini and Hitler in Germany, 1937. Hitler traveled to Rome in May 1938 to cement ties with Italy to form the Axis. Privately, the German and Italian leaders despised one another. Pope Pius XI left for his summer palace at Castel Gandolfo to avoid being at the Vatican during Hitler's visit. He did not want to see "the crooked cross of neo-paganism" flying over Rome.

President Roosevelt and Cardinal George Mundelein of Chicago, undated. Mundelein became one of the church's strongest critics of Nazism. In a 1937 speech, he derided Hitler as an "Austrian paper-hanger, and a poor one at that." Both Roosevelt and the pope supported Mundelein, who traveled to Rome as Roosevelt's official emissary in November 1938.

Jan Masaryk, undated. John LaFarge met with Masaryk, the Czech ambassador to Britain, in May 1938, as Britain sought to appease Hitler by ceding the majority-German region of Czech Sudetenland to German control. Meeting with LaFarge, Masaryk, son of the late Czech president Tomáš Garrigue Masaryk, predicted an alliance between Hitler and Stalin.

CONFÉRENCES DE LA CITÉ

Sous la Présidence d'Honneur de M. ABEL BONNARD, de l'Académie Française

Vous êtes prié d'assister à la conférence de

MONSIEUR LE R. P. LA FARGE S. J.

SUR

LA DÉMOCRATIE AMÉRICAINE
SA RÉUSSITE ET SES PROBLÈMES

qui aura lieu à la Maison de la Chimie

28, RUE SAINT-DOMINIQUE, 7ᵉ

LE MARDI 17 MAI 1938, A 21 HEURES

LE PRÉSIDENT :
BERNARD FAŸ

Participation aux frais :
10 francs

Invitation to LaFarge's speech before a group of intellectuals and politicians in Paris on May 17, 1938. LaFarge, who spoke about U.S. politics and issues of democracy, often found himself questioned about U.S. policy toward Europe and whether the United States would fight alongside France and Britain against the Nazis.

LaFarge in New York in 1938 after returning from Europe. LaFarge kept secret his work on the pope's encyclical. He delivered the draft encyclical to Superior General Ledóchowski in Rome, who said he would deliver it to the pope. On his return from Europe, LaFarge spoke out about themes of war and anti-Semitism.

British prime minister Neville Chamberlain; Benito Mussolini; Lord Halifax, the British foreign minister; and his Italian counterpart, Count Galeazzo Ciano, left to right. Chamberlain and Halifax visited Rome in January 1939 but had no success in improving relations with Italy. They also met with the pope, who reiterated his strong rejection of Hitler and Mussolini.

Gustav Gundlach, a German Jesuit, was LaFarge's main collaborator on the encyclical. Gundlach wrote to LaFarge in October 1938 that Ledóchowski refused to see him or discuss the document and suspected that as the pope grew ill, Ledóchowski was purposely withholding and delaying publication of the anti-Hitler declaration.

Charles Coughlin, the Radio Priest, undated. The Catholic priest's weekly national broadcasts in the 1930s became increasingly right-wing and anti-Semitic. He took an anti-Roosevelt, extremist political stance in defiance of the Vatican, gathering an audience of millions. He was eventually silenced amid FBI investigations of his contacts with Germans and of his sources of funding.

John LaFarge, circa 1954. LaFarge became editor of *America* magazine in 1944 and continued to speak out against anti-Semitism during World War II. In his 1954 memoir, *The Manner Is Ordinary*, LaFarge did not reveal the story of his time working with the pope. He promoted human rights for the rest of his life, wrote a series of books, and won a number of media and human rights awards.

LaFarge joined Martin Luther King Jr. at the march on Washington in August 1963, optimistic about the course of civil rights. The issue, he said, "concerns the fundamental rights of all of us . . . are all involved in this question of right and wrong."

Bishop Joseph Hurley and Pope Paul VI at the Vatican, circa 1964. Hurley was banished from the Vatican by Pope Pius XII after speaking out strongly against Hitler and Nazism in 1940. He was named bishop of St. Augustine, Florida, where he served for twenty-seven years.

visit was dampened by the pope's health. He did preside on November 13 in Mundelein's presence at the beatification ceremony of Mother Cabrini; however, he had to be propped up on his specially designed platform chair. Mundelein emerged from a private meeting with the pope saying that Pius appeared vibrant and healthy. Nevertheless, the pontiff's energy was draining away.

Ambassador Phillips left Rome for his long-delayed consultations in Washington on November 12 while Mundelein was still in town, but after the diplomatic portion of his visit. Caroline Phillips stayed on and recorded details of the rest of Mundelein's visit. She described the following day in her diary the beatification ceremony at St. Peter's for Mother Cabrini and saw the pope was not well.

"It was truly a marvelous sight," she wrote. She was seated behind

rows of Cardinals and Bishops in scarlet and violet robes, handsome Chamberlains of the pope in black Spanish costumes of the 16th century, white ruffs around their necks, gold chains across their black velvet breasts, short sword and knickerbockers, knights of Malta resplendent with gold cross and order on their black velvet and plumed hats. . . . we waited and finally flares of beautiful silver trumpets followed by wild cheers and waving of handkerchiefs announced the arrival of the pope.

He came seated in his red velvet . . . embroidered chair carried high by men in red cassocks and preceded by Cardinals and priests and acolytes. He was sitting there very wearily but with immense dignity and peace blessing the crowds on either side of him with his right hand. He had a fine, spiritual, intellectual face but looked very feeble.

Mundelein's visit ended with concern about the pope, and for a time he even delayed his departure for fear that the pontiff's illness might have been terminal. There was another underlying sadness and anxiety beneath events in Rome. Germany had fallen to a new level of terror in the Nazi campaign against Jews.

Berlin, November 9, 1938

Early on the morning of October 28, 1938, Nazi storm troopers in Hanover, Germany, rousted an old Polish tailor, Zindel Grynszpan, and his wife, Rifka, from their bed and forced them onto a train out of the city bound for Poland. Along with an estimated twelve thousand other Jews, they were denied entry and huddled instead in a refugee camp on the German-Polish border. Grynszpan contacted his seventeen-year-old son, Herschel, saying they were trapped in the harsh, overcrowded camp with no prospects of escape; the family had been left penniless. The young man was outraged and distraught.

A week later, on November 7, he walked into the German embassy in Paris and asked to speak with a diplomat. When an undersecretary named Ernst vom Rath stepped forward, Grynszpan shot him at close range. Vom Rath, a member of the SA Nazi storm troopers, died two days later.

The incident gave the Nazis an excuse to carry out a coordinated attack on Jews that was more violent and widespread than anything before it. Joseph Goebbels reported that Hitler had decided "demonstrations should be allowed to continue. The police should be withdrawn. For once the Jews should get to feel the popular anger."

The night of November 9 would be known as Kristallnacht, the Night of the Broken Glass. The marauding Nazis killed at least ninety-one people, raped and tortured many more, and burned at least 270 synagogues throughout greater Germany, which now also included Austria and the Czech Sudetenland. They smashed seventy-five hundred Jewish businesses and sent thirty thousand Jews to concentration camps. The organized bands were joined by others who looted merchandise and wrecked stores, carrying away clothing and shoes amid cries of "Perish Jewry" and "Kill the Jews."

The terror was boundless. Liesel Kaufmann, a fifteen-year-old girl, could not escape the memory of that night, "the flames, the smoke, and the chants," she recalled. "The next day, the synagogue was still burning and a crowd was still shouting. They said, 'Burn them—kill the Jews.' I still hear those voices."

Bystanders stood by silently and powerless, shocked as the plain-clothed marauders hunted down Jews and trashed and torched their synagogues and stores. The bands sometimes erroneously trashed non-Jewish establishments but tried to avoid that damage and to leave foreign businesses intact. There was looting; shoes were stolen from wrecked displays, and children wandered with their faces smeared with filched chocolate bars.

"'Move on,'" a policeman warned Otto D. Tolischus of the *New York Times*, "'there are young comrades of [our Aryan race] inside who have some work to do.'"

President Roosevelt condemned the attacks, expressed shock on behalf of all Americans, and said he could "scarcely believe that such things could occur in a twentieth century civilization." He then announced he was recalling the U.S. ambassador to Germany.

The ailing pope did not issue a statement on Kristallnacht; it was not clear if news about the attack reached him immediately or whether any statement he might have made could have gotten past Pacelli and the others surrounding him. The Vatican newspaper was also silent.

While Pius's voice was not heard, churchmen closest to him

beyond Rome spoke out. Cardinal Alfred Schuster, the archbishop of Milan, the pope's home city, said the racism preached by Mussolini and Hitler was heresy. Despite the calls for "peace and avoiding international conflict at any cost," Schuster said, the racist policies "constitute a forge upon which are formed the most murderous weapons for war to come."

"A kind of heresy has been abroad," Shuster said, "and is spreading elsewhere that not only attacks the supernatural basis of the Catholic Church but is materializing the spiritual concepts of individuals, the nation and the fatherland in human blood, denies to humanity every other spiritual value and thus constitutes an international danger no less than that of Bolshevism itself. It is so-called racism."

There were echoes of Pius's words elsewhere as well, especially among American bishops and cardinals, many of whom repeated the pope's earlier attacks on the Nazis.

New York, November 20, 1938

LaFarge's magazine, *America*, condemned Kristallnacht in a sharp editorial. "Germany, once counted among the civilized nations, has put herself beyond the pale. . . . We have no words to express our horror and detestation of the barbarous and un-Christian treatment of Jews by Nazi Germany. It forms one of history's blackest pages."

American Catholic leaders repudiated the savagery of Kristallnacht. Catholic University organized a high-profile, prime-time coast-to-coast radio broadcast, featuring a live hookup with bishops from around the country, with the rector of the university and with Governor Alfred E. Smith of New York. Rev. Maurice Sheehy, a professor at Catholic University, set the tone, saying that church leaders "raise their voice not in mad hysteria, but in firm indignation against the atrocities visited upon the Jews in Germany, because as Pope Pius XI has pointed out, we are all spiritual Semites."

Despite the condemnation from religious leaders, one widely known American priest presented a different message. Father Charles Coughlin, a onetime New Deal Democrat, had a one-hour weekly national radio broadcast that was steeped in demagoguery, virulent criticism of Roosevelt, and underlying support for Adolf Hitler. A forty-seven-year-old parish priest at the National Shrine of the Little Flower Church in Royal Oaks, Michigan, Coughlin had been broadcasting the weekly program since 1926. His power and influence had begun to falter under persistent criticism from the church hierarchy, but he still reached a loyal audience estimated at as many as fifteen million.

Coughlin took to the microphone at 4 P.M. on November 20 for his weekly Sunday address. That evening, he said his goal was to submit Kristallnacht to the lens of "scientific analysis." The result was rhetorical tripe and lies. Why did the Nazis lash out at Jews? His answer: Jews are aggressive and wily and the atheists among them are responsible for a worldwide conspiracy that led to the Russian Revolution and the onset of Communism.

After the anti-Jewish rant, his flagship radio station, WMCA in New York, threw him off the air as did many other stations. The next week he continued in the same vein, saying he only asked "that an insane world will distinguish between the innocent Jews and the guilty Jews as much as I would ask the same insane world to distinguish between the innocent gentile and the guilty gentile."

Prior to these broadcasts, Catholic officials and priests in the United States often had difficulty confronting Coughlin head-on. LaFarge, among others, was uncomfortable speaking about him in public because they feared his power. "He has tremendous influence among Catholics and non-Catholics," LaFarge said in an interview shortly after he had arrived in England in May 1938. "This influence reaches the most inaccessible places, in fact wherever there is a radio. I think on the whole his influence is good, though I don't agree with a lot of what he says."

Coughlin also had important friends, including the anti-Semitic and pro-Nazi head of the Ford Motor Company, Henry Ford, who was thought to be bankrolling the radio priest's political activities.

Unsurprisingly, Coughlin had become a darling of the Nazis and the Fascists. One of Mussolini's staunchest propagandists, Roberto Farinacci, called him an "apostle of Christianity." Joseph Goebbels wondered sarcastically about what had happened to the touted U.S. media and their famed freedom of the press.

More than a year later, an FBI investigation determined that Coughlin had been in touch for some time with German agents in the United States. He was finally forced off the air in May 1940, a year and a half after his Kristallnacht anti-Semitic broadcasts; by April 1942, when his newspaper, *Social Justice*, was banned from distribution, Coughlin was effectively silenced.

Three weeks after Kristallnacht, LaFarge resumed speaking out against racism in the United States and more prominently compared it to what was happening to Jews in Europe. At a dinner on November 29 in LaFarge's honor after he returned from Europe, he proclaimed that U.S. racism is the "pale but venomous elder cousin" of Nazi racism. "Racism, like the other destructive ideologies, cannot be understood and interpreted merely in terms of fear and dislike for its victims. In Europe racism is so closely associated with anti Jewish propaganda that one is included to ask whether the whole racist idea has any other aim or object than that of expressing spite against the Jews."

The speech reflected the tone and language he had assembled for the pope's encyclical, yet no one at the dinner had a hint that this was part of the Vatican's most important statement ever on anti-Semitism.

The Vatican, November 25, 1938

The pope woke up at his normal hour on the morning of Friday, November 25, feeling as well rested as he had in recent days. He ate breakfast and walked out of his private apartments toward the elevator to begin his workday. But then he suddenly faltered, and before his aides could react, he lost his balance and fainted to the floor. Two Vatican physicians, Aminta Milani, the chief of the Vatican health service, and Filippo Rocchi, the junior member of the medical staff, raced to the pope. Attendants carried him to his bed. Milani administered oxygen and an injection of camphor oil, which had been used for decades as a stimulant in such cases.

For hours, the pope did not regain consciousness. The pope's heart had been damaged in the attack he suffered in late 1936, and those surrounding him were gravely worried. The priests and cardinals had been told he could not survive a second attack. Word spread around Rome that the pope was near death. Lorenzo Lauri, the first of the cardinals to appear, administered the sacrament of Last Rights when Milani described the gravity of the situation.

Pius's heartbeat was irregular and Milani continued to administer oxygen. Cardinal Pacelli soon arrived and sent word to church officials around the world that the pope was ill and to expect the worst. He ordered all but the doctors and closest aides to stay away from the papal bedroom. People gathered at the Vatican as word spread. The mood was black and somber. Prayers were issued worldwide.

The pope's heart rate was alternately weak and fibrillating; he did not move. After a while, just as Milani was giving up hope, the pope's heartbeat grew stronger again and the fibrillation stopped. By late morning, the doctor reported that pope was improving. Around 3 P.M., Pius opened his eyes, smiled, and appeared well. He asked for something to drink, and Milani called for some hot broth. The pope's sister, Donna Camilla Ratti, and his nephew, Count Franco Ratti, who had raced down from Milan on first word of the pope's illness, were soon allowed to enter Pius's bedroom to sit with him. By the end of the day, the pope was weary, but the scare was over.

An official Vatican communiqué reported the pope had suffered an attack of cardiac asthma, a symptom of what would later be called congestive heart failure, but had improved significantly in the course of the day. "It is a question now of knowing whether a true improvement occurred," the communiqué said, "or whether the improvement was merely the effect of the remedies administered to sustain the Pontiff's heart."

The pope was fully alert by the next morning. Although he understood the severity of what had happened, he went back to work and tried to minimize the danger. "Do not think of me," he said. "Too many others are suffering today. May God help them all and bring peace to them all."

Meanwhile, the pope summoned a trusted friend from Milan, Dr. Domenico Cesa-Bianchi, who was chairman of the medical institute at the University of Milan. Cesa-Bianchi had assembled a team of doctors at the Milan Institute, most of them anti-Fascists who were working quietly against Mussolini. Among them was the thirty-five-year-old Jewish heart specialist, Massimo Calabresi, who had been imprisoned by the Italian regime as a student. Calabresi had just finished a text on advances in cardiology and received a nationwide prize for the best medical book of the year. The pope wanted the best medical care available as he fought for time.

Within days, papal audiences and speeches resumed. "The Pope must be a Pope, he must not stay in bed," Pius said. On Sunday morning, November 27, the pope surprised everyone by speaking to four hundred Hungarian pilgrims. One said the pope appeared "very pale but he appeared the master of his strength and unhesitating in his motions."

"Since that date," added a U.S. embassy official reported to Washington, "the Pope has not deviated from his normal schedule."

The pope had averted death once more, but his collapse added to the perception that these might be his final days. Through December it was understood that private audiences would be shortened. His secretaries insisted that the pope take longer breaks and rest frequently. Some of the time, at least, he complied.

CHAPTER TEN

A New Year and an End to Appeasement

The Vatican, Christmas 1938

DESPITE THE POPE'S amazing recovery, Pacelli took the incident as an opportunity to take over more responsibilities at the Vatican than ever before. The pope was attentive and authoritarian about the issues that mattered most to him, but he could not do everything.

On December 18, a cold, rainy day three weeks after his health crisis, the pope went out to the Vatican gardens to deliver a speech to the Pontifical Academy of Science. He addressed a pet theme, the relationship between religion and science, and had invited several Jewish scientists, now banned by Mussolini from working at Italian universities, to become members of the academy. Diplomats and prominent scientists attended the event, including Alexis Carrel, a French-born Nobel Prize–winning physician and pioneer in vascular surgery. Carrel, based at the Rockefeller Institute for Medical Research in New York, had been working on methods involving open-heart surgery and had been collaborating with the great aviator Charles Lindbergh on the development of a pump foreseen as something that others thought to be impossible—an artificial heart. Carrel and Lindbergh had been featured on the cover of *Time* magazine in June 1938.

After a forty-five-minute address, the pope returned to the Vatican and spent the next day in bed. Dr. Milani, the head of the Vatican health office, came to visit but denied rumors the pope was ill once more. Carrel, who in later years became a good friend of John LaFarge, apparently was not called in for a consultation with the pope.

Days following, the pope often suffered from night pains, coughing attacks, and insomnia. Some mornings he fell asleep while almost sitting up in bed so he could breathe better. He often woke up before dawn, tossed and turned, and then slept some more. Nevertheless, he was up every morning for breakfast. After that, he went to his office at 8 A.M. and met with Pacelli for an hour starting at 9:30 A.M. He took long rests in the afternoon and was given occasional injections of camphor oil as prescribed by Milani, who came to see him several times a day.

GUNDLACH HAD BEGUN to hear from his sources at the Vatican that the pope had requested information more than once about the encyclical. But it is not known if he ever confronted Ledóchowski and demanded immediate delivery. Vatican reporters were told the pope was still working on an encyclical dealing with "world problems." That report was transmitted by news services and published in the United States. A report in the *New York World Telegram* on November 28 said the pope "would soon issue an encyclical . . . It was believed . . . that he was anxious to reaffirm his position on various world problems such as his condemnation of armed conflicts and Communism and his plea to leading statesmen to cooperate for peace." The Associated Press added "there were reports, which were without confirmation, that the Pontiff might issue a Christmas Encyclical on world affairs, inspired by Nazi and Fascist racial policies." However, the report said that the papal document "might have been delayed indefinitely by his illness."

Gundlach noted Pacelli's ascendant role in the wake of Pius's recent medical crisis. As Gundlach told LaFarge: "Things seem to be proceeding in such a way that he [the pope] gets only what others want him to get; he is supposed still to be in good psychological condition, to be sure, but not able to do very much on his own."

The Italian government's sources at the Vatican were passing along word about the pope's precarious health. Neither Hitler nor Mussolini had forgiven the pope's intransigence and repeated harping against the racial policies. Il Duce told Ciano that he hoped the pope "will die very soon." Mussolini fumed, but backed off each time from doing what he wished he could do, rallying a popular revolt against the Vatican and putting padlocks on all the churches in Italy. But he told Ciano it was better "to not provoke a crisis with the Vatican at the present time."

During the pope's annual Christmas greeting to the College of Cardinals, he again said that Italy's laws about racial purity and attacks on Jews violated the Lateran agreement between the Vatican and the Mussolini government. The pope said he had negotiated the document with the king of Italy, and "his incomparable Minister"—Mussolini. Without mentioning Il Duce's name, he mocked Mussolini as if he were subordinate of the king. The Fascist press dealt with the pope's criticism by rewriting and censoring the negative connotation.

The pope continued his speech and referred once again to his "crooked cross" speech during Hitler's visit to Rome in May: "the recent apotheosis in this very city of a cross which is the enemy of the cross of Christ" in pushing cold-blooded laws on racism. "We at least hoped our white hair would be respected. Instead they rudely went ahead."

Germany reacted within days of the pope's Christmas speech, suggesting once again that the pope himself was Jewish or wanted to be. The Nazi newspaper *Angriff* attacked the pope, saying the Vatican was "occupying itself solely with the Jewish question to the extent of giving an impression of complete solidarity between Jewry and the largest Christian church."

Osservatore Romano, meanwhile, closed the year with a commentary that stated emphatically the pope's position on why Germany is a greater enemy than the Soviet Union. "While Russia simply has atheism without a substitute for religion, things are different in National-Socialist Germany. In the National-Socialist world the negation of Christianity, no less obstinate, is transformed into a neo-pagan and pantheist mysticism which pretends to protest against atheism and even stands as a defender of faith and religion . . . This work of religious destruction is all the more dangerous because it leads to error and is more deceitful than openly proclaimed and attempted atheism."

New York, December 29, 1938

LaFarge had still not heard anything about the encyclical. As he waited, he started raising his profile as someone who spoke out about race and anti-Semitism.

"This past year belonged to a great turning point in history," he had written in *America* on December 21, summarizing his European tour. He said world leaders had not sufficiently recognized the threat of Hitler's armies, and Hitler's speech at the Sportpalast, followed by Chamberlain's capitulation at Munich, "acquainted the world with a mixture of method and madness."

The task ahead was to avert war while defending freedom at all cost. "Our problem is to keep the torch of democracy and true liberty alight in the world," he wrote.

The next week, LaFarge spoke to an audience that extended far beyond his magazine's readership. He took the stage at Town Hall on West Forty-third Street in New York City at 9:30 P.M. on Thursday evening, December 29, 1938. The event was part of a nationally broadcast radio program called *America's Town Meeting on the Air*, which had become a major forum for public affairs nationwide. The program drew an estimated audience of two million, who sat around their radio consoles as the celebrated announcer, Milton Cross, signed on:

"Welcome to historic Town Hall in New York City for another free and open discussion of one of the great problems facing civilization today." The subject tonight: "How should religion deal with totalitarianism?"

This was LaFarge's opportunity to present the themes he had written about for the pope and to define the role of the church.

"There is, I believe, comparatively little that religion can directly accomplish to check the course of totalitarianism in other countries than our own," LaFarge said. "The dictators, unfortunately, do not appear beneath the pulpits of New York or Philadelphia, and they pay little attention to long distance communications. I am sufficient [sic] of an interventionist to agree to the use of force where it is the last and sole means of liberating people in another country from acute injustice." The time would come to apply armed force, he said, "if or when a totalitarian power might see fit to launch a physical attack upon our shores."

He also called on his audience to uphold the "dignity of all human persons—Jew, Negro, Catholic, or Indian . . . Let us denounce persecutions abroad, by all means, whether they are persecutions on a religious or national basis . . . let us prevent persecution by any means in our power."

Also on the program was Rabbi Morris S. Lazaron of the Baltimore Hebrew Congregation, and a member of the executive committee of the National Conference of Jews and Christians. Lazaron said the Nazis were in the process of challenging all religions and all freedoms. "Today it is hatred of the Communist or radical; tomorrow the Jew; the next day the Mason, the Catholic or the Protestant. Make no mistake about this: destroy the liberty of the least among us and you destroy the principle that guarantees liberty to all."

During the question and answer period, a member of the audience in Town Hall asked LaFarge whether and how Father Coughlin could be silenced. LaFarge remained cautious and said only that Coughlin's direct superiors had the ability to discipline him. Unfortunately, Coughlin enjoyed the same freedom of speech enjoyed by all Americans. Coughlin's superiors "in the end will give a fair and equitable judgment which will satisfy every reasonable man. That is our tradition and you can be perfectly sure it will be carried out in this or any other instance."

The rabbi added a point on Coughlin: "No responsible Jewish leadership will take the position that there should be censorship of the ether waves and that Father Coughlin should be ruled off the air. That would not be the way to fight what he is doing."

When the hour was up, Cross signed off the air followed by the three-toned chimes of NBC.

BY THE START of 1939, it had become clear that two world leaders had been most outspoken in condemning the dangers of Nazism. One was the pope; the other was Franklin Roosevelt, who listed freedom of religion in his State of the Union Message on January

4, 1939, atop three values threatened in the world. "All about us rage undeclared wars—military and economic," the president said. "Storms from abroad directly challenge three institutions indispensable to Americans, now as always. The first is religion. It is the source of the other two—democracy and international good faith.

"Religion, by teaching man his relationship to God, gives the individual a sense of his own dignity and teaches him to respect himself by respecting his neighbors.

"Where freedom of religion has been attacked, the attack has come from sources opposed to democracy. Where democracy has been overthrown, the spirit of free worship has disappeared. And where religion and democracy have vanished, good faith and reason in international affairs have given way to strident ambition and brute force."

Religious and political leaders praised both Roosevelt and the pope for taking their prominent stance against Nazism. "If pessimism is the dominant mood at the close of the year 1938," said Rabbi Israel Goldstein, a key Jewish leader in New York, a founder of Brandeis University, and later the head of the New York Board of Rabbis, "the valiant espousal of human rights by President Roosevelt and Pope Pius is the brightest page among the few bright pages in the doleful volume of the year."

LAFARGE RECEIVED bad news from Rome some time during the second week of January 1939. Zacheus Maher, Ledóchowski's American secretary, sent word that said publication of the encyclical "is for the moment 'in suspense,' and so we cannot look for immediate publication."

For the first time LaFarge had a real reason to doubt that the papal message would ever be published. John Killeen, who was returning to the United States, had just turned the matter over to

Maher. Killeen had briefed Maher before leaving Rome and said he had no information of his own. "I have not had the opportunity of speaking about it to His Paternity [Ledóchowski]." However, Maher had met with Gundlach, who kept pressuring for information about the papal document. According to Maher, Gundlach "was relieved to know that the German, the French and the English version are in my [Maher's] care."

LaFarge could easily see that the pope still did not have the encyclical.

Even more ominous was Maher's warning that LaFarge not try to contact the pope. Maher said he knew Gundlach had urged LaFarge to reach out to the pope. But, Maher wrote, "May I say that I do not think it would be well under present circumstances to so write."

Maher was obviously out of the loop. He also said LaFarge had given the encyclical to Gundlach for delivery, which was not true. Maher was obviously not in the inner circle at the Vatican. This was possibly good news because Maher and Ledóchowski apparently did not know LaFarge had already written to the pope. But that could possibly mean that the pope had not gotten the letter.

Finally, Maher said, "You may rest fully at ease in what you have done so far and be sure that all will be properly cared for. All you have done is greatly and gratefully appreciated." Maher was telling LaFarge that the matter was no longer his affair. But LaFarge was not comfortable with that order and awaited further word from Gundlach.

Rome, January 13, 1939

Caroline Phillips recognized the need to behave appropriately and with diplomatic grace in her role as wife of the U.S. ambassador to Italy. Sometimes, however, she was summoned to step outside those limited duties. On the evening of January 13, she and her husband arrived around 10:30 P.M.—fashionably late—at the British embassy for a reception with Prime Minister Neville Chamberlain and the British foreign minister, Lord Halifax. The avenue outside the embassy was a jumble, "cars running into each other from all directions and dozens of hapless policemen all issuing unrelated directions," she remembered.

No one knew exactly why Chamberlain and Halifax had come to Rome or what they hoped to achieve. Perhaps Chamberlain hoped to establish more of a relationship with Benito Mussolini, whom he hadn't had the opportunity to spend time with during the Munich accord process.

When Caroline and her husband entered the receiving room, she easily spotted the guests of honor across the room. Lord Halifax was "the most interesting and attractive looking, very tall and distinguished, with the face of an intellectual." Caroline, an astute analyst of politics and personality, was much more impressed by Halifax than Chamberlain; she thought Chamberlain appeared to be "more of the practical middle class man of business and morals."

She knew that proponents of appeasement continued to applaud Chamberlain's peace efforts. Commenting on Chamberlain's visit to Rome, the *Times* of London explained that "Great Britain has to live side by side with these countries and means to do so on a basis of equality and cooperation." If Chamberlain's talks with Mussolini "have a successful outcome," the British newspaper said, "they will undoubtedly not be of benefit to Great Britain and Italy alone."

Even Chamberlain knew by this point that the Munich Agreement had collapsed and he had failed. His foreign minister, Lord Halifax, told Roosevelt secretly in a meeting in the United States that "as early as November 1938, there were indications which gradually become more definite that Hitler was planning a further foreign adventure for the spring of 1939."

If Chamberlain had hoped to sway Mussolini from his support of Hitler after several hours of meetings, that didn't happen. A *New York Times* reporter was blunt: "Put in plainer language than diplomacy's jargon adopts, this means that this much heralded conference has closed . . . without changing anything whatever. In the United States it might be termed a washout."

Caroline, in personal terms, deemed the evening diplomatic reception for Chamberlain disastrous and close to appalling. Her husband, William, took her arm and asked her to accompany him to chat with Mussolini. After all, she spoke fluent Italian—it would be a rewarding effort. "I followed him a couple of steps as far as Ciano, to whom I said good evening," she wrote in her diary that night.

By this time, Mussolini was looking in Caroline's general direction as he chatted with the wife of German ambassador Baron Konstantin von Neurath. Caroline took a few steps more, but simply could not follow through. She turned away quickly, trying not to attract attention. "I could not bring myself to break into that alien atmosphere of Jew-baiting, bombastic, odious 'superiority complex,'" she said. "And what could I talk to him about? I yielded to my instinct of flight, much to William's horror."

Earlier in the day, Chamberlain and Halifax had met with the pope, who stood to greet them, smiled and welcomed them for a chat. Joseph Hurley was their interpreter. Halifax was pleased to see Hurley; they had known each other a decade earlier when both were posted to India—Hurley for the Vatican secretariat of state and Halifax as the British viceroy. The pope generally had been limiting the length of his audiences, but Chamberlain had been briefed ahead of time to expect a longer visit.

The pope reiterated his position that Nazi Germany had taken the place of Communism as the church's most important enemy. The British officials were impressed by the pope's forceful presentation. He had sharp words for Chamberlain. The effort to appease Hitler by giving him what he wanted had been an obvious failure; the pope had said so all along, and Chamberlain now had to admit that was true.

Pius repeated once more: it is not Communism that poses a threat to humanity; Nazism and Fascism and their march toward domination and racist attacks are the greatest danger the world has ever seen. If Britain and the Vatican agreed with this perspective, they could work together.

The pope stressed the need for united efforts to stop Hitler. The British ambassador, summarizing his own impressions, said the pope "has shown great courage. He finds himself now in open conflict with the totalitarian States . . . It is natural that he should look for support to the great Democracies . . . The Pope is an [sic] old and probably a dying man; for whatever reasons he is following a policy in international affairs which on the major issues of principle corresponds very closely indeed with our own."

Hurley reported back to the U.S. ambassador about the gist of the papal meeting—which ended up being more valuable than the failed diplomacy with Mussolini. Chamberlain, Halifax, and the pope saw eye to eye. The meeting had clarified the pope's view on Hitler, who he described as "a sick man." Halifax later said the three men had agreed they both had an "aversion" to the "brutal and totalitarian ideology of Hitlerism." In addition, Halifax later wrote, the pope "in the end realized that the more immediate menace to the Christian order of Europe was from the Nazis themselves."

When Chamberlain left Rome on January 14, Mussolini grudgingly went to the train station to bid Chamberlain farewell, both sides knowing full well that nothing had been accomplished. Il Duce was mildly amused when some British subjects present at the departure broke into a chorus of "For He's a Jolly Good Fellow." It must have had deep meaning, because, according to Ciano, "Chamberlain's eyes filled with tears when the train started moving."

Mussolini was baffled. "What is this little song?" he asked.

CHAPTER ELEVEN

Will There Be Time?

Vatican, January 21, 1939

THE POPE TRACKED down the encyclical in mid-January despite Ledóchowski's efforts to conceal and delay its delivery. Pius directed Pacelli's subordinate, Domenico Tardini, to tell Ledóchowski that he knew he had the encyclical and that the Holy Father wanted it immediately. Without further recourse, Ledóchowski delivered a version of the encyclical on January 21, 1939, almost exactly four months after he had received it from LaFarge.

Ledóchowski's cover letter to the pope admitted that he had held back the original. The superior general said that the prominent Jesuit editor Enrico Rosa had begun rewriting the encyclical before he became ill. Ledóchowski gave no explanation of why the matter had languished four months, including the two months since Rosa had died. He now proposed redrafting the encyclical from scratch and discarding LaFarge's version altogether.

WILL THERE BE TIME? 171

*I take leave to send immediately to Your Holiness the draft
by Father LaFarge concerning nationalism and the various
notes made by him. It seemed to me and to Father Rosa that the
draft, as it was, did not meet with what Your Holiness had in
mind. Father Rosa began to compose another draft, but he did
not have the energy to complete the job.*

*Your Holiness knows that I am always at your disposition,
most ready to be able to render whatever small task you might
desire. If Your Holiness would want in fact that I perform
a similar effort, it would be perhaps well to continue in the
manner which has shown to work well in the past, that is: to
first produce a short outline, second details from Your Holiness,
present it afterwards to Your Holiness, and only after that the
observations are received to process the first draft and submit it
once more to Your Holiness, to be able to compose the final draft.*

Ledóchowski's act and letter to the pope were disingenuous
on several grounds. First, he neither referred to the proposed title
of the encyclical, *The Unity of the Human Race*, nor could he even
bear to use the words *racism* or *anti-Semitism*. He presented it as a
treatise on nationalism, which it had not been, at least in its original form. There also was no indication the pope had deputized
Ledóchowski to rework the document without submitting it first
to the pope.

He was asking the pope to accept a different document entirely,
prepared the same way all other encyclicals had been prepared.
The pope did not want to do that. He had directed its preparation
personally and had told LaFarge to write it secretly and in the
pope's name, "as if you were the pope."

Now the question was whether the pope could summon the
strength to edit the encyclical and publish it quickly. The cold cal-

culation among dissenters at the Vatican made it clear that the issues of racism and anti-Semitism, Pius's singular focus, might be abandoned by the next pope, whoever it might be. Ledóchowski was playing for time until Pius died.

The general was a secretive man by nature who hid and often destroyed written communications of substance. In fact, one Jesuit researcher, Father Robert Graham, was told that Ledóchowski "burned all the preliminary drafts of the encyclical" and submitted an already-edited version. The Jesuit general had left one single letter to be read by the pope and then filed for anyone else who might see it in the future. He made it appear as though he was innocently trying to follow protocol. But that was not true.

Knowing none of this, Gundlach wrote desperately to LaFarge on January 28 and said he felt he was being treated like an "immature child." He didn't even have an original copy of the encyclical and feared it would be lost forever. Even if the text was never used by the pope, he hoped it could be resurrected in some other form. "I have, as you know, no carbon of the German text and also not of the table of contents," Gundlach wrote. "I have only the unabbreviated text in French of the first and second parts." With the originals, he hoped their project could at least become a book.

"This situation is easier for you to bear," Gundlach told LaFarge. "For you have a public activity with many relationships at home. But one of us (me) sits here within four walls in a foreign atmosphere and has to rely on the big brass as to whether they want to say something to me or not, indeed, whether they want to even answer a question."

Zacheus Maher, Gundlach said, had promised him a month earlier that he would speak to Ledóchowski the following day— "tomorrow" about the encyclical. Nothing happened. "That was the end of December," Gundlach said. "He would then let me know about it. I'm still waiting to hear."

Rome, January 23, 1939

In late January, Italian foreign minister Ciano told Mussolini that the Vatican had invited him to an event on February 11 to commemorate the tenth anniversary of the Lateran Accords. Mussolini rejected the notion out of hand, agreeing with Ciano that it sounded like a trap staged by the pope to confront and embarrass him.

Mussolini was becoming deeply concerned about the pope's possible next moves. Rumors circulated around Rome concerning the February 11 celebration, especially because the pope had scheduled an extraordinary meeting at the same time, summoning all 280 Italian bishops to the Vatican.

Vatican sources stirred the concern by telling reporters that the pope would take the opportunity to emphasize "Church-State differences that had developed since inauguration of Italy's anti-Semitic program."

Mussolini and Ciano began to worry about what the pope had in mind. Would the pope formally declare that the Lateran agreements had been broken? Would he even go to the extent of excommunicating Mussolini, Hitler, or both? Ciano demanded answers from his informants within the Vatican, but no one knew. "I do not know, because the Holy Father does not tell anyone what he will do," said Monsignor Francesco Borgongini-Duca, who as the papal nuncio to Italy was close to the center of power. But he added ominously: "it is clear that he will do something big."

Ciano wrote in his diary: "The atmosphere for the celebration of the tenth anniversary is becoming murky . . . we must be sure the Pope avoids some of those sharp statements he is known to make when he speaks to the bishops if we are to accept invitations to St. Peter's."

Mussolini was fixated on the dangers of what the pope might

do; the question was how far Mussolini would go to stop the pope from creating a serious rift between the Vatican and the Italian government. How could he stop the pope?

While concealing the details, the pope spoke cryptically about his plans on one public occasion. He met at the end of January with representatives of the Italian Federation of Catholic University Students. The students, whose organization included two future prime ministers, Aldo Moro and Giulio Andreotti, had faced tough times. They were in the vanguard of young Italians who opposed Mussolini and Fascism. One of them was Bianca Penco, a leader based in Genoa. At the age of ninety-one in 2008, almost three-quarters of a century later, she could still recall the pope's warmth and commitment that day.

The pope told Penco and the other student leaders he was determined to make one last great statement. He acknowledged the troubles faced by the students and compared it to his own struggle against Fascism. He believed the church must "speak out for freedom," she recalled in an interview with the Italian magazine *Il Secolo XIX*. "He spoke to us passionately about the persecution that our organization and other groups had suffered" for their opposition to Fascism, "as a betrayal of the Lateran Treaties." He then told the students he was preparing "a very tough speech: he was determined, spoke with gravity as he was accustomed to do, and was fully prepared to challenge Mussolini and Hitler. He appeared to be in perfect health."

The pope was consumed by writing the speech to the bishops those last days of January and first days of February. His secretaries saw him writing, reviewing, and editing the document to the exclusion of most other work. He drafted it with pad and pencil and showed it to no one until he was finished. He then gave the handwritten copy to his loyal personal secretary, Monsignor Confalonieri, who typed it in its final form. Only then did the pope show it to Pacelli, who hardly made a mark on the copy, even though the subject was provocative and certain to raise controversy. It was as if he suspected the pope would never deliver the discourse.

The pope was also worried that he might be incapacitated and not able to read the speech to the bishops. He told Confalonieri to have enough copies printed so that each bishop could get one. He wanted the event to be perfect and managed every detail, even discussing the menu for the lunch that was to be served. Pacelli, who otherwise was running routine affairs of the Holy See, repeatedly asked the pope to rest more and to delay the bishops' meeting. Pius refused.

At first, Ciano informed the Vatican that not only would Mussolini not attend or visit the Vatican, he would not even acknowledge the anniversary. Finally, however, Ciano said Mussolini decided that not attending at all would be too much of a diplomatic slight; Ciano would attend the event himself "in order to avoid giving offense to the Pope."

Everyone knew the pope had considerable leverage in his dealings with Mussolini. Despite the rancorous relationship, the criticism, and his own threats and saber rattling, Il Duce was concerned about public reaction and didn't really want a break with the Vatican.

New York, January 30, 1939

LaFarge continued to maintain a high profile. On January 26, he told a New York radio audience that the use of military force was justifiable under some circumstances. "Most people are stirred up over the political threat," he said. "They are scared not so much at racism itself as at the political and military force of the nation or nations which have made racism a national philosophy. If a racist

176 THE POPE'S LAST CRUSADE

power attacks us with boats and guns or any other weapon, let us by all means defend ourselves against them on sea and land."

Adolf Hitler delivered a major speech before the German Reichstag on January 30, 1939, casting himself as the determined leader of a peaceful nation. He claimed that warmongers abroad incited by the "Jewish press" were forcing the issue. And should the German Reich be drawn into a war, "if international financial Jewry within and without Europe should succeed in throwing the nations into another world war the result will not be the bolshevization of the earth and therewith a victory for Jewry, but the extermination of the Jewish race in Europe."

He said that calumnies were being cast upon Germany by agitators, including the likes of Winston Churchill and President Roosevelt's secretary of the interior, Harold Ickes, who had referred repeatedly to Nazism as tyranny. Ickes was also seeking a resolution to Jewish emigration from Germany by suggesting resettlement in the wide-open spaces of Alaska.

A day after Hitler's tirade, President Roosevelt proposed that the United States begin arming France and England for war. The Vatican said Hitler was practicing "the propaganda of hate." It also stated that German newspapers were conducting "an anti-religious campaign that spares neither God nor the Redeemer nor the Gospel nor the Church . . . the Pope is dragged with the Bishops and clergy . . . through a sea of insults and immoral caricatures on pages that concede the right of asylum to every most incredible audacity."

The Vatican, February 5, 1939

Still fine-tuning his speech to Italian bishops, the pope spent a quiet weekend. He knew that questions about the substance of the speech had created buzz around the Vatican, but he had kept his plans confidential. The pontiff met with old friends, Tomaso Gallarati Scotti on Friday, February 3, and Cardinal Eugene Tisserant on Saturday, February 4. Gallarati Scotti, a Catholic writer, was a generation younger than the pope and was his one-time student. Both men said the pope appeared to be in good health and discussed the world situation and the dangers around them.

Pius continued to harp on Mussolini and Hitler. Later, he retired to his rooms, where he read and listened to the latest news on Vatican Radio. The broadcast was a litany of tensions in Europe, including distressing news about Italy and its relations with Germany.

The pope turned from the news to word from his aides that the chief Vatican doctor, Aminta Milani, a constant visitor at the Vatican, was now sick at home with a bad case of the flu. Such illnesses were dangerous and contagious, especially in the winter chill. The pope's confessor, Father Lazarini, was also in ill health and had been taken to the hospital for surgery. The pope said Mass in his private chapel and went to bed.

He did not sleep well on Saturday night. His attendants heard him coughing during the night. On Sunday morning, February 5, Pius continued with as much of his schedule as he could. He had a brief talk with a group of children who had won a school catechism contest, but retired early. Monday morning, Cardinal Pacelli canceled the pope's regular meetings and called in house doctors and specialists. With Milani in bed, Filippo Rocchi, the junior member of the five-doctor Vatican health corps, was on duty. The pope told Rocchi that he felt "inexorable and widespread pain." His health deteriorated over the course of the day with fever, exhaustion, trouble breathing, and aches and pain. Rocchi issued an internal medical report.

"The condition of the circulatory apparatus of the Holy Father returned to cause preoccupation in the sense of a return of the signs of left ventricular insufficiency with bradiarhitmia," Rocchi wrote, saying the pope's pulse was in the range of forty to forty-four beats per minute. "To this is added traccheobronchial catarrh with light thermic movement, probably secondary to the circulatory conditions, and disturbances of retention which have imposed permanent drainage. The psyche is perfectly lucid and prompt to attention as habitually normal."

In layperson's terms, the pope was running a fever and he had a chest cold that was impacting his heart problems.

The Vatican press office, under orders from the pope, made no public mention of his health on Monday, February 6, the seventeenth anniversary of his election to the papal throne. Diplomats and church leaders who came to St. Peter's were invited to sign a register of greetings and congratulations to honor the pope, but Pius did not receive visitors. As congratulations came in by telegram from around the world, the press office reported that the pope had spent the day "by kneeling long in prayer in his private chapel" and the rest of the time "was conserving his strength." It was likely that he stayed in bed most of the day.

The pope was alert though weak on Wednesday morning, February 8. He feared that any announcement about his health would damage preparations for the bishops' meeting on Saturday. Pacelli asked the pope one last time to cancel the bishops' conference, saying it would be too tiring for him.

The pope refused with a single "No."

He ordered his secretary, Confalonieri, to maintain silence about his condition. No medical bulletin was issued during the day. "The pope on his own account desired to avoid the diffusion of alarming news," Confalonieri said, and he limited announcements to saying the pope was canceling audiences for the day.

By Thursday, February 9, nevertheless, word of the pope's condition had spread. The Vatican merely said the pope's schedule had been canceled again so he could rest and prepare for his meeting with the bishops. The bishops kept to their itineraries and began arriving in Rome from around the country, though many started to doubt whether the Saturday event would take place. An official statement on Thursday repeated "that the Pope was feeling well but by the counsel of his doctors had canceled again the audiences to be in condition to receive the Italian Episcopate on Saturday," Confalonieri recalled. "A similar notice was published in the evening edition of *Osservatore Romano*." The pope rested and the doctors said he was a good patient. He had only one repeated request in the form of a demand: he wanted to be kept alive through Saturday.

Joseph Hurley told Ambassador Phillips at the U.S. embassy that, characteristically, the pope insisted on trying to get up on Thursday morning, repeating the same stubborn words his aides were accustomed to, "A Pope is never ill." But the pope had suffered a relapse in the early afternoon and was forced back to bed. "From that time on he was conscious off and on," and seemed to be dozing, Hurley said.

From then on, multiple versions of events circulated about the pope's condition and what happened in the course of the night. Some said the pope, displaying a great air of spirituality, was resigned to whatever might happen and remained conscious all the while and that he prayed and blessed those around him. Others, more objective and less melodramatic in describing events, said the pope did not regain consciousness beyond the afternoon of Thursday, February 9.

Starting that afternoon, the sequence was never pinned down. There were multiple accounts, some focused on medicine, others on prayer and divinity. All might have been partially true; some might not have been true. The pope's state of health weakened to

the point that Last Rites were administered on Thursday afternoon. Hurley said the pope had nodded that he understood what
was happening as the prayers were recited. Hurley did not report his
sources for this information; it was not likely he had been present
at the pope's bedside. Pacelli, Hurley's superior at the Secretariat of
State, was once again the gatekeeper at the pope's chambers.

The other sources of information about the following day were
Monsignor Confalonieri, the secretary; Zsoldt Aradi, a biographer
who worked under the auspices of Francis Spellman; and reporters for major newspapers and magazines, many of whom quoted
unnamed Vatican sources.

The main differences in the versions involved who actually was
present at the pope's bedside and whether the pope was conscious
at different points during the overnight period from Thursday
night into Friday, February 10. The question of who had access
to the pope during those hours would later be a significant issue.

All agreed that doctors from the Vatican health office inter-
vened with consultation from various outside doctors. One basic
element ran through all variants; the pope, who had seemed
healthy and well on February 4, had caught a cold or the flu. The
chief of the medical office, Milani, had also contracted the flu.
He was sick enough and contagious enough to remove himself
from the case those first days of February. About the same time,
the pope was also coming down with a virus, which the Vatican
described as a "mild catarrh." It had grown progressively worse
and it was evident that an eighty-one-year-old with a heart condition had few defenses.

Confalonieri, who was present and assembled a chronicle of
events months later, said Doctor Rocchi had remained close by. He
said Rocchi gave the pope an unspecified injection on the afternoon of February 9 because the pope seemed to have grown weak
and pale. According to some Vatican sources, the injection was

camphor oil, the stimulant used on other occasions that seemed to help rally the pope's recovery.

The version written by Zsoldt Aradi had Rocchi becoming concerned and summoning Milani despite his illness. Aradi said Milani got up from his sick bed, came to the Vatican, and decided to give the pope an injection of adrenaline. "After the injection, the Pope fell asleep. As no immediate crisis was anticipated by the physicians, everybody left the room. Around 2:30 A.M. the next morning, one of the Franciscan monks nursing the pope, Brother Faustino, was alone in the sickroom with the Pontiff, when he became alarmed and called the doctors, the secretaries and Cardinal Pacelli."

Whatever the injection was and whichever doctor administered it, the pope had slipped into a coma. The pope's secretary, Confalonieri, said, "After eleven o'clock that night, the temperature, almost normal, began to rise rapidly beyond 39 degrees centigrade [102 Fahrenheit]. Professor Rocchi shook his head sadly and with a typical gesture, saying nothing, gave indication that at length all had come to a finish."

The *New York Times* report on February 11 differed in significant ways. The *Times* said that Rocchi, not Brother Faustino, spent the night in the Pope's bedroom. At 4 A.M., the report said, Rocchi noticed that the pope's pulse rate had weakened and he, not Milani, had "immediately tried injections of stimulants, but the Pope failed to react to them." The *Times* attempted a medical explanation at this point, saying that Rocchi "took the great personal responsibility of giving an injection of camphorated oil—a heroic measure in the circumstance because myocarditis is a dysfunction of the heart muscles that causes the organ to alternate between deficient and excessive action. Any stimulant, though giving immediate relief, may therefore prove fatal. Just as he had reacted to an injection of camphorated oil during his last attack in

November, the Pope reacted well yesterday, regaining conscious-ness about half an hour later."

The *New York Times* report included sources who contra-dicted Confalonieri—the only witness who wrote a public ver-sion of events—and said the pope was awake all the evening of the ninth. It said the pope summoned all present to be close to him and that he had asked to be able to confess to Cardinal Lauri and take Communion. "A few minutes later, it being evident that the effect of the stimulants was evaporating and the end approaching, Extreme Unction [last rights] was administered."

The *Times* of London correspondent also reported the pope as conscious and that Pacelli asked Pius for a blessing. The pope "raised his right hand from the bed-covers and went through the motion of giving the apostolic blessing, at the same time mumbling the ritual formula." This version added another element, that the pope rallied one more time, dramatically making "another attempt to regain his hold on life. He opened his eyes . . . at the same time giving a weak imitation of a smile."

"Finally, with what evidently was a very great effort, he raised himself in his bed and mumbled a few words that were almost com-pletely incomprehensible to the majority who heard them. Those nearest to him report that he said, 'God bless you, my children,' followed more weakly by 'Let there be peace.' "

The *Times* of London correspondent also reported that the pope had asked that Last Rites be administered at 4:00 A.M. on February 10 in the presence of Pacelli, Cardinal Camillo Caccia-Dominioni who was the pope's protégé and master of ceremonies; various prelates of the papal household; the governor of Vatican City; Count Franco Ratti, the pope's nephew; and a "little group of doctors, attendants and penitentiary monks." Dr. Milani had been summoned again from his sick bed and he administered oxygen at around 5:00 A.M. The pope did not respond to that treatment.

In a fifth version of the story, *Time* magazine provided a moment by moment rendering of what had happened. It said that the doctor had roused Brother Faustino and another Franciscan, not the other way around. It listed Pacelli as being present late into the night, along with "Caccia-Dominioni, Count Franco Ratti, the Pope's nephew, Governor Camillo Serafini of Vatican City," Rocchi, and Milani.

It said the injection "rallied Pius XI" for a time and that the pope was alert. The pope, it said, "propped up by pillows, whispered his confession, received absolution for his sins." Even in the throes of death, according to *Time* magazine, "In deep emotion Cardinal Pacelli cried: 'Holy Father, give us your blessing!'

"In an agony of effort, while the others wept, the Pope summoned his strength to make this last, supreme gesture. He lifted his right hand, mumbled a blessing. Falteringly his hand signaled its last apostolic benediction, fell back on the bed. He mumbled something. To some it seemed that he said: 'Jesus and Mary . . . Peace to the world.' Others thought they heard him say: 'In our Last Rites . . . Sister Therese and the Infant Jesus . . . art near to us. God is merciful. May His will be done.'

"But all were agreed that earlier, the Pope's last articulate words had been: 'I still have so many things to do.'"

But it wasn't true that everyone agreed. Stories also did not coincide on who had said Last Rites and when they were administered. One biographer said Cardinal Lorenzo Lauri, the grand penitentiary of the Holy Roman Church, was the designated person, but could not be found. The biographer said instead that Monsignor Alfonso de Romanis, the sacristan and parish priest of the Vatican, administered the Last Rites toward the end. *Time* magazine said Lauri was present for the Extreme Unction ceremony, but that de Romanis had conducted the ceremony anyway. Confalonieri made no mention of Lauri's presence and said that other family members had been present the afternoon before, when the pope prayed with them, and then lapsed into a coma, after uttering his last words at around 3:30 P.M. "I breathe forth my soul in peace with you." Confalonieri said another important prelate was present, Monsignor Giovanni Battista Montini, the undersecretary of state.

No one could say exactly what happened in the papal apartments that night. Reporters pieced together the story from sources that were most immediately available on deadline. *Time* magazine had a few more days to report its story on February 20. Aradi was writing in 1957 to commemorate the one hundredth year of Pius XI's birth. Of all those who reported directly, only Confalonieri had been present, and though he might not have reported accurately or remembered every detail of who was present, he likely would have remembered whether or not the pope had been unconscious. He published his book about the pope some years later and included his account of the deathbed scene. In any case, all the stories arrived at the same terminus.

The pope died before dawn on Friday, February 10, 1939. He appeared to have breathed his last breath at 5:31 A.M., and Milani declared he was dead. Then, according to long church tradition, Cardinal Pacelli, the *camerlengo*, followed a prescribed ritual. He knelt beside the pope, the *Times* of London reported, and "drew back the veil from the face and in a loud voice called the dead man three times by his baptismal name, 'Achille, Achille, Achille,' at the same time tapping his forehead gently with a silver mallet."

Thus satisfied he was able to declare: "The Pope is truly dead."

CHAPTER TWELVE

Change Overnight

Trastevere, Rome, February 10, 1939

EARLY ON THE morning of Friday, February 10, a ringing telephone woke Cardinal Eugene Tisserant at his apartment on
Via Mercadante in the Trastevere section of Rome. Monsignor
Carlo Grano, a member of the Vatican staff, was relaying a message
from Monsignor Giovanni Battista Montini (later Pope Paul VI)
that the pope was alive, but "gravely ill and had received Extreme
Unction." Tisserant was saddened by this but still held out hope
that his friend, the pope, would survive. After all, he had been
given Last Rites twice before and recovered.

Tisserant was one of the pope's few friends. They had known
each other for more than twenty-eight years, since 1910 when they
worked together at the Vatican Library. The pope, then Monsignor
Ratti, was fifty-three years old and had just been appointed assistant director of the library by Pope Pius X. Tisserant, who was
twenty-six, was curator at the library.

"I must say from the first meeting we were in very friendly
terms," Tisserant recalled.

Ratti and Tisserant began taking regular evening strolls from St. Peter's on the Via della Consolazione, along the Tiber and then along the river to the Palace of Justice. They had a lot in common; both were scholars and voracious readers and were dedicated to the preservation of old books.

Ratti's background as a famous mountain climber made him unusual among leaders of the Roman Catholic Church, and Tisserant also had an unorthodox past. He took leave from the priesthood in 1914 to enter the French Army as a cavalry officer and served in the Dardanelles and Palestine. He later served as a logistics and military intelligence officer until the end of World War I and in 1919 returned to the Vatican Library.

Tisserant said he and the future pope had corresponded frequently. Ratti "used to write me about every month," Tisserant told a friend, "and I have still twenty of His letters [sic], one from Milan of 1913, three from Warsaw after the war, the others from Rome in wartime." When Ratti became pope, they remained close. "When He became a Pontiff," Tisserant said in a letter a month after the pope died, "I felt that His affection for me remained unchanged."

By the time Tisserant had gotten ready to leave his apartment for the short walk to the Vatican, the bells of St. Peter's began to toll. Within moments, church bells resounded throughout Rome. The news was broadcast everywhere that Pope Pius XI had died.

When Tisserant arrived at the Vatican, he was told that the pope had died at 5:31 A.M. Tisserant had looked at the clock when the phone woke him up. He did not understand how he could have received a message that the pope was alive forty-nine minutes after he had been pronounced dead? He did not think the call was a mistake; he thought he had been given false information. He did not know why.

*   *   *

AS WAS customary after the death of a pope, Cardinal Pacelli as *camerlengo* ordered the pope's offices and files sealed. Most of the files would not be available to the public for at least seventy-five years, long after almost all witnesses to the pope's life and death had also died. Pacelli then withdrew to his own Vatican office and began communicating with cardinals and apostolic offices around the world.

He also sent Joseph Hurley on a special mission to inform U.S. ambassador William Phillips formally that Pope Pius XI was dead. When Hurley got to the embassy, he made it clear that this meeting was official, quite different from his normally informal chats with Phillips. He told Phillips he had come "by instruction of Cardinal Pacelli, the Secretary of State, who during the interim directs the affairs of the Vatican." Hurley said that other nations had been contacted in writing, "but in the case of the United States, he was instructed to make an oral communication."

Pacelli interrupted his work later in the day when he received word that Foreign Minister Ciano was on his way to the Vatican.

Ciano had already met with Mussolini and told him the pope had died. Il Duce was "completely indifferent," Ciano said, and "mentioned the death only in order to inform me that this evening he will postpone the meeting of the Grand Council out of respect for the memory of the Pope, and also because the public is much too concerned with the mourning to be interested [in anything else]." Several days later Mussolini expressed his own view of the pope's death: "At last that stiff-necked man is dead."

Since the pope was head of state and Italy had diplomatic relations with the Vatican, it was proper protocol for Ciano to express sympathy in person. As he crossed the Tiber in his car, then rode directly to St. Peter's, he saw that mourners were already gathering in the square.

Ciano walked with Pacelli to the Sistine Chapel, where the pope had been placed on a catafalque. "I conveyed the sympathy of the Italian government and of the Fascist people," Ciano wrote, "and I said that the deceased pope had forever tied his name to history through the Lateran Treaty. They liked my expressions very much."

This was the highest-level meeting between the Vatican and the Italian government in some time, and Ciano had not planned to bring up political issues. But Pacelli did and hinted at an agenda to come. Pacelli acknowledged that relations with the Fascist government had not been good but indicated that things were about to change. Pacelli "spoke to me about the relationship between State and Church with very agreeable and hopeful expressions," Ciano wrote in his diary. He was encouraged but gave no details of what was said.

Pacelli and Ciano approached the catafalque in the chapel. "Of the Pope himself we could see nothing—only his enormous white sandals and the hem of his robe; but the atmosphere created was one of infinity."

It was too early to make predictions about the pope's successor or how relations between church and state would change in that new regime. For the moment, whatever the pope had planned to do or say at the upcoming meeting with Italian bishops had been postponed.

Now the Italian government's focus was to make sure that the pope's plan for that day would never be carried out. Il Duce had been increasingly troubled about the bishops' meeting. Had Pius been preparing to excommunicate Il Duce or Hitler or both? Would there be further embarrassments or challenges by the church? Persistent rumors said that the content of the pope's speech might have been "devastating for Fascism." The reports said the pope had worked fervently on the speech and had hoped to deliver it himself or to be present while it was read to the bishops. The rumors now were that the speech might be distributed as a tribute as his final statement to the world.

Mussolini wanted to know the status of the speech and what it said. Ciano had told him about the meeting with Pacelli and his hint that relations with the Vatican would improve. But what did that mean in practical terms? Pacelli, who was solely in charge of the church, might have a copy of the speech. Mussolini ordered his sources at the Vatican to either get a copy of the speech or information about it.

But Mussolini should not have been so concerned because Pacelli had already dealt with the issue when he impounded the pope's desk and its contents. Among the papers were three important pieces of business. One was the speech to the bishops, in printed form as well as the original version that was handwritten in pencil. The second document was Ledóchowski's cover letter to the pope, along with a third larger file, the one-hundred-page draft encyclical, with versions in French, German, and Latin— *Humanis Generis Unitas*, written in the pope's name by John LaFarge.

Pacelli might not have read the encyclical, but he knew all about the pope's planned speech to the bishops. The *camerlengo* told his deputy, Monsignor Montini, to make sure all versions of the pope's final speech were confiscated. The pope's assistants were to "hand over all the material he has regarding the discourse [and] that the printer destroy all he possesses relative to the same discourse," according to notes taken by Monsignor Domenico Tardini.

Montini deputized Tardini to carry out Pacelli's orders, and Tardini then passed along word to the late pope's secretary, Confalonieri. Confalonieri did as he was told and then telephoned Tardini to say "that the vice-director of the print shop was himself taking care to destroy all the material that had been prepared so that there did not survive 'not even a line.'" Mussolini received word through channels that Pope Pius XI's document would never appear in any form.

WHEN WRITING ABOUT the pope's death, the Fascist press did not mention anything about the pope's protest against Fascism and Nazism and presented sanitized version of relations between Pius XI and the government. Newspapers reported that Mussolini and his government lamented the pope's passing and said the pontiff died a day before he was going to announce a full reconciliation between the church and the Italian government.

Some Vatican spokesmen participated in this deception and transmitted Mussolini's version to the foreign press. The *New York Times* reported four days after the pope died that Pope Pius "had reached a satisfactory solution of various controversial points on which the Church had differed with the Italian Government. It is presumed that a *modus vivendi* was reached also on the racist question, which has been the most important reason for dissent between the Italian government and the Vatican."

The *Times* story also said: "It is reported in Vatican circles, in fact that the Pope intended to make a speech, of which peace was to have been the keynote. . . . The Pope was most anxious to deliver this speech and repeatedly begged his physicians to prolong his life at least until he could attend the meeting."

Of course, a small group of people knew it was a lie, among them Confalonieri and Pacelli, who had each read the speech.

The speech was far from a reconciliation between the Vatican and the government; it was an angry warning to the bishops of Italy and criticized the government, words that might have led to a permanent rupture between church and state. Conflict and overt confrontation between Mussolini and the Vatican ended within hours of the pope's death. His final words were erased from the public record. However, at least one version of the pope's speech did survive and was found in the Vatican Secret Archives by Italian academic researchers more than half a century later.

He may have been sick and limited in his ability to reach the outside world, but a speech written and delivered by the pope would have broken through and had an impact.

The pope wrote in his speech to the bishops:

> *You know, dear and venerable brothers how the words of the pope are often construed. There are some, and not only in Italy, who take Our allocutions and Our audiences, and alter them in a false sense [and] have Us speak incredibly foolish and absurd things. There is a press capable of saying most anything that is opposed to Us and Our concerns, often twisting in a perverse way the recent and more distant history of the Church, arriving even at the persistent denial of any persecution in Germany and adding to that the false accusation of Our engagement in politics . . . They arrive at true irreverence; and these things are said while our press is forbidden to contradict or correct them.*

He warned the bishops to be on guard against distortions about what they say. "Dear Brothers you must take care not only about the abuse of what you say in public but also about what you say in private, especially if you . . . speak with individuals holding a government or party office."

Furthermore, he voiced aloud his concerns about treachery inside the Vatican, warning that there were spies on behalf of Italy and Germany around him. "Do not forget that often there are observers and informers (you would do well to call them spies) who, of their own initiative or because charged to do so, listen to you in order to condemn you."

Beyond informants, governments were listening in to communications as well. "Do not ever speak on the telephone words that you do not want to be known," the pope wrote. "You may believe that your words are traveling to your distant correspondent and yet at a certain point they may be noticed and intercepted."

The pope referred one last time to the subject of racism. Humanity, he said, is "joined together and all of the same blood in the common link of the great human family."

His final words saw the likelihood of war, but with a prayer: "peace, peace, peace for all the world that instead seems seized by a homicidal and suicidal folly of weapons. Peace demands that We implore the God of peace and hope to attain it. So be it!"

The pope had planned to follow his Saturday speech with what he called a "dialogue" with the bishops about the political situation. Since the pope was known for making emotional statements beyond the scripted word, his conversation with the bishops could have set off sparks that went beyond the text.

The Vatican, February 13, 1939

Twelve abreast, people filed past the bier that held the pope's body on Monday, February 13. All day they came, thousands and thousands every hour, perhaps two hundred thousand by the end of the day. So many crowded into St. Peter's Basilica that Cardinal Pacelli decided to leave the doors open so everyone could be accommodated. The Vatican had to ask the Italian government for help with crowd control. That morning the first of nine funeral Masses was celebrated.

Pius XI was buried on Tuesday, February 14, in a crypt at St. Peter's carved from marble that had been used to build the Milan Cathedral.

The Latin inscription on the tomb said: "The body of Pius XI, Supreme Pontiff. He lived eighty-one years, eight months and ten days and he was the head of the Universal Church for seventeen years and five days. He died February tenth of the Year of Our Lord 1939."

He had died a day too early.

Funerals were held for nine days from February 12 to February 20. One day was reserved for diplomats, another for the Italian government. Ambassador William Phillips was among the mourners on February 16; the next day, Mussolini, Ciano, and the Italian cabinet were at the Vatican. The king of Italy and his wife also were present. Mussolini had declared a day of national mourning in keeping with the impression that he and his government were saddened that Pope Pius XI was gone.

Public reaction to the pope's death outside Italy focused on his political stance against Fascism and Nazism. No pope had ever been mourned in such a way, a testament to the times and his role as the leading voice against the fanaticism of Hitler and Mussolini. In Germany, the pope's death was treated with dismissal. As expected, the Nazi newspaper *Angriff* dismissed Pius as "a political pope" who did not understand the ability of Fascism and Nazism to protect the world from Communism.

In Washington, Congress convened an unprecedented joint session in memoriam and then adjourned for the day in the pope's honor. A declaration praised the pope "who exerted the most challenging and sincere efforts for world peace, who manifested the broadest tolerance toward all nations and creeds, and who pleaded for the protection of oppressed minorities." Secretary of State Cordell Hull cabled Pacelli on behalf of President Roosevelt, expressing sorrow at the death of the pope whose "zeal for peace and tolerance won him a place in the hearts of all races and creeds."

Reaction from Jewish leaders reflected a broad understanding of what Pius XI had sought to do. Rabbi Edward L. Israel of Baltimore, a rising voice in American Jewry, expressed the significance of the pope's actions. Pius XI was "the first of all Christian voices in Europe to be raised against the general anti-Semitic policy of Nazism in all of its ramifications. . . . The hope and prayer of the entire world . . . is that the College of Cardinals by divine guidance, may be led to place upon the papal throne one who through his love of peace and justice and brotherhood may become a worthy successor to the lamented Pius XI."

Francis Talbot spoke for *America* magazine when asked about the death of the pope. Interviewed by the *New York Times*, he focused on the pontiff's special role in world politics and praised Pius XI's "continuing enunciation of tyranny which endeavored to destroy natural political and religious rights of men in countries hurt by Fascism and Communism."

LAFARGE WROTE to Gundlach on February 16, asking if there was any news about the encyclical, but he and Gundlach knew that now they had to wait for a new pope to be elected and see if he felt the same way Pius did about these issues. Gundlach said in his reply that he thought there was a chance the pope's successor would follow through in the aftermath of Pius's death and issue the encyclical against racism.

But Ledóchowski was still vacillating on the question of whether Nazism or Communism was the most dangerous. He seemed to change his political perspective depending on the audience. Sometimes, "he proclaims to anyone who will listen that National Socialism is at least as dangerous as Communism." The next moment, Gundlach wrote, Ledóchowski changes his tune—when someone hears reports from the United States about a Communist threat there. When such "reports about Communism come in from America," Ledóchowski says, "Communism is once again the sole true enemy!"

LaFarge still remembered Ledóchowski's odd reaction when they listened to Hitler's speech on the radio in September 1938. And Gundlach was once more questioning Ledóchowski's reliability concerning the encyclical. The final decision would come from the new pope.

Rome, March 1, 1939

Cardinals from around the world began arriving at the Vatican throughout the mourning period for Pius XI. Pacelli declared that the conclave to choose the new pope would begin on March 1. Speculation was rife, and Vatican sources fed the rumors that any of the sixty-two cardinals had a chance, even the twenty-seven who were not Italian. The question seemed to be: Would the new pope be a "political or spiritual pope"? A political pope would match Pius XI's confrontations with Hitler and Mussolini. A spiritual pope would be circumspect and impartial and tend to his mission as the Holy Father of the Roman Catholic Church.

Sources at the Vatican did not discourage talk that a liberal cardinal from the United States or a Frenchman such as Tisserant could be viable candidates. The British and French governments immediately favored Pacelli. They thought he had been groomed by years of diplomatic service in Germany and as secretary of state. They said he had been a faithful subordinate to Pius XI, whose forthright rejection of the Nazis had been attractive. And finally, Germany and Italy had publicly made negative comments about Pacelli's candidacy, which British officials said was a point in Pacelli's favor. If the Italians and the Germans didn't want Pacelli, he must be a perfect choice.

It also was possible that a counterpropaganda campaign had been under way all the while. Publicly, via Nazi and Fascist newspapers, Germany and Italy did signal that the Pacelli's election would mean the Vatican was still taking a political, confrontational approach. Pacelli had been Pius's enforcer and had repeatedly criticized their governments. Ciano in particular was reported to be lobbying against Pacelli with Italian cardinals.

But behind the scenes some German and Italian officials said something different. Ciano had already had successful contacts with Pacelli early on that signaled a difference in Vatican relations with the Fascist state and had also sent word that the pope's troublesome final speech had been erased.

The German ambassador to the Vatican, Diego von Bergen, reported to Berlin that he thought Pacelli would be a good choice because he was a Germanophile who spoke German and had spent a long time in the country as a diplomat.

U.S. diplomats, meanwhile, concluded that Pacelli could not be a serious candidate. Rarely in history had a Vatican secretary of state been named pope. Ambassador Phillips apparently did not have an inside line from Monsignor Hurley, whose role at the Vatican was certain to change with the death of Pius XI, his protector. Phillips reported to Washington that while a number of candidates had been mentioned, the information about candidates was "purely speculative."

Caroline Phillips had actually spent more time speaking with Pacelli than her husband had, and she might not have discarded his candidacy so easily. She was not only insightful, she also spoke fluent Italian. She found Pacelli to be charming and at the same time a great diplomat.

The French ambassador, François Charles-Roux, made the rounds among diplomats in Rome in support of Pacelli. Charles-Roux urged Phillips to speak with the American cardinals about papal candidates. Phillips refused, saying that lobbying in favor of any candidate was improper for a diplomat.

Charles-Roux, nevertheless, did lobby the French cardinals in favor of Pacelli; only one was inexorably and vehemently opposed to Pacelli: Cardinal Eugene Tisserant, who said he would not even consider the possibility, though he would not say exactly who he would vote for.

As the day of the conclave approached, Italian police and military monitored all arrivals in Rome, searching for weapons, bombs, or anyone they considered suspicious. There had been no specific warning of trouble, just a general suspicion because, over history, conclaves had sometimes been accompanied by violence. Mussolini pretended to be disinterested, but privately he pressed for inside information once more. He ordered his intelligence apparatus to track the proceedings as a top priority and issued an order to intelligence agents commanding that they pursue "penetration of and contact with the Vatican authorities, work which needed maximum delicacy."

By March 1, the Italian government had gathered firsthand information from high levels at the Vatican. Italian agents were tracking all correspondence and all communications and had planted middle-level operatives inside the Vatican. Some were priests, bishops, or higher and in reality were spying for the Fascist government.

Charles-Roux made an eleventh-hour attempt to change Tisserant's mind about Pacelli. He was committed to the importance of the conclave and lobbied hard. He argued that "this is the election which could best maintain the Papacy on the high moral level to which Pius XI had raised it." The French cardinal agreed with that and the argument appeared to steel him even more against Pacelli, whom he would never vote for. Tisserant's position was so odd in Charles-Roux's view that he thought something else must have been at play. "It is influenced by a personal antipathy towards the former Secretary of State," the French ambassador wrote in a memoir, "an antipathy probably born of the relations during their careers."

Tisserant remained suspicious about the pope's death and developed two theories. Tisserant had told his friend Monsignor George Roche that he believed Pius XI was murdered. He concluded that the evidence had been hidden during the interval between his death and the phone call Tisserant received. "They killed him and we know who did it," the cardinal told Roche. Tisserant told Roche, according to newspaper reports, that the pope's face "showed bluish marks unusual in cases of death by natural causes."

Roche said Tisserant blamed Doctor Francesco Saverio Petacci for accelerating Pius's death, even though the pope was gravely ill. Tisserant contended that the lag between the phone call and the tolling of the church bells had given someone with access the opportunity to hide evidence that the pope had been murdered. When Tisserant's suspicions were made known in 1972, a Vatican spokesman told reporters the idea was too "fantastic" to consider serious. The Vatican also said Petacci could not have been involved in such a thing because he had no access to the pope before or after his death.

Although Doctor Petacci was the second-ranking physician at the Vatican, accounts of the pope's final hours did not mention him at the pope's bedside. The Vatican not only denied Petacci was present but also said he had no access. One question could have been asked: Why wasn't he at the pope's bedside? There were five doctors on the Vatican medical staff, each listed in order in the Vatican yearbook. Milani was the boss, and Petacci was listed number two. Why would the number two physician at the Vatican not be present or have access when the pontiff was gravely ill? Instead, after Milani became ill with the flu, the physician with least seniority attended the pope in his final days. Why would the Vatican say Petacci had no access to the pope?

Petacci was the father of Clara Petacci, Mussolini's mistress and a well-known subject of scandals and gossip around Rome. She recorded pillow talk with Il Duce in her diary and Mussolini had often complained about the pope. At the height of the pope's attacks on Italian anti-Semitic laws, Clara recorded one such outburst: "You have no idea of the bad this Pope is doing toward the Church," Mussolini had said. "Never has there been such an ill-omened Pope towards religion. There are committed Catholics who detest him. He has lost virtually everyone. Germany completely. He doesn't know how to keep them and he has made mistakes in everything."

Doctor Petacci had a long history with the Vatican. A relative, perhaps his father, Giuseppe, had been Pope Pius X's personal doctor at the Vatican from 1906 to 1912. The Petaccis were a middle-class family who had acquired influence and power by their proximity to Mussolini. Various stories said Mussolini, married and fifty years old, met Clara in 1933. She was barely twenty-one years old and Mussolini, various stories said, met her at a party or perhaps spotted her on the road one day while she was driving with her fiancé, an Italian Air Force officer. In either case, Mussolini was smitten and telephoned the Petacci house. Clara's mother answered the call and was happy to arrange their first romantic tryst. Less than a year after that, an affair blossomed. Clara married the air force officer for propriety's sake, and it was a major social event. One of those who attended was Cardinal Eugenio Pacelli. Not long after the wedding, the air force officer was shipped off as a military attaché to Tokyo, and Clara moved to her own private suite in Mussolini's Palazzo Venezia.

Two of Doctor Petacci's other children benefited from their proximity to power and were considered corrupt power brokers in Rome those years. A son, Marcello, also became a doctor, and it was said that he had passed his medical exams with a "recommendation" from Il Duce. Marcello frequently traveled with his sister on Mussolini's official visits as a way of lending a veneer of propriety to the proceedings. A daughter, Maria, became an actress, changed her name to Miriam Day, and married into nobility.

Decades later, when Tisserant's charge was publicized, one of the surviving members of the Petacci family, Marcello Petacci's son, Ferdinando Petacci, said his grandfather Francesco was being slandered by such charges. He rejected Petacci's involvement in any such plot and said the doctor had admired Pope Pius XI. "My grandfather was an exceptionally capable, humble doctor who had high moral values . . . incapable of even hurting a fly," he said. In addition, he said, Doctor Petacci had opposed his daughter's liaison with Mussolini. "Personally, I do not think that Pope Pius XI was killed. He was an old man and he was very sick."

Doctor Petacci died in 1970 at the age of eighty-three. He had outlived two of his children. Clara and her brother Marcello were executed by Communist partisans in northern Italy along with Mussolini on April 29, 1945.

There were other scenarios in which Pius XI could have met an untimely death. Doctors Milani and Rocchi, who attended the pope in his last hours, practiced techniques that were common in the day that might have been damaging without them realizing it. They were alternately giving the pope injections of camphor oil and adrenaline, compounds to stimulate the heart and increase the pulse rate. Camphor had been used as a traditional medicine for some time, but there had been published reports of fatal camphor poisoning.

The timing of the pope's death did add to the suspicion of foul play. Mussolini was worried to the point of obsession about the February 11 speech. Even if Mussolini's informants hadn't seen the document, they knew how much emphasis the pope was placing on his speech.

It was also feasible that someone could have substituted, contaminated, or otherwise altered a medicine prepared for the pope. The Vatican categorically said the story from Tisserant was false, based on "statements and insinuations already amply denied on the basis of irrefutable testimony." It did "concede that Cardinal Tisserant may have recorded it, together with other hearsay and gossip, in his diaries," the *New York Times* reported in 1972.

Others who had seen the pope in his last days were also suspicious. Bianca Penco, the student leader of the anti-Fascist Catholic youth organization FUCI, was probably the last surviving person to have met and spoken to Pius XI. At the age of ninety-three in 2011, she held to her impression of a meeting with the pope on January 31, 1939. She said in the 2008 interview published in *Il Secolo XIX* that she and her fellow student leaders were shocked when they heard the pope had died just a few days after their audience.

"Especially because of the atmosphere surrounding the speech and the pope's attitude in the meeting," she said. "We had the agonizing thought that his death was not an accident. To our insistent inquiries for explanations and clarifications about the document that [the pope had spoken about], [the church] replied that no such thing had been written. It is a question that has never been resolved."

Doctor Massimo Calabresi, the Milan heart specialist who had been consulted previously on the pope's illness through his patron Doctor Cesa-Bianchi, heard the rumors of foul play. Calabresi was an ardent opponent of Mussolini, a militant protester who had been imprisoned for his anti-Fascist activities. But he told his son,

Guido—who eventually became dean of the Yale Law School and a U.S. circuit court judge—that he was also an honest man. He saw no indication of foul play. "He said he would have liked to have blamed it on the Fascists, but it would not be true. The pope was a very, very sick man."

The pontiff's state of health was so precarious that he could have died at any time. Tisserant acknowledged as much in a letter to a librarian friend in the United States less than a month after the pope died. He said the pope appeared vibrant and well on February 4, six days before the death. "Nothing was inspiring the fear of a near end," Tisserant said on February 27, 1939, "although we knew well that the end would come abruptly."

Tisserant died on February 21, 1972, before he could follow through on plans to edit and publish his memoirs. Selected citations from Tisserant's diaries were published several months later in major international magazines and newspapers. Tisserant's niece had started legal proceedings against the Vatican for the return of twelve suitcases of the cardinal's notes and diaries. The Vatican claimed that all the material belonged to the church, but the niece, Paule Hennequin, was also Tisserant's secretary and said that she was her uncle's sole executor.

At the same time, Monsignor Roche, Tisserant's friend, said he had taken at least some of the cardinal's papers out of Italy, presumably to safekeeping in France. Those documents have not been found. A doctoral candidate at Indiana University, Nicola Mattioli Hary, said that some of the cardinal's papers had been secreted away to the French Pyrenees. Church historians said the bulk of Tisserant's papers are likely still held at the Vatican Secret Archives. Part of the reason Tisserant's files were removed has been attributed to his sometimes turbulent relationship with Pope Paul VI. Speculation about their disagreement focused on the administration of the church. Paul VI issued a decree in November 1970 that cardinals reaching the age of eighty were no longer eligible to vote in papal conclaves. Tisserant, then eighty-six, thought the measure was among several specifically aimed at forcing his retirement.

By 1958, Tisserant was the dean of the College of Cardinals and acted as *camerlengo* himself. In the papal conclave that followed, some considered the French cardinal a candidate to replace the pope and he was said to have received a small number of votes in early balloting. Again, it had been unlikely that a non-Italian would be chosen. Cardinal Angelo Roncalli was elected on October 28, 1958, and chose the name Pope John XXIII. There were eleven ballots over four days. Tisserant was present when John XXIII died of stomach cancer on June 3, 1963, and he celebrated the funeral Mass.

All that was publicly known about Tisserant's sentiments and concerns after his friend's death are contained in a handful of diplomatic reports and letters he wrote to friends. In a letter to a librarian friend in Michigan several weeks after the pope died, he expressed only sorrow and concern about how the next pope would deal with the world situation.

Pius's death was "a great loss for me, and a great pain. . . . Now we have the awful responsibility to choose a Pope, and in the most difficult circumstances since the time of the French Revolution. Evident signs of a hastened preparation of Germany to war are known: Would the next Pope be able to do something for preventing that horrible thing, war?"

CHAPTER THIRTEEN

The New Regime

The Vatican, March 1, 1939

JOURNALISTS WERE ALLOWED to visit the Sistine Chapel on the night before the sixty-two cardinals were going to be sequestered there. Plush velvet seats had been arranged in a horseshoe against the frescoed walls of biblical scenes such as *Moses Leaving to Egypt* and *The Delivery of Keys* by Perugino; *The Temptation of Christ* and the *Punishment of the Rebels* by Sandro Botticelli; and *The Last Supper* by Cosimo Rosselli. But all of them were crowned by Michelangelo's vault ceiling fresco, completed in 1512; some of the images were cracked and clouded from the passage of years, but the eye still sought out the *Creation of Adam*—God reaching down to the first man from on high, humankind's life for all eternity never quite touching the divine.

On leaving the chapel just as the cardinals were arriving, Camille Cianfarra, the *New York Times* correspondent, spotted Monsignor Joseph Hurley, who had been an excellent source for many American reporters. Cianfarra asked Hurley for his assessment of who would be chosen. "You shall know fairly soon I think," he told Cianfarra. "I should not be surprised if you have the answer tomorrow."

Of the sixty-two cardinals, fifty-five were European; thirty-five of those were Italian. Even if the Italians voted in a bloc, they needed votes from other countries to provide the requisite forty-two votes. There were three cardinals from the United States, one from Quebec, one from Asia, and two from Latin America. The Latin Americans were last to arrive: Sebastiano Leme da Silveira Cintra of Brazil and Santiago Luis Copello of Argentina. Everyone believed the new pope would be an Italian. There had not been a non-Italian since Adrian VI, an Englishman, was chosen in 1522. This did not appear to be a moment for experimentation, although Tisserant and some American cardinals were still being mentioned as candidates.

There was no escaping the presence of Nazi Germany as the cardinals arrived in Rome. A swastika fluttered on a ship's mast in Naples harbor when Cardinal George Mundelein of Chicago and Cardinal Dennis Dougherty, the archbishop of Philadelphia, arrived. The third American cardinal, William O'Connell, could see another swastika waving over his hotel balcony in central Rome where Nazi and Fascist members of the National Women's Organization were also housed.

A crowd at St. Peter's cheered that afternoon as the cardinals arrived to open the conclave. Outsiders were allowed in for a time during the late afternoon prior to the traditional opening. Cardinal O'Connell, seventy-nine years old and ailing, was last to enter and had to be helped up the steps by attendants and colleagues. O'Connell, the archbishop of Boston since 1906, had officiated at the marriage in 1914 of Joseph P. Kennedy and his bride, Rose Fitzgerald.

At around 6:00 P.M. the bells of St. Damasus signaled the

final moments before the cardinals were to be sequestered. *"Extra Omnes!"*—Everyone out—the Latin cry echoed from the Vatican halls. Swiss Guards searched every room and walked the periphery of the chapel to ensure that no people but the cardinals were present. At 6:17 P.M., the doors of the chapel swung closed. Three locks were heard turning on the door inside the Sistine Chapel, and a guard turned three locks from the outside as well.

So much importance was given to the event that reporters conducted a vigil from a rented apartment and set up a telescope that was fixed at the little tin chimney over the Sistine Chapel. After each vote, black smoke would signal no choice yet. White smoke meant a new pope had been chosen. Many assumed the conclave would last for days or even weeks.

The cardinals had assumed their places around the Sistine Chapel, now dressed in specially prescribed violet cloaks that buttoned in front. They did not take a first vote that evening. Swiss Guards outside the chapel could see candles burning in the opaque windows of the chambers where the cardinals were spending the night. They had retired relatively early.

The cardinals reconvened on Tuesday morning, March 2, which happened to be Cardinal Eugenio Pacelli's sixty-third birthday. Immediately Pacelli received thirty-five votes, seven short of the required two-thirds to elect a new pope. They voted once more in the late morning, and this time forty votes were his. The proceedings were then delayed because the stove used to burn the ballots became clogged up and smoke began pouring out into the Sistine Chapel. The cardinals were forced to break the seal of the room and called the Vatican fire brigade, who extinguished the flames and cleared out the smoke.

The cardinals returned to the chapel and voted once more in the afternoon. This time Pacelli had reached forty-two, and if he accepted, he would be the pope. Witnesses among the cardinals said the usually impassive Pacelli buried his head in his hands when he realized what had happened. There had never been serious opposition to Pacelli as the new pope, and all the speculation outside that room about other candidates had been meaningless. A Pacelli supporter said afterward: "We had against us nothing but a handful of dust."

Now the other cardinals turned to Pacelli and awaited his decision. Pacelli accepted and said, "I wish to be called Pius XII because all my ecclesiastical life, all my career has taken place under Pontiffs of that name and particularly because I have a debt of gratitude toward Pius XI, who always caused me to be indebted to him for his affection to me."

The conclave was now over; a pope had been chosen in record time, less than twenty-four hours and after only three ballots. Pacelli was right that he owed much to Pius XI's support. Ironically, however, his name choice would serve to obscure the name of his predecessor. With the history that came afterward, when lay-people heard the name Pope Pius pronounced, they assumed one referred to Pope Pius XII, Eugenio Pacelli.

Preparations were now made before the world was to be told. By ritual, the new pope was to be fitted quickly with his new robes. As he left the Loggia of Raphael after emerging from the Sistine Chapel, Pacelli walked down a stairway toward the Royal Hall. "Suddenly he missed his footing," the *New York Times* reported, "falling headlong down the last half-dozen steps." Luckily he was only lightly bruised, as he had been in the car accident several months earlier.

AMBASSADOR WILLIAM PHILLIPS felt like going down to St. Peter's Square on the afternoon of March 2 to see if smoke might rise from the roof over the Sistine Chapel. He had a "feeling that something was happening," he recalled, but he had just missed the white smoke emanating from the little tin chimney. "I found the Piazza San Pietro already two-thirds filled and a tapestry was being hung over the little balcony above the main entrance of St. Peter's." An amplified voice boomed over the crowd within moments—*Habemus Papam*—"we have a pope."

"Tremendous enthusiasm burst forth from the crowd," Phillips said. "Everybody waved his hat and the Piazza resounded with cheers. All faces were turned toward St. Peter's and then, led by the invisible Sistine choir a slow chanting began. It was an impressive moment."

In a few hours, night had fallen and a full moon cast shadows through the colonnade of St. Peter's. Attendants draped white-and-yellow bunting emblazoned with the papal crown over the balustrade before the pope's balcony. All attention focused there. Shortly after 6 p.m., Phillips watched as "the new Pope appeared on the balcony and the crowd knelt reverently." Dressed in white, Pope Pius XII blessed the crowd, both hands raised to the heavens. "As the balcony was not flood-lighted, it was difficult to see his face very clearly. The crowds were again enthusiastic," said Phillips. "There was a curious combination of reverence and cheering and waving of hats, but it was evident that the choice of Pacelli was a popular one."

The Vatican, March 12, 1939

Eugenio Maria Giuseppe Giovanni Pacelli was crowned with the papal tiara ten days later, on Sunday, March 12. Caroline Phillips was well situated to observe the coronation and record her observations. She wrote,

> *It was a delicious morning clear and sunny and not cold,*
> *and the clear soft pearly light of early morning as we drove*
> *across the Tiber and passed the tower of St. Angelo was*
> *breathlessly lovely. For me it will I hope ever remain a vivid*
> *picture of brilliant ecclesiastical pageantry, the central figure,*
> *tall emaciated, ascetic, calm and aloof with the closed eyes of an*
> *ancient Cambodian Budda [sic], drawing into himself all that*
> *was most mystic and holy and beautiful of that ancient ritual.*
> *He seemed to be moving in a world apart, living through*
> *within the depths of his soul a great spiritual experience.*

By this point, the United States had resolved a minor diplomatic problem regarding the new pope's coronation. Although Ambassador Phillips was in Rome, he was not accredited to the Holy See, and the United States had not yet decided to take up diplomatic relations with the Vatican. Both the Vatican and the United States wanted for their own reasons to avoid the appearance of too close relations between President Roosevelt and the Vatican.

Roosevelt decided that Joseph Kennedy, now the U.S. ambassador to Great Britain, would be the official American representative at the coronation. Phillips and Caroline were seated inconspicuously some distance from the official representatives, Ambassador Kennedy and his wife, Rose. Caroline had particularly noticed that one of the ambassador's dashing young sons was in town as well, John Fitzgerald Kennedy, a twenty-one-year-old junior at Harvard College. The Kennedys, including Jack and two of his sisters, Eunice and Kathleen, had come to dinner at the Phillipses' house the night before. Jack Kennedy had been spending considerable time with his father at the embassy in London, learning the trade of diplomacy and traveling around Europe when he was not studying.

The assembled dignitaries had waited for hours. At just after 10 P.M. the new pope could be seen entering. He walked slowly to the throne of St. Peter. "After His Holiness had taken his seat on the throne, his jeweled miter was replaced by a simple one of gold material," Ambassador Phillips said, comparing notes with his wife.

An unseen choir chanted throughout the Mass, which lasted two and a half hours. Then followed "the procession of all the cardinals to the throne each one kissing his ring . . . I noticed that the more important cardinals did not kiss the Pope's toe . . . Some of them were very old and feeble and had to be helped up and down the steps leading to the dais." By tradition, one prelate paused before the pope three times during the ceremony and intoned— *sic transit gloria mundi*—"thus passes the glory of the world"—a reminder to the pope that one day, too, he would die.

The new pope's first message made only the most indirect mention of world affairs. "We invite all to the peace of a conscience," he said, "tranquil in the friendship of God . . . peace between nations by way of mutual help, friendly collaboration and cordial understanding, for the higher interest of the great human family . . . We have before our eyes the vision of the vast evils with which the world is struggling and to which it is our duty, unarmed but relying on the help of God, to bring succor."

The media and various pundits engaged in much analysis of how Pacelli would act as pope. They drew threads from his repetition of the word *peace* twice in the same sentence; nothing more telling was available. The use of the word, they said, signaled that he intended to seek peace. But would he confront Hitler and Mussolini as Pius XI had? It appeared to be so. His choice of name, Pius XII, appeared to mean something. Many simply assumed that Pacelli—the pope's loyal servant and most visible understudy— would emulate old Pius's politics.

Analysts generally praised the choice of Pacelli. Ambassador Phillips expressed the opinion of many that "the fact that he has chosen the name of his predecessor is an intimation to the world that he intends to pursue the strong policy of Pius XI." Dorothy Thompson of the *New York Tribune* said his election was "not only in harmony with the spirit and policies of his predecessor [but] it is in harmony with his diplomatic career." That was also the impression in France. "The cardinals have marked the clear desire to pursue the politics energetically affirmed by Pius XI," editorialized the Paris daily *L'Epoque*, "against all doctrines of violence and those that may come in the future."

Yet there was significant diplomatic dissent. The American consul-general in Cologne, Germany, Alfred Klieforth, told the State Department that Pacelli, though a veteran diplomat, was deluded in his view of the Nazis. Klieforth reported to Washington on March 3 that Pacelli had told him he thought "Hitler was not a true Nazi and 'in spite of appearances would end up in the camp of the left-wing Nazi extremists where he began his career.'" Another critic, the former German chancellor, Heinrich Brüning, maneuvered out of office by Hitler in 1932, told the British Foreign Office that "he knows Cardinal Pacelli very well and considers that there is a great deal of naiveté" in his view of Hitler and Mussolini.

Dissenters also remained within the walls of the Vatican. Among them were Cardinal Tisserant, who had not only refused to vote for Pacelli, but also told a friend afterward that he had voted for the Jesuit cardinal of Genoa, Pietro Boetto, a wasted vote because a Jesuit had never been and would not be elected pope. Among the other silent critics were Joseph Hurley, who had always maintained a cool relationship with Pacelli; and Gundlach, who doubted that Pacelli as the new pope would ever publish a treatise that condemned anti-Semitism. Gundlach described what hardly anyone outside the Vatican wall realized. He saw the new pope as a wisp of a man, swaying like a thin reed in the breeze, and he feared that his voice would be just as thin.

Rome, March 15, 1939

Three days after the papal coronation, Hitler invaded the remaining independent portion of Czechoslovakia, seized Prague, and annexed the country. As with Austria, exactly a year earlier, the Nazi army met virtually no resistance. Czechoslovakia no longer existed, and Chamberlain's plan for peace in our time was dead, just as Pope Pius XI had predicted.

Pope Pius XII, who had wanted the previous pope to endorse the Munich Agreement, now did nothing to criticize the German invasion. Even before Pacelli's investiture, he made sure that the Vatican would avoid taking sides and stay impartial.

William Phillips noted that the Vatican newspaper, *Osservatore Romano*, had toned down its rhetoric and replaced vitriolic attacks on Italy and Germany with moderate language. Britain quickly saw the same. "Vatican policy changed overnight," wrote British historian Owen Chadwick. "Pius XI denounced the Nazi ill-treatment of the Churches, or countered Mussolini's anti-Semitic provisions, and generally stood up for justice and liberty. All these good objectives were suddenly seen as secondary to one supreme quest, that of helping the European powers not to destroy each other."

British officials had wrongly assumed that Mussolini would be unhappy with Pacelli as the new pope; it turned out that his congratulations had been genuine. Ciano told the French ambassador Charles-Roux he was "delighted with the election. I am on the best terms with Cardinal Pacelli . . . His election is a great success for Italy."

The new pope met with Ciano within a week of assuming office and said he planned to "follow a more conciliatory policy than Pius XI," Ciano wrote in his diary. Ciano's assessment was succinct: "I believe that we can get along well with this Pope."

The Germans were also enthusiastic. Pacelli was in touch almost immediately with the German embassy and sent a friendly letter to Hitler within days of his election. Heinrich Himmler spoke to Ciano about the prospects for improved relations. "They like the new Pope and believe that a *modus vivendi* is possible," Ciano said. "I encouraged him along these lines, saying that an agreement between the Reich and the Vatican would make the Axis more popular."

The new pope advocated peace negotiations with Hitler and Mussolini on one side and with the Western powers on the other. Critics said the peace negotiations initiated by the new pope did not point to peace. Everyone expected the pope, any pope, to support peace, "to use the authority of his great office to avert the threat of war in Europe," the *New York Times* said in an editorial in May 1939. But as the new pope sought to be a fair broker and intermediary between the Axis and the Allies, he faced the problem, the *Times* continued, of "creating a will to peace on the part of nations which have been ready to resort to violence in order to achieve their ambitions."

New York, March 12, 1939

John LaFarge wrote enthusiastically in *America* about the election of the new pope. He assumed that Pope Pacelli, as he was sometimes called, would follow the policies and the legacy of Pope Pius XI. LaFarge had never spoken with him and had seen him only twice, in Budapest and briefly in the courtyard at Castel

Gandolfo, yet he had every reason to be hopeful that his project still could be issued as an encyclical.

LaFarge had read the speculation about what exactly the new pope would focus on. "In a simple sense, of course, the new Pope is 'political.' He has for years occupied with brilliance a major political position . . . and he has dealt with the world's leading politicians," LaFarge wrote.

Yet in another sense, LaFarge repeated what Pope Pius XI had often said. The church is intrinsically not political. It guides and views politics as part of its spiritual mission. And that must be based on humanity and morality.

"For the totalitarian governments," LaFarge continued, "whether Communist, National Socialist or Fascist, it is practically impossible to see anything else in the Papacy than a rival to their own state-centered autocracy."

LaFarge wrote that civilization and humanity were at stake. The church creates "an unswerving devotion to human rights and to the common good," he said. "If we look back to the late Pope Pius XI, "we find this exemplified in his own life and utterances." LaFarge assumed the new pope would follow the same path.

At the Vatican, on Easter Sunday, April 9, or the following Monday, Pope Pius XII, the new leader of the Roman Catholic Church, met with the Jesuit superior Wlodimir Ledóchowski and considered the words of John LaFarge that condemned anti-Semitism as racism and a crime against humanity. Pope Pacelli indicated that he had never before seen LaFarge's draft encyclical. His good friend Ledóchowski told him that he thought the document was lacking in focus and was too extreme. The pope accepted the word of his friend. That was all Ledóchowski needed to hear.

Ledóchowski's assistant, Zacheus Maher, wrote to LaFarge on Monday and told him the new pope had rejected the encyclical. The Vatican no longer wanted it and banned any reference to it being a papal document. "If you wish, you may now profit by your recent work and proceed to its publication," Maher said. But "there shall not be the least allusion to the work as having in any way had any connection with anything requested of you by his late Holiness.

"The Lord will surely bless you for all the effort and anguish this work caused you even though it will not have the outlet at first anticipated."

LaFarge and Gundlach exchanged letters after they each received this news from the Vatican. LaFarge suggested to his German friend that they make a pact not to publish the encyclical on their own, even as an independent document. Perhaps in that case, the new pope might change his mind and publish it one day.

"Slim chance of that," Gundlach wrote back to LaFarge. But he agreed to hold on to the text. In his view, the "diplomatic" bloc within the Vatican—those who did not support the previous pope's confrontational style—had simply won out.

Gundlach also had received a letter from Maher on behalf of Ledóchowski and described it to LaFarge. "You can imagine that I was very shaken," Gundlach wrote, "less on account of the content of the note, which I after all had no longer expected in any other fashion, than on account of the peculiar way with which this affair and we ourselves have been handled.

"We are hoping here for the continuation of the true line that once was," Gundlach continued. But he could see that Pope Pacelli would not take sides in the battle against the rising tide of Nazism. Some defended the pope, Gundlach added, saying Pacelli would "in no way degrade himself and not go astray, even though his decisions and pronouncements be less spirited and more nicely balanced." Gundlach did not agree.

Gundlach summed up what he believed had happened with Pius XI's encyclical: Ledóchowski's strategy of delay had worked.

He blocked the previous pope, and he advised his close friend, Pacelli, the new pope, to discard the encyclical on racism and to silence those who produced it. "Our affair in any case meanwhile went the way of all flesh"—it died with the old pope.

Gundlach was bitter about how he and LaFarge had been treated, but he was mostly motivated by the conviction that the encyclical deserved to be published. He struggled in vain to find a positive side of the story—he thanked LaFarge for involving him in the drafting of the document and for his friendship. He also said how much he had enjoyed that summer working in Paris.

The two Jesuits came away from this experience with an understanding of the modus operandi of the new pope. This would be the course of the church in the midst of inevitable war—standing far back while Europe collapsed before an advancing German army and as the Nazis carried out their persecution of the Jews.

The Vatican, August 14, 1940

Cardinal Tisserant never spoke out in public against Pope Pacelli; he suffered in silence at first, then began to complain privately and directly to the new pope about his policy of neutrality. Some said the policy was intended to protect the Vatican and protect Catholics in Europe. Others said it was not the pope's role to make political statements. Tisserant vehemently disagreed. "I have insistently asked the Holy Father to issue an encyclical (condemning Nazism and Fascism)," he said in a letter to a fellow churchman. "I fear history will have to reproach the Holy See with having pursued a policy of convenience for itself, and not much more. This is extremely sad, especially for one who has lived under Pius XI."

Joseph Hurley, Pius XI's personal interpreter and conduit to the U.S. embassy, also thought that Pope Pius XII should speak out.

The European war had begun when Nazi Germany seized Poland in September 1939. Chamberlain resigned on May 10, 1940, the final acknowledgment that his policy of appeasement was a failure. He died of cancer six months later. On June 10, 1940, Italy entered the war alongside Germany. Four days later, Hitler's Wehrmacht marched triumphantly into Paris after conquering Belgium and Holland.

Hurley took his first open step toward a break with the Vatican when he issued a remarkable commentary on Vatican Radio in English on July 4, 1940, less than a month after Paris fell to the Nazis. The speech, monitored in Britain and the United States, declared that the time for pacifism was past. "We have sympathy for the pacifists but they are wrong," Hurley said. "No word in the Gospel or in papal teaching suggests that justice should go undefended, that it is not worth dying for. . . . The Church is no conscientious objector."

Hurley, the ranking American at the Vatican Secretariat of State, had spoken far beyond his brief, knowing well that the new pope did not like threatening remarks. Hurley's declaration was a throwback to the days of the previous pope—his beloved benefactor. The commentary came on the air without identifying Hurley, but Vatican reporters recognized his voice.

The *Times* of London reported on the commentary, saying that while "*Osservatore Romano* prints no war commentary nowadays," this particular report shows that "the Vatican still allows strongly worded broadcasts." Hurley's broadcast was most likely not authorized by the pope or other high-ranking officials at the Vatican. He was speaking as a loyal American and a man of moral force.

Hurley had never been a favorite of Pacelli, and his outspoken role was visible. He continued to work closely with U.S. officials in Rome, especially with Myron Taylor, who had been appointed as President Roosevelt's personal envoy to the Vatican. Hurley's role as intermediary with U.S. ambassador Phillips was thereby curtailed, much to both men's disappointment.

Phillips stayed on in Italy for another eighteen months, cooperating with Taylor in unsuccessful efforts to dissuade Mussolini from fighting alongside Hitler. But Phillips quit his Italian post in October 1941 and became station chief of the U.S. Office of Strategic Services in London. The OSS was the forerunner of the Central Intelligence Agency. Phillips continued to serve Roosevelt and President Truman in several diplomatic roles throughout the 1940s. He and his wife, Caroline, then retired to their home in Beverly, Massachusetts. Caroline maintained her diaries until her death at the age of eighty-four in 1965. Her husband, eighty-nine, died three years later.

Pope Pius XII's opportunity to oust Hurley came quickly. When word came on August 12 that Archbishop Patrick Barry of St. Augustine, Florida, had died, Hurley was unceremoniously assigned as his replacement four days later. The naming of a new bishop normally took months of deliberations. Hurley's elevation to bishop of St. Augustine was cast as a promotion and was carried out with praise and sweet words.

But the church hierarchy knew that Hurley was being banished. St. Augustine was considered a backwater assignment for such a high-ranking Vatican official. He was cast aside for daring to speak out against the Nazis in solitary tribute to his mentor, Pope Pius XI. One of the new pope's first acts had been to promote Francis Spellman, Hurley's predecessor, as the designated American at the Vatican; Spellman became archbishop of New York on April 15, 1939, en route to becoming a cardinal seven years later.

Even in Florida, Hurley drew attention in the United States as one of the most vocal church figures during World War II. He proudly spoke, for example, about U.S. war preparations on the CBS Radio Network on July 6, 1941, with the preface that his word did not carry "any mandate from the Vatican . . . only my own authority." He repeated Pius XI's condemnation of the "the crooked cross of National Socialism," a term Hurley had coined. The previous pope, he said, had warned that Nazi "intrigues had been laid bare which aim at nothing less than a war of extermination."

He did not criticize Pius XII, but rather praised his attempt to negotiate for peace. He did say it was time to prepare for the inevitable conflagration. "Pope Pius XII has not ceased to raise His voice against the evils of totalitarianism . . ." and for peace. "It is history, of course, that we failed," Hurley said. "We failed because one nation, confidently arrogant in its armored might, wanted war. This war is Germany's doing . . . We may not, we must not, wait for the start of hostilities . . . let us pray for peace but prepare for war."

After the war, Hurley was occasionally summoned back to temporary diplomatic duty at the Vatican, but he remained as bishop of St. Augustine until he died in 1967, embittered, disillusioned, increasingly conservative and as autocratic in his Florida domain as his beloved mentor Pope Pius XI had been at the Vatican.

EPILOGUE

New York, May 20, 1963

T HE RECREATION ROOM at America House had been silent except for John LaFarge's voice as he told the story of his summer in Europe in the days before the war began.

LaFarge was filling in the details of a story he had acknowledged in his 1954 memoir, *The Manner Is Ordinary*. At the time, he described his meeting with Pius XI as a discussion about racism and anti-Semitism. "He had read my book *Interracial Justice* and liked the title of it," LaFarge said. "'*Interracial Justice, c'est bon!*' the pope said, pronouncing the title as if it were French. He said he thought my book was the best thing written on the topic, comparing it with some European literature. Naturally, this was a big lift to me."

LaFarge promoted human rights issues for the rest of his life through books and commentaries in *America* and in speeches around the country. Awards showered upon him—the 1955 Catholic

International Peace Award; media awards; a social justice award from the Religions and Labor Council in 1957 shared with Martin Luther King; recognition in 1962 by the American Jewish Committee. He wrote a number of books, including *A Catholic Viewpoint on Racism* (1956) and *An American Amen* (1958). "A priest's life," he wrote in that book, "is not unlike that of a bridge between God and man." A final book, *Reflections on Growing Old*, was published in 1963.

And yet, his meeting with Pope Pius XI pulled at his conscience. LaFarge wrote in *The Manner Is Ordinary*: "If I were in Rome again, he said in conclusion, I should be sure to drop in to see him. He might like to talk to me again on the question and might have some further ideas." The pope had expected him to return that year in person with a finished encyclical.

Now, in 1963, he was revealing what really happened during his conversation with the pope.

LaFarge told his friends he had trusted Wlodimir Ledóchowski. His fellow Jesuits understood that his loyalty and deference to the Father Superior was tantamount. How could LaFarge have known that Ledóchowski was lying?

Ledóchowski had died at the age of seventy-six on December 13, 1942, midwar, about four years after the death of Pius XI. One Jesuit who worked with Ledóchowski said that the Jesuit superior general always covered his tracks and left no compromising documents.

Nevertheless, LaFarge knew he had failed. The pope had asked LaFarge to return personally and deliver the encyclical. But extenuating circumstances, sickness and death, and the pressure of Ledóchowski's personality had kept LaFarge from ever seeing the pope again.

Walter Abbott, one of LaFarge's longtime fellow Jesuits at America House, asked Uncle John one basic question about Ledóchowski's role.

"I asked him if he thought that the Father General sabotaged the encyclical," Abbott said.

LaFarge said yes; he did think Ledóchowski had blocked the encyclical. "I could not fathom why" Ledóchowski would do such a thing, LaFarge said. In any case, he added, it probably didn't matter by that time. LaFarge told Abbott he thought "Pius XI was weakened and too far gone" to follow through with the encyclical's publication.

LaFarge, tugged by obedience to Ledóchowski and by the personal need to be with his family, had made a difficult and, in some ways, defensible decision. He now regretted the decision to go home; he could have given the pope the encyclical in person. "I made a mistake by doing the right thing," LaFarge told the other Jesuits.

He then stood up and shuffled slowly off to his room for bed. After Uncle John had left, Abbott looked to the others. "He told us the whole story . . . JLF had us spellbound. I have lived with him for 20 years and this is the first time I'm hearing about this project."

A few weeks later, President John F. Kennedy invited LaFarge to the White House for a meeting of religious leaders to discuss "certain issues of this nation's civil rights problem. This matter merits serious and immediate attention and I would be pleased to have you attend the meeting to be held in the East Room of the White House."

The meeting was one step in the Kennedy administration's commitment to creating equal opportunity and job training for black Americans. In the ensuing months, never complaining about the pain in his legs or his weariness, LaFarge focused on the wave of civil rights legislation and preparations for Martin Luther King Jr.'s March on Washington. He was too frail to walk very far on the August day of the march, but he insisted on being present, so he was carried to the front of the line on the shoulders of other men. It was a fitting gesture; he knew that eventually King's dream would be accomplished by a new generation, where "children will not be judged by the color of their skin, but the content of their character."

Interviewed by a *New York Times* reporter, LaFarge said civil rights were central to the future and promise of the United States: "It concerns the fundamental rights of all of us—not merely the Negroes but the entire population. We are all involved in this question of right and wrong."

He joked with a niece about being carried that day, making light of the problem. "After all, the mechanism runs down after a while," he wrote. "Wonderful it has worked as long as it has."

THREE MONTHS LATER, on November 9, 1963, LaFarge stood with Martin Luther King one last time and introduced the civil rights leader at the Statler Hilton Hotel in New York City. King was awarded the St. Francis Medal, citing his work for peace through nonviolence. That was a rare appearance for LaFarge, who had begun turning down meetings and speaking engagements.

On November 22, 1963, LaFarge chose to stay home at *America* headquarters rather than serve as tour guide to a visiting priest, something he usually loved to do. At around noon, he heard the news that President Kennedy had been assassinated in Dallas. LaFarge was devastated. The Jesuits at America House, along with everyone in the country, watched the television story as it developed: the death of the young president; the body borne back to Washington; grieving tributes to Kennedy who lay in state in the Capitol rotunda; and the first public statement by the new president, Lyndon Johnson.

On Sunday morning, November 24, 1963, John LaFarge ate breakfast and then returned to watching the television coverage. He retired to his room for a nap at midday, probably before the shocking televised murder of the president's killer, Lee Harvey Oswald. The other Jesuits watched the drama throughout the day.

At around 4 P.M., one of younger Jesuits, C. J. McNaspy, went to look in on LaFarge. When he got no answer from his knocks on the door, McNaspy entered the room. LaFarge was fully dressed and lying motionless on his bed. He had taken off his glasses after having read the newspaper nearby. McNaspy realized what had happened and came running from the room.

"Uncle John is dead! Uncle John is dead!" he shouted to the others.

LaFarge had died quietly sometime during the afternoon.

The editor in chief of *America* at the time, Thurston N. Davis, said the grief among the Jesuits was so great that it seemed as if "the whole earth ached."

"I can't escape the feeling that the Dallas tragedy had something to do with it," Davis said. "One of the Fathers anointed him and called the police to get a doctor. When the police examined his person for 'valuables'—a routine procedure—they found two worn rosaries."

Cardinal Richard Cushing of Boston, who officiated at the funeral of President Kennedy two days earlier, said Mass on November 27, 1963, for John LaFarge of the Society of Jesus, who had chosen a path that would portray him to the world as an ordinary man. Cushing, a progressive force in Catholic-Jewish relations, had known LaFarge for at least forty years and focused on LaFarge's exhortation that Catholics join the civil rights movement.

"Let us cherish the memory of this great crusader for the truth. And we can do it best not only by our prayers but by perpetuating more and more the wonderful spirit of Catholic interracial work."

POPE PIUS XI'S last crusade against the Nazis was revealed after LaFarge's death. Priests reviewing LaFarge's papers found the draft encyclical against anti-Semitism and began speaking about it. The first major revelation was on December 15, 1972, with publication in the *National Catholic Reporter* of an extensive report about LaFarge and the encyclical by associate editor Jim Castelli.

"The encyclical, had it been published, would have broken the much criticized Vatican silence on the persecution of Jews in Europe, before and during the Second World War," Castelli wrote.

Vatican officials rejected the notion that the document could even be called an encyclical, arguing it was not clear the pope would finally have issued it. An official, the Reverend Burkhart Schneider, described the text in 1973 as "speculative, theoretical, and [having a] laborious style that more resembled Gundlach's manner of thinking than LaFarge's." Further, he said, the draft was submitted because Pius XI wanted "to commemorate the tenth anniversary of the Concordat" with Italy. But the pope's death "caused the text prepared, along with many others on different themes, to end up in the silence of the archives."

It is true that the pope would likely have edited and sharpened, even shortened the encyclical. He published thirty-two encyclicals during his pontificate, an average of two a year. Some of them were short, others as long as LaFarge's. The pope had reviewed and edited them all.

The *National Catholic Reporter*'s report quoted extensively from the encyclical text, which was being published for the first time. It cited letters between LaFarge and Gundlach and their secret mission and some other documentation.

The *NCR* article was based on research by a young priest, Thomas Breslin, who discovered the encyclical and correspondence among LaFarge's personal papers. Breslin contacted *NCR* after reading about Tisserant's charge that Pius XI had been killed. In 1995, Georges Passelecq and Bernard Suchecky wrote a book about the encyclical that was based in part on the material Breslin had found. The book, written in French, was translated into English in 1997, as *The Hidden Encyclical of Pius XI*. The book includes an English text of the encyclical, retranslated from the French version.

A number of elements of the story were unavailable then: the files of Pope Pius XI, which were opened by the Secret Vatican Archives in 2006, and the complete files of Edward Stanton at Burns Library, Boston College, which include previously unreported memos and documents from LaFarge's papers. Stanton, a Canadian Jesuit, wrote about LaFarge and the encyclical for his doctoral thesis. He continued to work on the story when he began teaching at Boston College in the 1970s, gathering material and additional research for a book that would go beyond the doctoral thesis. Stanton's file included original copies of LaFarge's draft of the encyclical in English, and papers and notes not seen before. Those include LaFarge's original draft letter to the pope on October 28, 1938, in French; and an undated note to Stanton from the Reverend Walter Abbott, LaFarge's longtime friend who was present on the evening of May 19–20, 1963, when LaFarge told his story to his fellow Jesuits.

The Vatican archives revealed for the first time a copy of Ledóchowski's transmittal cover letter with the encyclical on January 21, 1939, which, along with the pope's hints during his meeting with anti-Fascist students a week later, provides circumstantial evidence that Pius XI had the encyclical in hand.

Stanton died of a heart attack while jogging on March 13, 1983, and the LaFarge material remained unseen among his own personal papers, which are housed at the Burns Library at Boston College. The original draft of the encyclical in this file, which includes handwritten corrections by LaFarge, is similar but not identical to previously published versions of the document.

Sources also include the unpublished diaries of William Phillips, housed at Houghton Library, Harvard University, and from his privately published memoir, *Ventures in Diplomacy*. *The Diary of Caroline Drayton Phillips* was examined at the Schlesinger Library, Radcliffe Institute for Advanced Study, Harvard University.

Pope Pius XI's archives were opened to researchers in 2006. Material about the pope's relationship with other members of the curia and primary documents comes from the masterful scholarship of Professor Emma Fattorini of the University of Rome La Sapienza, who then began examining Pius XI's archives. Her efforts and the work of scholars, including David Kertzer, professor of history, Brown University; Robert Maryks, professor of history, City University of New York; Frank J. Coppa, professor of history, St. John's University; and Hubert Wolf, professor of history at the University of Munster, are based on dedicated years of research. I am indebted to them. The archives of the diocese of St. Augustine, Florida, house the papers of Bishop Joseph Hurley and were consulted as well.

It was evident in the course of assembling this book that some material has not yet been discovered. Hurley kept notebooks that amounted to diaries and random thoughts throughout his life. He made reference in a notation late in his life that he intended to gather up these notebooks with material to write a memoir. The notes are found in his papers at St. Augustine, but the Rome material appears to have been removed. Charles Gallagher, S. J., a former archivist at St. Augustine, and Professor Michael Gannon, a Florida-based historian and former priest who once was Hurley's assistant, said that Vatican authorities had been in contact with the St. Augustine diocese. Unspecified files of Hurley's papers were removed and apparently taken into Vatican custody some time after Hurley died. Gannon said that he had found the notebooks in Hurley's desk after the bishop died, but it was not clear where the Rome notes Hurley listed had ended up.

In the case of Cardinal Tisserant, there was no known follow-up to the 1972 *New York Times* story that reported a legal case involving his files. No trace of his papers has been found. The Vatican Secret Archives reported in 2010 that it is indexing files covering the papacy of Pope Pius XII, millions of documents that may provide more information. That material is expected to be available by 2015.

POPE PIUS XI'S attempt to use his words as a weapon remained a source of controversy seventy-five years after the fact. He has been overshadowed in history by his onetime secretary of state, Eugenio Pacelli, Pope Pius XII. Pacelli has been the object of both adulation and condemnation for his role during World War II. That role has not been the subject of this book but is amply debated in dozens of books, treatises, articles, and plays. One side of the argument said that Pope Pacelli could have done more. That argument was summed up by Albert Camus in 1948: "For a long time I waited during those terrible years, for a voice to be lifted up in Rome," he told a meeting of Dominicans. "It appears that this voice was raised, but I swear to you that millions of men, myself included, never heard it."

Pius XII once hinted at his own perspective. Once the war began, a reporter for *Osservatore Romano*, Edoardo Senatro, asked him if he would consider criticizing Nazi atrocities. Pope Pacelli replied: "You must not forget, dear friend, that there are millions of Catholics in the German army. Would you like to place them in the middle of a conflict of conscience?"

Pacelli's pursuit of political impartiality did not stop him from sheltering Jews and other refugees at Castel Gandolfo and endorsing other individual acts to save possibly tens of thousands of Jews. I walked through the gardens of Castel Gandolfo one fall day in

2011 and stepped into the brick-arched rooms where Jews were safe from the Nazis, thanks to Pius XII.

Criticism has focused, however, on what the Vatican might have done to stop the systematic killing of Jews by the Nazi regime. The Vatican had reliable information at least by February 1942 about mass executions taking place in Nazi concentration camps. The archbishop of Krakow, Poland, Adam Stefan Sapieha, sent a message through couriers to the Vatican that "We live in terror, continually in danger of losing everything if we attempt to escape, thrown into camps from which few emerge alive."

"To make the extent of the disaster clear," he added, "there is no difference between Jews and Poles."

After Pius XII died at the age of eighty-two on October 9, 1958, some criticism emerged. Domenico Tardini, the monsignor who at the direction of Pacelli helped destroy copies of Pius XI's final speech to bishops on February 11, 1939, said Pacelli "was, by natural temperament, meek and rather timid. He was not born with the temper of a fighter. In this he differed from his great predecessor, Pius XI, who rejoiced, at least visibly, in the contest. Pius XII visibly suffered."

Eight popes were elected in the twentieth century. The first of those to be canonized as a saint was Pope Pius X, who served from 1903 to 1914. Five others have been considered for sainthood, including John XXIII, Paul VI, and John Paul I. John Paul II, who died in 2005, was beatified by Benedict XVI in 2011, a step before canonization. Pius XII is en route to beatification, which requires evidence of miracles having been ascribed to him. The priest in charge of that process, Peter Gumpel, a German Jesuit, has said that such miracles can be attributed to Pius XII. The process has been surrounded by controversy and charges from critics that Pius XII did not do enough to fight Nazism.

Only two popes of the twentieth century are not in the process of consideration for beatification: Pope Pius XI and his benefactor and predecessor: Benedict XV.

Some scholars speculate that Pius XI's speech, if delivered on February 11 and followed by LaFarge's encyclical, would have led to a break with the German and Italian treaties with the Vatican. If he had died even a week later, such analysis says, Eugene Pacelli would not have been the front-runner to succeed him. An appeaser of the Nazis and the Italians would no longer have been able to restore relations.

Other scholars say, as well, that once such a break took place, and once condemnation from the Vatican rose, the world might have been different. It was possible that continued pressure from a strong-speaking pope would have blocked or weakened what eventually became Hitler's Final Solution for the Jews.

After Kristallnacht, Hitler felt "he could go to any length with the Jews, without fear of attack from any church," wrote Conor Cruise O'Brien, the Irish writer and politician, in 1989. "Had Pius XI been able to deliver the encyclical he planned, the green light would have changed to red. The Catholic Church in Germany would have been obliged to speak out against the persecution of the Jews. Many Protestants, inside and outside Germany, would have been likely to follow its example."

One strong piece of evidence emerged decades later within the Church to show that Catholic leaders had an influence on the behavior of the Nazis. In 1996, then cardinal Joseph Ratzinger, who became Pope Benedict XVI, recalled that his village in Germany "experienced a sense of liberation" when Cardinal Clement von Galen of Munich "'broke the silence and publicly defended the mentally ill' who were likewise earmarked for extermination by Hitler's Reich."

Ratzinger, forced under law into the Nazi Hitler Youth organization at fourteen years old in 1941 and into a military antiaircraft unit when he was sixteen, saw a fourteen-year-old cousin with Down syndrome dragged away by the Nazi eugenics program and later killed.

"Only a boldly public outcry could have halted the atrocities," Max Pribilla, a German Jesuit journalist, wrote in 1946. The implication was that a similar voice from the Vatican could have made a difference.

After its report on the encyclical in 1972, the editors of the *National Catholic Reporter* said this: "Considering that Hitler had only begun to move into full-scale persecution of the Jews, and had not yet begun planned extermination; considering that Italy had only begun to copy Germany's racial laws; considering the persecution of Jews throughout history; considering the difficulty, especially in Europe, of launching a similar wide-scale attack on Catholics; and considering the moral weight of the papacy, especially at that point in history—considering all this, we must conclude that the publication of the encyclical draft at the time it was written may have saved hundreds of thousands, perhaps millions of lives."

That can never be known. It was only clear that Pope Pius XI took a stance in favor of absolute morality and defended to his last breath his principles of decency and humanity, nothing more, nothing less.

ACKNOWLEDGMENTS

SPECIAL THANKS TO Charles Gallagher, S.J., assistant professor of history at Boston College, for his help, thoughtful analysis, and friendship in considering the issues surrounding the Vatican in Europe in the 1930s and 1940s, and for reviewing the manuscript. Thanks also to Robert Burruss for his maps and for reading early versions of the manuscript; Steve Christensen provided, as always, well-focused advice as did Henry Heilbrunn, Lynne Heilbrunn, and Madeleine Lundberg.

The Reverend Donald Conroy provided constant encouragement, insight, and historical and ecclesiastical context, and gave very helpful suggestions and impressions on an early version of the manuscript. My appreciation and gratitude to Ian Portnoy, who advised, encouraged, and followed me on this project all along.

I also thank Rector T. Frank Kennedy, S.J., at the Jesuit Community at Boston College, and the members of the community, who welcomed me and provided stimulating conversation, not to mention room and exquisite victuals during two visits.

Thanks to Miguel Pagliere, friend and photographer extraordinaire, and to Neal Levy for their encouragement. In Italy, I benefited from the insights of Professor Piero Melograni and am grateful for the help of my colleague in Rome, Sarah Delaney, for making things work so smoothly. We shared a wonderful welcome in the lovely town of Segni in Lazio by members of the archives at the Archivio Diocesano Innocenzo III; and thanks to the archive director, Alfredo Serangeli, for his time and expertise. During a long lunch in Segni, the archivists reminded me that memories endure of World War II and its consequences.

One highlight was a day trip to Castel Gandolfo where Brother Guy Consolmagno, S.J., an American research astronomer and planetary scientist, took us on an extensive tour of the papal grounds. It included a rare visit to the marvelous Vatican Observatory, its Zeiss telescope and breathtaking museum and library—complete with a four-hundred-year-old copy of Copernicus's *Astronomia Instaurata* (published about seventy years after his death).

The current pope was not there during our visit in October 2011, yet one could imagine the presence of Pius XI, pacing the balconies and feeling the wind whipping across Lake Albano. I am grateful to Brother Guy for his kindness; and also to my niece, Natalie Hinkel, who made the connections for that visit.

Sister Catherine Bitzer, archivist at the Catholic Diocese of St. Augustine, Florida, was of great help and my appreciation to her consideration; and to the members of her order, The Sisters of St. Joseph of St. Augustine, who hosted me for a week. My uncle and aunt Jerry and Joan Gropper and cousins Amy Gropper and David Futch provided the logistics. Thanks to David Futch for also helping review the archives of Bishop Joseph Hurley.

I enjoyed greatly my chats with The Honorable Guido Calabresi, Senior Judge, United States Court of Appeals for the Second Circuit, following the revelation that his family had a direct connection to some of the events that took place in the book. Thanks as well to the Rev. Michael P. Morris, M.A., M.Div., archivist of the Archives of the Archdiocese of New York, who graciously provided advice and access to relevant files in the archdiocese's archives.

Among others, thanks to a number of historians, Richard Breitman, Suzanne Brown-Fleming, Michael Gannon, David I. Kertzer, my colleague David Kahn, David Alvarez and Robert Maryks, and Michael R. Marrus; Thomas J. Reese, S.J; Thomas Brennan; and to Tomas Gergely, Martin Hosking, and Berle Cherney, for his photo expertise; Neal S. Levy; Matthew Budow helped connect me with an important archive at the University of Michigan through Adam Zarazinski, who tracked down a letter from Cardinal Tisserant there.

No one could have a better editor than Henry Ferris, whose logical choices and sensitivity are unparalleled and central to the book; my agent, Flip Brophy, is the dynamo that keeps things together. Many thanks to both.

None of this works without family support—my wife, Musha Salinas Eisner, partner, editor, and best critic; my daughters, Isabel and Marina, constant boosters; Maria Teresa Leturia, my aunt, and Amparo Maria Salinas are not only supporters, but are also assiduous copyeditors and critics. I always wish that Bernie, Lorraine Eisner, and Agricol Salinas Artagoitia could have stayed longer with us. *Sic transit gloria mundi.*

EXCERPTS FROM LAFARGE'S ENCYCLICAL

The following excerpts from John LaFarge's draft encyclical are from the files of Edward Stanton, S.J., Burns Library, Boston College.

Humanis Generis Unitas
(The Ineditum)
Pope Pius XI

The unity of the human race is forgotten, as it were, owing to the extreme disorder found at the present time in the social life of man. This disorder is seen whether we consider the smaller or the lesser groups of people, but especially when we look at the greater groups. This disorder is found not only in what people do, but still more in what they think. All varieties of catchwords are produced which are supposed to cure the state of things but their mere number furnishes telling proof of the confusion.

In one place a magical remedy is prescribed under the resounding formular [*sic*]: Unity of Nation; elsewhere people are roused to enthusiasm by a leader's intoxicating appeal to the Unity of the Race, while in the eastern European sky dawns a promise reddened with terror and blood of a new humanity to be realized in the Unity of the Proletariat.

In the name of the Unity of the State the obligations imposed by the political nature of community are added to the often incompatible demands of those diverse collectivities, Nation, Race, and Class.

RACE AND RACISM

111 When we come to the question of race we find most completely exemplified the harm that is done by the loose, sentimental, almost mystical manner of speaking which has been applied to the ideas of nation, people, and State. There is so little unanimity, whether in scientific or in practical usage, as to what is meant by the term race or racial bond that we find it is actually used now, and was formerly more used, merely to designate a nation or people. Apart from that, racial bond is used, in accordance with present-day scientific parlance, to denote the common participation of a group of human beings in certain definite, permanent physical qualities, and in association with the bodily constitution which is marked by these physical qualities are certain constantly observed psychological characteristics. If this and no more than this is meant and if, moreover, the constancy of all the individual racial characteristics is not extended over too long a period of time, the usage of the term "race" remains within the limits of verifable [*sic*, meaning verifiable] observation.

Denial of human unity

112 But so-called racism wishes to imply much more than this. It contradicts the negative conclusions which we already established in this Letter based upon the teachings of the Faith, the testimony of philosophy and of other sciences and experience as to every genuinely human form of separation in the social life of man. Theoretically and practically it contradicts the principle that no type of separation can

be genuinely human, unless it shares in that which forms the common bond of humanity. The theory and practice of racism which makes a distinction between the higher and lower races, ignores the bond of unity whose existence is demonstrated by these three sources of knowledge or at least it robs it of any practical significance. It is incredible that in view of these facts there are still people who maintain that the doctrine and practice of racism have nothing to do with Catholic teaching as to faith and morals and nothing to do with philosophy, but is a purely political affair.

Denial of human personality

113 The surprise at such people increases when the three criteria that were proposed in connection with these negative conclusions are applied to the doctrine of Racism. The first criterion showed that the inner unity and free-will of the human person was indispensable for the creation of any truly human society. But if the racial community is to be the source of all other forms of society, this inner unity and free-will of the human person must be guaranteed. But no justice is done by racism to the significance of the human person in the formation of society. According to racism the common blood stream drives individuals with compulsive force into a community of physical and psychological qualities. Otherwise there is no explanation of the absolutely hopeless position which racism assumes as to the so-called inferior races; its complete assurance as to the so-called superior races; the mechanics of its legislative procedure, which judges all individuals of a given race according to the same ethnic formula.

Religion is not subject to race

120 But Racism is not content with denying the validity of the universal moral order as a benefit that unifies the whole human race; it likewise denies the general and equal application of essential values in the field of economic welfare, or art, of science and, above all, of reli-

gion. It maintains, for instance, that each race should have its own science, which should have nothing in common with the science of another race, particularly of an inferior race. Although the unity of the sum of human culture is a matter of concern for Catholic faith and morals, let us touch here only upon the relation between race and religion. In this connection We have recently drawn attention to a false proposition of racism, which declares: "Religion is subject to the law of race and must be adapted to that law." Scholars, however, of reputable standing who in their researches have made comparison of the various peoples and of the various phases of development of individual peoples, declare that there is no immediate connection between race and religion and that the result of their studies points rather to the religious unity of humanity.

Racism destroys the structure of society

123 Respect for reality, as it is consistently manifested by the divine Revelation, by the various sciences and by experience, does not permit the Catholic to remain silent in the presence of racism; for respect for that which is must always be an essential trait of the Catholic. Therefore it must be said that Racism likewise fails to stand the test of the third of the negative criteria. According to this criterion a group which claims for itself extensive totality, that is to say, which judges the content of all other purposes and values from the standpoint of its own purpose and fundamental scale of values, destroys the basic structure of humanity as a true unity in true diversity and thereby betrays its own inner falsity and worthlessness. But this is precisely what is done by Racism, both theoretical and practical. It places the fact of racial grouping in such a central position, assigns to it such exclusive significance and efficacy, that in comparison therewith all other social bonds and groupings have no distinct, relatively independent individuality or juridical foundation for the same. Through the extension of racial values the entire life of society becomes a single mechanically unified totality; it is

robbed precisely of that form which is given it by the spirit; true unity is true diversity.

124 The central race value oversimplifies, confuses, obliterates everything besides itself. Through its extensive Totalitarianism it effects a type of society which is entirely similar to that Internationalism which Racism affects to reprove and which is combated by Us. Its concept of the world is too simple, primitively simple. Youth that is brought up in this concept of the world will be fanatical as long as it accepts it, and nihilistic once it rejects it; and either of these developments is possible if mind and heart have lost the ability to appreciate the manifold riches of the True and the Good, riches which in all their breadth and unity can only be communicated by a truly spiritual life.

Evil Effects on Youth and Education

125 Wretched youth, wretched parents, wretched teachers to whom the fundamental law of racist education permits naught but the prospect of fanaticism or nihilism. Let Us lay before the whole world this shameful educational principle, which We recently stigmatized as false: "The aim of education is to develop the qualities of the race and to inflame the mind to a glowing love of one's own race as the supreme good." For youth menaced through such racist doctrine with spiritual destitution and decay We cannot pray fervently enough to Him who is the divine Teacher, who in His own Person gave a perfect example, uniting the supernatural and the natural in unparalleled breadth and universality, saying "I will that they shall have life and have it more abundantly."

The diversity of races

126 Would that the world were free of this mistaken and harmful Racism with its assumption of a rigid separation of superior and inferior races and aboriginal, unchangeable differences of blood. Certainly, there exist today some more or less perfect or more or

less perfectly developed races, if we measure them by the outward manifestations of cultural life. But these differences come from and are determined by the environment, in the sense that only through the influences of the environment—apart from what is caused by the exercise of man's free will—could original racial tendencies develop in one or the other manner and still continue to develop. Even if we grant that the various original, as well as later racial tendencies, impose a certain definite direction and even limitation upon that development and upon the influence of the environment, they afford as yet no basis for an essential difference between the individual races in the capacity for religious, moral and cultural life. This is shown by the teachings of Revelation as well as by those of philosophy and of the other sciences.

Influence of environment

127 For these teachings point to the original and essential unity of the human race; in accordance with which the various original racial tendencies are not to be ascribed to original differences of blood, but only to the influence of the environment, including also the spiritual environment. To such an influence certain great isolated groups have been exposed over long periods of time. In that respect the positive development of various racial tendencies, through the diversity of particular races, occurs in exactly the same way as the development of other elements shaping human communities. These tendencies put on the whole the clear stamp of a vital individuality, and enrich the life of humanity as a whole. The only influence in this fertile and positive development of different races in the world today—again, apart from the influence of human freedom—is in the favorable or unfavorable disposition of the past or present environment.

The Jews and anti-Semitism (religious separation)

131 Those who have placed race illegitimately on a pedestal have

rendered mankind a disservice. For they have done nothing to advance the unity to which humanity tends and aspires. One naturally wonders if this end is faithfully pursued by many of the principal advocates of a so-called racial purity or if their aim isn't rather to forge a clever slogan to move the masses to very different ends. This suspicion grows when one envisages how many subdivisions of a single race are judged and treated differently by the same men at the same time. It is further increased when it becomes clear that the struggle for racial purity ends by being uniquely the struggle against the Jews. Save for the systematic cruelty, this struggle, in true motives and methods, is no different from persecutions everywhere carried out against Jews from antiquity. These persecutions have been censured by the Holy See on more than one occasion, but especially when they have worn the mantle of Christianity.

The actual persecution of the Jews

132 As a result of such a persecution, millions of persons are deprived of the most elementary rights and privileges of citizens in the very land of their birth. Denied legal protection against violence and robbery, exposed to every form of insult and public degradation, innocent persons are treated as criminals though they have scrupulously obeyed the law of their native land. Even those who in time of war fought bravely for their country and the children of those who laid down their lives on their country's behalf are treated as traitors and branded as outlaws by the very fact of their parentage. The values of patriotism, so loudly invoked for the benefit of one class of citizens, are ridiculed when invoked for others who come under the racial ban.

　　In the case of the Jews, this flagrant denial of human rights sends many thousands of helpless persons out over the face of the earth without any resources. Wandering from frontier to frontier, they are a burden to humanity and to themselves.

NOTES

SOURCE ABBREVIATIONS

ACDSA Archives of the Catholic Diocese of St. Augustine
BLBC Burns Library, Boston College
GUL Georgetown University Archives
HLHU Houghton Library, Harvard University
NARA National Archives and Records Administration, Washington
NYT *The New York Times*
SLRH Schlesinger Library, Radcliffe Institute for Advanced Study,
Harvard University

Prologue

1 **"If by chance . . ."** Robert A. Hecht, *An Unordinary Man. A Life of Father John LaFarge, SJ* (Lanham, MD: Scarecrow Press, 1996), 242.

2 **"that great flame . . ."** John LaFarge, *The Manner Is Ordinary* (New York: Harcourt Brace, 1954), 194.

2 **"Once the light of science . . ."** John LaFarge, *Interracial Justice* (New York: America Press, 1937), 11.

2 **Sometimes he appeared** Hecht, *Unordinary Man*, 251.

3 **One night, LaFarge began** Walter Abbott, S.J., to Edward Stanton, S.J., undated, Stanton Papers, BLBC.

Chapter One: Nostalgia Confronts Reality

8 **"Although there are differences . . ."** "Religious Leaders Unite for Austria," *NYT*, March 23, 1938.

10 **He turned once more** LaFarge, *Manner Is Ordinary*, 76.

11 **To his horror** Ibid., 254.

12 **A quick cab ride** John LaFarge, "Europe Revisited," *The Month*, London, March 1939, 215.

13 **"Catholics in the Vienna diocese . . ."** "Cardinal Makes Appeal," *NYT*, March 13, 1938.

13 **The Vatican secretary of state** Emma Fattorini, *Hitler, Mussolini and the Vatican* (Malden, MA: Polity Press, 2011), 140.

13 **Hitler's trip on May 2** "Rome Ready for Hitler, An Elaborate Welcome," *The* (London) *Times*, May 2, 1938, 1.

14 **Ambassador William Phillips, accompanied** William Phillips diaries (MS AM2232), HLHU, 2539.

14 **"I only hope the poor wretches . . ."** William Phillips letter to FDR, May 8, 1938, William Phillips diaries (MS AM2232), HLHU, 2539.

14 **The *Times* of London described the event** "Dictators Meet," *The* (London) *Times*, May 4, 1938, 1.

15 **LaFarge's newspaper also reported** "Rome Ready for Hitler, An Elaborate Welcome," *The* (London) *Times*, May 2, 1938, 1.

15 **"What a curious sensation . . ."** LaFarge to Margaret, May 3, 1938, LaFarge Papers, GUL, 38-3.

16 **"I suppose he exploded!"** Ibid.

16 **"Just as I had anticipated"** Ibid.

16 **He was haunted** LaFarge, "Europe Revisited," 215.

17 **"Britain has written off . . ."** Robert F. Post, "British Bid Czechs to Give Nazis More," *NYT,* May 3, 1938, 13.

17 **"If Great Britain . . ."** LaFarge, *Manner Is Ordinary,* 255.

18 **"If I send . . ."** LaFarge to Talbot, May 17, 1938, GUL, 21-2.

Chapter Two: A "Crooked Cross"

19 **"Sad things appear . . ."** Carlo Confalonieri, *Pius XI, A Close-Up* (Altadena, CA: The Benzinger Sisters Publishers, 1975), 303.

20 **The Great War, as World War I was known** Arnaldo Cortesi, "Pope Pius Avoids Meeting Hitler," *NYT,* April 30, 1938, 31.

20 **The newspaper reported facetiously** Confalonieri, *Pius XI,* 303.

22 **A *New York Times* reporter said** "Pope Canonizes Three Saints," *NYT,* April 18, 1938, 1.

23 **"Despite his eighty years . . ."** Ibid.

23 **Cardinal Carlo Salotti told him** The passage about the pope's medical treatment comes from Thomas B. Morgan, *A Reporter at the Papal Court* (New York: Longman, 1937), 287–292.

24 **Milani, a respected physician** E-mail correspondence with Alfredo Serangeli, director Archivio Storico "Innocenzo III," Segni, Italy, February 5, 2012.

24 **The pope's American** Morgan, *Reporter at the Papal Court,* 288–289.

24 **"we cannot look upon . . ."** Confalonieri, *Pius XI,* xv.

25 **The pope had clashed** Frank J. Coppa, "The Papal Response to Nazi and Fascist Anti-Semitism: From Pius XI to Pius XII," in *Jews in Italy under Fascist and Nazi Rule, 1922–1945,* ed. Joshua

D. Zimmerman (London: Cambridge University Press, 2005), 265–286.

25 **Vatican commentaries . . . censured Nazi regulations** Ibid.

26 **The encyclical,** *With Deep Anxiety* Nazism, http://www.vatican.va.

26 **He vowed retaliation** Otto Pies, *The Victory of Father Karl* (London: Victor Gollancz, 1957), 39–40, cited in Joseph M. Malham, *By Fire into Light: Four Catholic Martyrs of the Nazi Camps* (Brussels: Peeters Publishers, 2002), 160.

26 **"Our brothers were . . ."** Arnaldo Cortesi, "Pope Foresees Break with Reich and Plans Appeal to the World," *NYT*, June 21, 1937, 1.

27 **The pope planned to broaden** Fattorini, *Hitler, Mussolini and the Vatican*, 51.

27 **Mountain climbing involved** The pope's early years, mountain climbing, and descriptions are based on and quoted from Morgan, *Reporter at the Papal Court*, 57, 81–83, 111–126. For more on the Alps, see Nicholas Shoumatoff and Nina Shoumatoff, *The Alps: Europe's Mountain Heart* (Ann Arbor: University of Michigan Press, 2001).

32 **"There are two crosses . . ."** Charles R. Gallagher, *Vatican Secret Diplomacy: Joseph P. Hurley and Pope Pius XII* (New Haven: Yale University Press, 2008), 75.

33 **The world would know** Confalonieri, *Pius XI*, 303.

34 **"You must be Father LaFarge . . ."** Draft copy of article prepared for *America*, July 1938, GUL 38-3.

34 **His opinion was sought after in Paris**, GUL, 21-2.

34 **"It is hard to explain . . ."** Anne O'Hare McCormick, "A Human Enigma Casts a Long Shadow," *NYT*, May 8, 1938.

Chapter Three: The Imposition of the Reich

36 **"Bleiben Sie Hier, bitte,"** LaFarge Papers, GUL, 38-3, and LaFarge, *Manner Is Ordinary*, description of trip from Paris until Rome, 253–284.

37 **"One glance out the window . . ."** LaFarge undated notes, LaFarge Papers, GUL, 38-3.

42 **Before dawn that Saturday morning,** Edward L. James, "Europe Boiling Again, Czech Election Today," *NYT,* May 22, 1938, 59.

43 **"We are living through . . ."** Ibid.

43 **When Sir Neville Henderson** Robert P. Post, "Rebuff to Britain by Reich," *NYT,* May 21, 1938, 34.

43 **All this was going on** Description of Czech train ride, LaFarge, *Manner Is Ordinary,* 264.

43 **"Half paralyzed with fear . . ."** Ibid.

44 **LaFarge "slept amid maps . . ."** Ibid.

44 **But the Nazi newspaper** . . . The Associated Press, "Press Issues an Appeal," *NYT,* May 22, 1938, 34

45 **" 'The Führer . . . knows . . .' "** David Irving, *Goebbels— Mastermind of the Third Reich* (London: Parforce Ltd, 1996), 457.

45 **"In all this excitement . . ."** LaFarge, *Manner Is Ordinary,* 265, and LaFarge letter to Talbot, May 15, 1938, GUL, 21-2.

46 **"IMPOSSIBLE EXAGGERATE . . ."** LaFarge cable, May 27, 1938, LaFarge Papers, GUL, 38-3.

46 **"It has been a common . . ."** "Nazi Terror Drive Goes on in Vienna," *NYT,* May 23, 1938, 1.

47 **Attending the Eucharistic Congress** Frederick T. Birchall, "Catholics Worship in Danube Pageant," *NYT,* May 28, 1938, 8.

48 **Jesus, he said** . . . Moshe Herczl, *Christianity and the Holocaust of Hungarian Jewry* (New York: New York University Press, 1993).

48 **LaFarge saw Pacelli** LaFarge, *Manner Is Ordinary,* 265–266.

48 **The medieval citadel** The hill is named for St. Gellert who set out to convert Hungarians to Catholicism. Hungarians did not prove to be receptive; in the year 1046, pagans hurled him, his carriage and his horses into the Danube from the hill that now carries his name.

48 **The candlelight shimmered** LaFarge, *Manner Is Ordinary,* 266, and Birchall, "Catholics Worship," May 28, 1938.

49 **"A city and a nation . . ."** LaFarge, *Manner Is Ordinary*, 266.

49 **He prayed for peace** "The Pope's Broadcast to Budapest," *The* (London) *Times*, May 30, 1938.

49 **As he spoke those words** Reuters in *The* (London) *Times*, May 30, 1938.

Chapter Four: The Pope's Battle Plan

50 **"The story isn't told . . ."** Anne O'Hare McCormick, "A Human Enigma."

51 **"to all races and conditions . . ."** LaFarge, *Interracial Justice*, 194.

52 **"Magnificent slogans . . ."** LaFarge, *Manner Is Ordinary*, 270–272.

53 **"You know, we were having . . ."** Ibid., 270.

53 **"Nothing I had seen . . ."** Ibid., 271.

53 **"Mosquitoes have been abolished . . ."** Ibid.

53 **Mussolini's construction projects** Borden Painter, *Mussolini's Rome: Rebuilding the Eternal City* (New York: Palgrave Macmillan, 2007), 94.

54 **On Wednesday, June 22** "Memo on Conversation with Holy Father, June 25, 1938," LaFarge Papers, GUL, 38-3.

54 **McCormick had asked** Ibid.

55 **McCormick and LaFarge entered** "Visit to Castel Gandolfo, June 22, 1938," LaFarge Papers, GUL, 38-3.

55 **Then two days later** "Memo on Conversation with Holy Father, June 25, 1938," LaFarge Papers, GUL, 38-3.

56 **LaFarge was overwhelmed** John LaFarge, "The New Holy Father Will Face Grave Problems," *America*, February 25, 1939, 490.

56 **"I was mystified . . ."** LaFarge, *Manner Is Ordinary*, 272.

56 **"a sense of wonder . . ."** Ibid.

58 **After a while, an attendant** An account of the meeting is in LaFarge, *Manner Is Ordinary*, 272–274; also see Jim Castelli, "Unpublished Encyclical Attacked Racism, Anti-Semitism," *National Catholic Reporter*, December 15, 1972, 8; memos June 22, 1938, and June 25, 1938, GUL, 38-3; and memo of LaFarge to Talbot, July 3, 1938, GUL 38-3; Edward S. Stanton Collection, BLBC.

59 **"a natural vigor . . ."** LaFarge, "The New Holy Father Will Face Grave Problems," *America*, February 25, 1939, Ibid.

59 **LaFarge went further** LaFarge, *Interracial Justice*, 11.

62 **"The Rock of Peter . . ."** Memo of LaFarge to Talbot, July 3, 1938, 38-3.

63 **Pius XI envisioned** Herbert Matthews, "Papal Summer Home Nearly Completed," *NYT*, February 5, 1933, E2.

64 **"Always the twentieth century . . ."** *Popular Mechanics* 56, no. 5 (November 1931): 722–727.

65 **"This is the first . . ."** Arnaldo Cortesi, "Pope Speaks to World in Greatest Broadcast," *NYT*, February 13, 1931, 1.

65 **The pope's first words** "Latin Text of Pope's Speech," *NYT*, February 13, 1931, 14.

65 **"Listen all people . . ."** "Text of Pope's Radio Talks," *Washington Post*, February 13, 1931, 5.

65 **When he was done** The Associated Press, "Pope's Talk Translated," *NYT*, February 13, 1931, 14.

65 **"Listeners in the United States . . ."** "150 Stations Carry Program to Nation," *NYT*, February 13, 1931, 15.

66 **"Few events in the history . . ."** *New York Herald*, February 13, 1931, http://www.vatican.va/news_services/radio/multimedia/storia_ing.html.

67 **During Hitler's visit to Rome** The Associated Press, "Führer and Duce Political Talks Ended," *NYT*, May 7, 1938.

Chapter Five: The Flying Cardinal

68 **President Roosevelt was keenly interested** For a discussion
of Phillips as undersecretary of state and of other U.S. diplomats
dealing with Germany during the period, see Erik Larson's *In the
Garden of the Beasts* (New York: Crown Publishers, 2011).

69 **Like so many others** For a look at State Department treatment
of Jews in the period, see Peter Eisner's "Bingham's List: Saving
the Jews from Nazi France," *Smithsonian Magazine*, March 2009,
http://www.smithsonianmag.com/history-archaeology/Binghams-
List.html.

70 **News media had been calling** John Cornwell, *Hitler's Pope: The
Secret History of Pius XII* (New York: Penguin, 2008), 177.

71 **The White House reported** "Pacelli Lunches with Roosevelt,"
NYT, November 6, 1936.

71 **The president recalled the meeting** The FDR anecdote is from
Charles R. Gallagher, *Vatican Secret Diplomacy: Joseph P. Hurley and
Pope Pius XII* (New Haven: Yale University Press, 2008), 87.

72 **Two days later** "Cardinal Pacelli Departs for Rome," *NYT*,
November 8, 1936, 1.

72 **Suddenly, Pope Pius XI** The Associated Press, "The President's
Speech," *NYT*, October 5, 1937.

72 **Even if "the Pope . . ."** Owen Chadwick, *Britain and the Vatican
During the Second World War* (Cambridge: Cambridge University
Press, 1986), 17–19.

72 **Eugenio was born in 1876** Cornwell, *Hitler's Pope*, 19.

73 **"I am of average height . . ."** Ibid.

73 **He began his religious studies** Ibid., and Hubert Wolf, *Pope and
Devil. The Vatican Archives and the Third Reich* (Cambridge, MA:
Belknap Press of Harvard University, 2010), 33–37.

74 **"was a devotee of [Richard] Wagner's . . ."** Unpublished notes
of Bishop Joseph P. Hurley Papers, ACDSA.

76 **Pius, who never conducted business on the telephone** Chadwick, *Britain and the Vatican*, 50.

77 **"National Socialism is more menacing . . ."** Dorothy Thompson, "On the Record," *Washington Post*, February 13, 1939, 9.

77 **"Perhaps your Holiness . . ."** Fattorini, *Hitler, Mussolini, and the Vatican*, 65.

78 *Divinis Redemptoris* **did criticize** See http://www.vatican.va/ holy_father/pius_xi/encyclicals/documents/hf_pxi_enc_19031937_ divini-redemptoris_en.html.

78 **Your Holiness, he told the pope** Fattorini, *Hitler, Mussolini and the Vatican*, 66.

78 **"For not only . . ."** Ibid., 69.

78 **"Verify!". . . .** Ibid.

79 **The pope told a French bishop** Ibid., 78.

79 **"Jesuits obeyed . . ."** Undated notes, Hurley Papers, ACDSA.

80 **"People look to us . . ."** LaFarge letter to Talbot, June 8, 1938, GUL, 38-3.

80 **"It was fortunately . . ."** LaFarge memo to Talbot, July 3, 1938, GUL, 38-3.

81 **"every government in Europe . . ."** Ibid.

82 **"If people get nosey . . ."** Unpublished manuscript, 53, Edward Stanton, Stanton Papers, BLBC.

83 **"Remember, you are writing . . ."** Hecht, *Unordinary Man*, quoting Walter Abbott, 120.

83 **"I had a curious sensation . . ."** LaFarge, *Manner Is Ordinary*, 273.

Chapter Six: A Democratic Response

84 **"We had a splendid view . . ."** Account of the Paris visit is in LaFarge, *Manner Is Ordinary*, 277–278.

85 **"Two hours before their arrival . . ."** United Press, "Paris Acclaims Royal Visits," *Miami News*, July 19, 1938, 1.

85 **"I found my French . . ."** LaFarge, *Manner Is Ordinary*, 277–278.

85 **"A forced migration . . ."** "U.S. Spurs Nations to Prompt Action at Refugee Parley," *NYT*, July 7, 1938, 1.

86 **"such deep sympathy . . ."** Quoted in Walter F. Mondale, "Evian and Geneva," *NYT*, July 28, 1979, 17.

86 **"It is well not to be . . ."** LaFarge letter to Margaret, May 3, 1938, LaFarge Papers, GUL, 38-3.

87 **"suddenly finding a hundred reminders . . ."** LaFarge, *Manner Is Ordinary*, 280.

87 **"I was never part . . ."** Ibid., 3.

87 **"The background of my boyhood . . ."** Ibid., 37.

88 **When LaFarge was quite young,** Ibid., 30.

88 **shared "her problems . . ."** Ibid.

88 **"I was glad to know . . ."** Ibid.

88 **A critical appraisal,** The Ascension by LaFarge, *NYT*, September 27, 1888.

89 **Henry Adams, in his autobiographical** Henry Adams, *The Education of Henry Adams: An Autobiography* (Boston: Mariner Books, 2000; originally published 1918), 161.

91 **The preface had even quoted the pope,** LaFarge, *Interracial Justice*, vi, viii, and xi.

91 **LaFarge added that** Ibid., vi.

91 **LaFarge and Gundlach divided** Castelli, "Unpublished Encyclical," 8.

91 **"a certain degree of historical . . ."** JLF to Pope Pius XI, October 28, 1938, Stanton Papers, BLBC.

92 **In 1930, Gundlach had** Georges Passelecq and Bernard Suchecky, *The Hidden Encyclical of Pius XI* (New York: Harcourt Brace, 1997), 47.

93 **Nevertheless, three years before** Ibid., 48–49.

93 **"Every now and then . . ."** LaFarge letter handwritten to Talbot, GUL, 32-3.

93 **"You are the one best equipped . . ."** Talbot to LaFarge, July 13, 1938. Stanton Papers, BLBC

94 **"As I remember it . . ."** Passelecq and Suchecky, *Hidden Encyclical*, 173–174.

95 **"If we go back to the beginnings . . ."** Draft encyclical, Papers of Edward Stanton, BLBC.

95 **"The Mechanistic-Atomistic . . ."** Ibid.

95 **"Men of good will should do everything . . ."** Ibid.

96 **One Jesuit recounted** Passelecq and Suchecky, *Hidden Encyclical*, 174.

96 **Ledóchowski caused a stir** Passelecq and Suchecky, *Hidden Encyclical*, 61, and Ledóchowski to LaFarge, July 17, 1938, LaFarge papers, GUL.

97 **TALBOT SEVERE WARNING** Stanton Papers, BLBC.

98 **The German Foreign Office** David Kahn, *Hitler's Spies* (New York: DaCapo Press, 2000), 185.

98 **The Vatican also had** David Alvarez, *Spies in the Vatican* (Lawrence: University Press of Kansas, 2002), 130–172.

99 **They apparently were** Ibid., 156.

99 **By the end of** Ibid., 166.

99 **Now suddenly,** Passelecq and Suchecky, *Hidden Encyclical*, 60–61.

100 **"The whole time . . ."** Henrich Bacht, quoted in Passelecq and Suchecky, *Hidden Encyclical*, 57.

Chapter Seven: In the Heat of the Summer

101 **The pope denounced** Frank Coppa, "The Papal Response to Nazi and Fascist Anti-Semitism: From Pius Xi to Pius XII," in *Jews in Italy Under Fascist and Nazi Rule 1922–1925*, ed. Joshua D. Zimmerman (London: Cambridge University Press, 2005), 274.

101 **"We should ask ourselves . . ."** Giorgio Angelozzi Gariboli, *Pius XII Hitler E Mussolini: Il Vaticano Fra Le Dittature* (Milano: Mursia, 1988), 81.

102 **"To say that Fascism"** Arnaldo Cortesi, "Mussolini Defies Vatican Warning in Racist Dispute," *NYT*, July 31, 1938.

102 **"Enemies . . . reptiles," he complained** The Associated Press, "Lover's Diary: Mussolini Wanted to Destroy Jews," November 16, 2009, http://www.msnbc.msn.com/id/33973018/ns/world_news-europe/t/lovers-diarymussolini- wanted-destroy-jews/#.TtY9VLIr2nA.

103 **Pius, however, could not be** Fattorini, *Hitler, Mussolini and the Vatican*, 160.

103 **"the pope would not retract . . ."** Phillips unpublished diary, 2697.

103 **Ambassador Phillips sent a report** Phillips, unpublished diary, HLHC, 2675.

103 **Hurley, as the token** Hurley's biography comes from Gallagher, *Vatican Secret Diplomacy*, esp. 71–92.

106 **"If the Reds would . . ."** LaFarge, *Manner Is Ordinary*, 279–280.

106 **LaFarge's notes** Draft copy of article prepared for *America*, July 1938, GUL, 38-3.

106 **The pope had criticized Franco** United Press, " 'Useless massacre of the civil population . . .' Vatican Paper Joins in Bombing Protests," *NYT*, June 10, 1938.

107 **LaFarge grieved** LaFarge, *Manner Is Ordinary*, 281–282.

107 **"I had so hoped to be . . ."** Ibid., 282.

107 **"I said Mass for your brother . . ."** Talbot to LaFarge, August 8, 1938, GUL, 21-2.

108 **"Some days before his death . . ."** Ibid.

108 **Bancel's "last hours were of great peace . . ."** LaFarge, *Manner Is Ordinary*, 282.

108 **"About other things at home . . ."** LaFarge letter to Talbot, GUL, 38-3.

109 **"Contrary to what people believe, . . ."** Galeazzo Ciano, *Diary, 1937–1943* (New York: Enigma Books, 2002), 117.

109 **"During the Ethiopian War, . . ."** "Purge Extension Is Urged in Italy," *NYT*, September 3, 1938, 15.

109 **As expected, Mussolini's decision** "Italy Exiles Jews Entering Since '19," *NYT*, September 2, 1938, 1.

109 **"Anti-Semitism is a hateful movement . . ."** Susan Zuccotti, *Under His Very Windows* (New Haven: Yale Nota Bene, 2002), 45.

110 **"The Germans are mistaken in . . ."** Gallagher, *Vatican Secret Diplomacy*, 63, and cf. 241.

111 **At breaks from the writing,** LaFarge letter to Bacht, October 22, 1948, LaFarge Papers, GUL.

111 **LaFarge had included** Draft encyclical, Stanton Papers, BLBC, 132.

112 **War was a constant theme** LaFarge, "The Munich Agreement Demands Further Adjustments," *America*, November 5, 1938, 100.

112 **"for a 'button to be pushed' . . ."** Ibid.

112 **He felt himself to be "exhausted to the very limit . . ."** Letter to Bacht, GUL.

113 *Humanis Generis Unitas* Draft encyclical, Papers of Edward Stanton, BLBC.

113 **"In one place a magical remedy . . ."** Ibid.

114 **"When we come to the question of race . . ."** Ibid.

115 **"is not content with denying the validity . . ."** Ibid.

116 **He sent a message** LaFarge to Talbot, September 18, 1938. GUL.

118 **There was speculation** "Reich's Envoy Sees Pacelli," *NYT*, September 24, 1938.

118 **Soon after they pulled away** "Pacelli Is Bruised in Motor Accident," *NYT*, September 25, 1938.

Chapter Eight: The Pope's Discontent

120 **"I reminded Ciano that . . ."** Phillips, unpublished diary, 2696.

121 **"I play [*sic*] the same . . ."** Ciano, *Diary*, 120.

121 **"So far as I was concerned, . . ."** Phillips, unpublished diary, 2696.

121 **"A long war might again . . ."** Ibid.

121 **"If we get the idea . . ."** Phillips, *Ventures in Diplomacy*, privately published, 219–220.

122 **"I reminded Hurley that . . ."** Phillips, unpublished diary, 2705.

122 **The United States was gratified** Summary of Dispatch, January 21, 1939, Department of State, Division of European Affairs, NARA, RG 84, Italy, U.S. Consulate and Rome, General Records, 1936–1964.

123 **Hurley ran a considerable risk** Gallagher, *Vatican Secret Diplomacy*, 78–79.

123 **"You can rely on your people . . ."** The Associated Press, "Text of Chancellor Adolf Hitler's Speech on the Czechoslovak Situation Yesterday, Sept 26, 1938," *NYT*, September 27, 1938.

124 **"Father Ledóchowski seated himself . . ."** LaFarge, *Manner Is Ordinary*, 276.

124 **William Shirer, the Berlin correspondent** William L. Shirer, *The Rise and Fall of the Third Reich* (New York: Simon & Schuster, 1960), 397–398.

124 **He found the führer to be a master** Phillips unpublished diary, HLHC, 2717.

125 **Hitler had begun in a gentle** LaFarge, *Manner Is Ordinary*, 276.

125 **trading on the New York Stock Exchange** "Market Seesaws to Hitler's Speech," *NYT*, September 27, 1938.

126 **"That evening Hitler burned his bridges . . ."** Shirer, *Rise and Fall*, 398–399.

126 **Jan Masaryk, the Czech ambassador** The Associated Press, "Masaryk Shocked," *Washington Post*, September 27, 1938, x7.

126 **"The full import . . ."** LaFarge, *Manner Is Ordinary*, 276–277.

127 **"For the first time in all the years . . ."** Shirer, *Rise and Fall*, 398–399.

127 **"And the bell rang . . ."** LaFarge, *Manner Is Ordinary*, 276.

128 **"And sure enough . . ."** Ibid.

128 **"Let the Lord of life and death . . ."** "Pope Calls on All for Peace Prayer," *NYT*, September 30, 1938.

129 **Soon after the formal announcement** "Pope Overjoyed at Agreement," *NYT*, October 1, 1938, 2.

129 **"Don't you understand? . . ."** Fattorini, *Hitler, Mussolini and the Vatican*, 174.

129 **"This is all warmed-over . . ."** Ibid., 170.

129 **Subordinates sought to tone down** Ibid., 175.

130 **Franklin Roosevelt shared** Phillips, *Ventures in Diplomacy*; letter from Roosevelt to Phillips, 219.

130 **"I cannot forget . . ."** Fattorini, *Hitler, Mussolini and the Vatican*, 176, and fc. 63, 245.

130 ***Osservatore Romano* editorialized** U.S. embassy memo to State Department, November 4, 1938, Phillips, NARA, RG 84, Italy, U.S. Consulate and Rome, General Records, 1936–1964.

130 **U.S. ambassador William Phillips, monitoring** Ibid.

131 **SAILING OCTOBER 1** Telegram LaFarge to Talbot, September 29, 1938, LaFarge Papers, GUL, 1-10.

131 **"War-scares, like hurricanes . . ."** John LaFarge, "The Munich Agreement Demands Further Adjustments," *America*, November 5, 1938, 100.

132 **"The impression of a foreigner in Paris . . ."** Ibid.

133 **Chief among his critics** Churchill, http://www.winstonchurchill.org/learn/speeches/speeches-of-winston-churchill/101-the-munichagreement.

133 **"That fellow [Chamberlain] has spoiled my entry . . ."** Shirer, *Rise and Fall*, 427.

134 **In keeping up with his and LaFarge's plan** Gundlach letter to
JLF, October 16, 1938, Stanton Papers, BLBC.

135 **There was no precedent** Joseph F. Keaney, S.J., to Rev. Edward
S. Stanton, S.J., May 13, 1971, Stanton Papers, BLBC.

135 **"The Jews are merely guests . . ."** "Cattolicismo e Nazismo: Idee
chiare e pericolosi equivoci," *Osservatore Romano*, June 10, 1938.
Quoted in Zuccotti, *Under His Very Windows*, 25.

136 **"I was here . . ."** Gundlach letter to JLF, October 16, 1938,
Stanton Papers, BLBC.

136 **"This is the situation . . ."** Ibid.

138 **Killeen followed Gundlach's letter** Killeen to LaFarge, October
28, 1938, BLBC.

138 **Killeen also told LaFarge** Ibid.

139 **"I was not a good sailor"** LaFarge, *Manner Is Ordinary*, 283.

139 **Unknown to LaFarge** "Alien Moneys Fall; Gold Receipts Huge,"
NYT, October 11, 1938.

140 **"Father Talbot and I met him . . ."** Miss Frances S. Childs to
Edward S. Stanton, S.J., December 3, 1973, Stanton Papers, BLBC.

140 **"Alas, just as I was about to . . ."** LaFarge, *Manner Is Ordinary*,
284.

Chapter Nine: Shame and Despair

142 **The cardinal is one of those** Papers of Caroline Drayton
Phillips, November 12–13, 1938, MC560SLRH, 47–48, 21.2

143 **"And tell that, Father, to Mussolini himself! . . ."** Fattorini,
Hitler, Mussolini and the Vatican, 163.

143 **Foreign Minister Ciano reported** Ciano, *Diary*, 143.

144 **"A mob of 1500 Nazi youths . . ."** Phillips diary, HLHC, 2785.

144 **"It is a lie—we repeat . . ."** Cardinal Innitzer, "Abroad Column,"
NYT, October 16, 1938.

145 **"Nowadays mail often has a curious fate . . ."** Gundlach to LaFarge, November 18, 1938, Stanton Papers, BLBC.

145 **"With the heavy responsibility . . ."** Translated from the French, LaFarge letter to the pope, October 28, 1938, Stanton Papers, BLBC.

146 **While LaFarge could not be sure** Gundlach to LaFarge, November 18. LaFarge's original draft of the letter, written in French, is in the Stanton Papers. Another version was found in the archives of *Civilta Catolica*. See Giovanni Sale, *Le Leggi Razzziali In Italia E Il Vaticano* (Milan: Editoriale Jaca, 2009), 269.

147 **In 1936, he had said** "Mundelein Sees Church Menaced," *NYT*, January 16, 1936, 12.

147 **"How is it that . . ."** "Mundelein Scorns Nazi Government," *NYT*, May 19, 1937, 11.

148 **"This is all most interesting . . ."** Phillips unpublished diary, Wednesday, October 26, 1938, 2805, HLHU.

148 **Hurley agreed that the ambassador's involvement** Phillips diary, Saturday, October 15, 1938, 2785

148 **Phillips welcomed** The Associated Press, "Roosevelt Requested Honors," *NYT*, November 5, 1938.

148 **Nazi newspapers reviled** Otto D. Tolischus, "Berlin Sees Election Deal," *NYT*, November 6, 1938.

149 **"It was truly a marvelous sight"** Caroline Drayton Phillips, diary, 49–50, SLRH, 21.2.

150 **Early on the morning** http://www.holocaustresearchproject.org/holoprelude/grynszpan.html.

150 **Joseph Goebbels reported that** Martin Gilbert, *Kristallnacht: Prelude to Destruction* (New York: Harper Perennial, 2007), 29.

150 **The marauding Nazis killed** Kristallnacht: A Nationwide Pogram, November 9–10, 1938, http://www.ushmm.org/wlc/en/article.php?ModuleId=10005201.

151 **The terror was boundless** Jill Huber, "Eyewitnesses Remember 'Night of Broken Glass,'" *New Jersey Jewish News*, http://

njjewishnews.com/njjn.com/111308/moEyewitnessesRemember
.html, November 18, 1998.

151 **"'Move on,'" a policeman warned** Otto D. Tolischus, "Bands
Rove Cities," *NYT*, November 10, 1938, 1.

151 **President Roosevelt condemned** Jean Edward Smith, *FDR* (New
York: Random House, 2007), 426.

151 **While Pius's voice was not heard** The Associated Press, "Milan
Cardinal Sees Racism 'A Danger,'" *NYT*, November 17, 1938.

152 **"A kind of heresy . . ."** Ibid.

152 **"Germany, once counted among civilized nations . . ."**
"Beyond the Pale," *America*, November 26, 1938, 181.

152 **American Catholic leaders** http://archives.lib.cua.edu/education/
kristallnacht/index.cfm.

153 **Despite the condemnation** See Donald Warren, *Radio Priest*
(New York: Free Press, 1996).

153 **Coughlin took to the microphone** Charles Coughlin, radio
broadcast, November 27, 1938, http://ia600304.us.archive.org/11/
items/Father_Coughlin/FatherCoughlin_1938-11-20.mp3.

154 **"He has tremendous influence . . ."** *Catholic Herald*, May 20,
1938, London, LaFarge papers, GUL.

154 **Unsurprisingly, Coughlin had become a darling** "Nazi Papers
Come to Aid of Fr. Coughlin," Associated Press, Berlin, November
26, 1938.

154 **"Racism, like the other destructive ideologies . . ."** "Price of
Racism in United States Held a Peril by Catholic Writer," *NYT*,
November 30, 1938, 378.

155 **The pope woke up at his normal hour** Arnaldo Cortesi, "Pope
Suddenly Striken, But Condition Improves; His Doctors are
Hopeful," *NYT*, November 26, 1938, 1.

156 **"Do not think of me"** Ibid., 4.

156 **Meanwhile, the pope summoned** Telephone interview with
Judge Guido Calabresi, September 29, 2011.

157 **Within days, papal audiences** The Associated Press, "Pope Pius Resumes Normal Activities," *Montreal Gazette*, November 29, 1938, 1.

157 **"Since that date,"** U.S. Embassy Report, December 2, 1938, Edward C. Reed Charge, NARA, RG 84, Italy, U.S. Consulate and Rome, General Records, 1936–1964.

Chapter Ten: A New Year and an End to Appeasement

158 **On December 18, a cold, rainy day** The Associated Press, "Pope Presides at Session of Academy of Science," *NYT*, December 19, 1938, and http://archive.catholicherald.co.uk/article/12th-january-1940/5/jews-expelled-from-rome-university-to-attend-ponti.

159 **Carrel and Lindbergh** http://www.time.com/time/covers/0,16641,19380613,00.html.

159 **He took long rests** "Pontiff Attends Chapel Services," *NYT*, November 29, 1938.

159 **A report in the *New York World Telegram*** Castelli, "Unpublished Encyclical," 13.

160 **Gundlach noted** Gundlach letter to LaFarge, GUL, 22-2.

160 **Il Duce told Ciano** Ciano, *Diary*, 165–166.

160 **The pope continued his speech** Arnaldo Cortesi, "Pius XI Deplores Fascist Hostility; Reveals Incidents," *NYT*, December 25, 1938, 1; U.S. Embassy memo Rome to the State Department, December 30,1939, NARA, RG 84, Italy, U.S. Consulate and Rome, General Records, 1936–1964.

161 **Germany reacted within days** "*Angriff* Assails Vatican," *NYT*, December 28, 1938; "Jews Guide U.S. Policies Toward Nazis, Gayda Says," The Associated Press, December 27, 1938.

161 **"This past year belonged . . ."** John LaFarge, "Of Peace and Conflict Through Both Hemispheres," *America*, December 21, 1938, 292.

162 **"Welcome to historic Town Hall . . ."** Transcript, *America's Town Meeting on the Air*, December 29, 1938, 3, in LaFarge Papers, GUL.

164 **"All about us rage undeclared wars . . ."** http://www.presidency.ucsb.edu/ws/index.php?pid=15684#axzz1eRWtJTw5.

164 **"If pessimism is the dominant mood . . ."** "Rabbi Hails Pope for 1938 Appeals," *NYT*, January 1, 1939.

164 **LaFarge received bad news** Letter from Maher to JLF, January 3, 1939, Stanton Papers, BLBC.

166 **When Caroline and her husband** Caroline Drayton Phillips, diary, January 13, 1939, SLRH, 21.2, 21.3. and William Phillips diary, HLHU.

166 **"Great Britain has to live side by side . . ."** "Mr. Chamberlain for Rome," *The (London) Times*, November 29, 1938, 15.

166 **Even Chamberlain knew** U.S. embassy memo, to State Department, January 13, 1939, NARA, RG 84, Italy, U.S. Consulate and Rome, General Records, 1936–1964.

167 **A *New York Times* reporter was blunt** Frederick T. Birchall, "Rome Parleys End Without Results; Chamberlain Firm," *NYT*, January 13, 1939, 1.

167 **"I followed him a couple of steps . . ."** Caroline Drayton Phillips, diary, SLRH, 21.3.

168 **Pius repeated once more** . . . Chadwick, *Britain and the Vatican*, 25.

168 **the pope "has shown great courage . . ."** Ibid., and Gallagher, *Vatican Secret Diplomacy*, 75–76.

168 **Hurley reported back** Gallagher, *Vatican Secret Diplomacy*, 76, and cf. 244.

169 **Mussolini was baffled** Ciano, *Diary*, 177.

Chapter Eleven: Will There Be Time?

170 **The pope tracked down the encyclical** Castelli, "Unpublished Encyclical"; and Sale, *Le Leggi Razzziali*, 271.

171 **"I take leave . . ."** Translated from the Italian, Sale, *Le Leggi Razziali*, 271.

172 **In fact, one Jesuit researcher** Stanton Papers, manuscript, 56, BLBC.

172 **Knowing none of this** Gundlach letter to LaFarge, January 28, 1939, Stanton Papers, BLBC.

173 **In late January, Italian foreign minister** Ciano, *Diary*, 184.

173 **Vatican sources stirred the concern** "Duce's Sharp Speech," *The (London) Times*, January 23, 1939, 11; and The Associated Press, "Pope Calls Bishops to Discuss Treaty," *NYT*, January 31, 1939.

173 **Ciano demanded answers** Fattorini, *Hitler, Mussolini and the Vatican*, 192; Wolf, *Pope and Devil*, 208.

173 **Ciano wrote in his diary** Ciano, *Diary*, 184; see Fattorini, *Hitler, Mussolini and the Vatican*, 179–180.

174 **The pope told Penco** http://www.ilsecoloxix.it/p/genova/2008/09/21/ALJLtk5Bmussolini_hitler_scontro.shtml;jsessionid=686EED918E004BB680AD6E1D1DACA2A8.

174 **The pope was consumed** Fattorini, *Hitler, Mussolini and the Vatican*, 180–187.

175 **Finally, however, Ciano said** Ciano, *Diary*, 185.

175 **"Most people are stirred up . . ."** "Threat of Racism," LaFarge, January 27, 1939, WMCA Radio transcript, GUL.

176 **He claimed that warmongers** Otto D. Tolischus, "Hitler Demands Stolen Colonies," *NYT*, January 31, 1939, 1.

176 **The Vatican said Hitler** "Hitler Is Disputed by Vatican Organ," *NYT*, Feburary 3, 1939.

176 **Still fine-tuning** Fattorini, *Hitler, Mussolini and the Vatican*, 193–194.

177 **The pope told Rocchi** Confalonieri, *Pius XI*, 314.

177 **"The condition of the circulatory apparatus . . ."** Ibid., 316.

178 **The Vatican press office** The Associated Press, "Pope Marks Anniversary," *NYT*, February 7, 1939, 12.

179 **An official statement on Thursday** Confalonieri, *Pius XI*, 317.

179 **Joseph Hurley told Ambassador Phillips** Phillips unpublished diary, HLHC, 2979.

181 **"After the injection . . ."** Zsolt Aradi, *Pius XI: the Pope and the Man* (Garden City, NY: Hanover House, 1958), 249.

181 **Whatever the injection was** Confalonieri, *Pius XI*, 322.

181 **The *New York Times* report** Camille M. Cianfarra, "Death at 5:31 a.m." *NYT*, February 11, 1939, 1.

182 **The *Times* of London correspondent** "Death of the Pope," *The* (London) *Times*, February 11, 1939.

183 **In a fifth version of the story** "Religion: Death of a Pope," *Time*, February 20, 1939.

183 **Confalonieri made no mention** Confalonieri, *Pius XI*, 322, quoting the pope's last words in Latin: *Spiritus in pace con Voi l'anima mia.*

184 **Thus satisfied he was able to declare** "Death of the Pope," *The* (London) *Times*, February 11, 1939, 1.

Chapter Twelve: Change Overnight

185 **Monsignor Carlo Grano** Castelli, "Unpublished Encyclical."

185 **"I must say from the first meeting . . ."** Tisserant letter to Mr. Bishop, February 27, 1939, Bentley Historical Library, University of Michigan.

186 **He took leave from the priesthood** http://archive.catholicherald .co.uk/article/25th-february-1972/1/cardinal-with-common-touch-dies-aged-87.

186 **Ratti "used to write me . . ."** Tisserant letter to Mr. Bishop.

186 **When Tisserant arrived** Castelli, "Unpublished Encyclical."

187 **He also sent Joseph Hurley** Phillips unpublished diary, HLHC, 1979.

187 **Ciano had already** Ciano, *Diary*, 188–189.

188 **Now the Italian government's** Fattorini, *Hitler, Mussolini and the Vatican*, 197 and Ciano, *Diary*, 189.

189 **The pope's assistants were "to hand over . . ."** Fattorini, *Hitler, Mussolini and the Vatican*, 189–190.

190 **The *New York Times* reported** Camille M. Cianfarra, "Pope Pius Made Peace with Italy, Plans for Mass in Rome Indicate," *NYT*, February 14, 1939, 1.

191 **The pope wrote in his speech** Fattorini, *Hitler, Mussolini and the Vatican*, 190–192, and text of speech, 210–215.

192 **The pope had planned** Fattorini, *Hitler, Mussolini and the Vatican*, 190.

192 **Pius XI was buried** Camille M. Cianfarrra, "Pope Pius Buried in St. Peter's Crypt with Splendid Rite," *NYT*, February 15, 1939, 1.

193 **In Germany, the pope's death was treated** Otto D. Tolischus, "A 'Political Pope' Is Reich Comment," *NYT*, February 11, 1939.

193 **In Washington, Congress convened an unprecedented** Edward T. Folliard, "Congress to Break Precedent to Honor Memory of Pius XI, *Washington Post*, February 12, 1939, 1.

194 **Pius XI was "the first of all Christian voices . . ."** Religious News Service, Rabbi Edward L. Israel, February 17, 1939.

194 **Francis Talbot spoke for *America*** "Pope's Leadership in Campaign for Peace of the World Is Widely Hailed," *NYT*, February 11, 1939.

194 **Sometimes, "he proclaims to anyone . . ."** Gundlach letter to LaFarge, March 16, 1939, Stanton Papers, BLBC.

196 **The French ambassador, François Charles-Roux** Phillips diary, 2990.

197 **As the day of the conclave** Chadwick, *Britain and the Vatican*, 33.

197 **Charles-Roux made an eleventh-hour attempt** Ibid., 43.

198 **He concluded that the evidence had been hidden** Peter
Nichols, "Support for Theory of 1939 Killing of Pope," *The
(London) Times*, June 23, 1972, 1; Fattorini, *Hitler, Mussolini and the
Vatican*, 198 and cf. 34, 247; *Paris Match*, May 13, 1972, 81-82.

198 **When Tisserant's suspicions were made known** Paul
Hofmann, "Cardinal's Notes Cause a Dispute," *NYT*, June 12,
1972, 13.

198 **There were five doctors on the Vatican** Annuario Pontificio,
Archivio Storico "Innocenzo III," Segni, Italy, February 5, 2012.

199 **"You have no idea of the bad . . ."** Nick Pisa, "Hitler He's just a
big softie: The diaries of Mussolini's lover that show what Italian
dictator really thought," *The Daily Mail* online, November 17,
2009.

199 **A relative, perhaps his father** "POPE PIUS IMPROVING;
'Seems Another Man,' Says Dr. Petacci," *NYT* August 12, 1911, 1.

199 **Various stories said Mussolini** . . . See Jasper Ridley, *Mussolini: A
Biography* (New York: St. Martin's, 1998), 289.

200 **Decades later . . . Massimo Petacci's son** http://
ferdinandopetacci.blogspot.com/2006/02/francesco-saverio-
petacci_114065949615039054.html.

201 **The Vatican categorically said** Nichols, "Support for Theory."

201 **It did "concede that Cardinal Tisserant . . ."** Hofmann,
"Cardinal's Notes."

201 **"Especially because of . . ."** http://www.ilsecoloxix.it/p/
genova/2008/09/21/ALJLtk5Bmussolini_hitler_scontro.shtml;jsess
ionid=686EED918E004BB680AD6E1D1DACA2A8.

202 **"He said he would have liked . . ."** Interview with Guido
Calabresi, September 29, 2011.

202 **"Nothing was inspiring the fear . . ."** Tisserant letter to Mr.
Bishop, February 27, 1939, Bentley Historical Library, University
of Michigan, Bimu C410, Michigan University Library Papers,
1837–1957 Box 46, 1936-41, Cardinal Tisserant.

202 **Speculation about their disagreement** . . . Paul Hofmann, "Strains Between Pope and Late Cardinal Reported," *NYT,* July 2, 1972.

203 **Pius's death "was a great loss . . ."** Tisserant letter to Mr. Bishop, February 27, 1939, Bentley Historical Library.

Chapter Thirteen: The New Regime

205 **"You shall know fairly soon . . ."** Gallagher, *Vatican Secret Diplomacy,* 83.

205 **At around 6:00 P.M.** Camille M. Cianfarra, "Vatican Door Shut on 62 Cardinals as Conclave Opens to Elect Pope," *NYT,* March 2, 1939, 1.

207 **A Pacelli supporter said afterward** Chadwick, *Britain and the Vatican,* op. cit. 46.

207 **"I wish to be called Pius XII . . ."** "Pius XII Was Calm During the Voting," *NYT,* March 4, 1939, 3.

207 **"Suddenly he missed his footing"** Ibid.

207 **Ambassador William Phillips** Phillips diaries, HLHC, 3018–3020.

209 **"It was a delicious morning . . ."** Caroline Drayton Phillips, diary, 47-48. SLRH, 21.5.

210 **"After His Holiness had taken his seat,"** Phillips, *Ventures in Diplomacy,* 253.

210 **An unseen choir** Ibid.

210 **"We invite all to the peace . . ."** "Pope's First Message," *New York Herald Tribune,* March 4, 1939.

211 **Ambassador Phillips expressed . . . "the fact that . . ."** Phillips, unpublished diary, HLHC, 3020.

211 **his election was "not only in harmony . . ."** Dorothy Thompson, "On the Record: Pius XII—The Former Diplomat," *Washington Post,* March 6, 1939, 9.

211 **"The cardinals have marked . . ."** News roundup in *Journal de Geneve*, March 4, 1939, 10, http://www.letempsarchives.ch/.

211 **"Hitler was not a true Nazi . . ."** Gallagher, *Vatican Secret Diplomacy*, 88, and cf. 246.

211 **"he knows Cardinal Pacelli very well . . ."** Chadwick, *Britain and the Vatican*, 57.

212 **Pope Pius XII . . . now did nothing to criticize** Ferdinand Kuhn Jr., "Invasion No Shock to British Leaders," *NYT*, March 15, 1939, 1.

212 **"Vatican policy changed overnight . . ."** Chadwick, *Britain and the Vatican*, 57.

212 **Ciano told the French ambassador** Ibid., 47.

213 **"I encouraged him along these lines . . ."** Ciano, *Diary*, 204.

213 **Everyone expected the pope** "A New Approach," editorial, *NYT*, May 10, 1939.

214 **"the new Pope is 'political' . . ."** John LaFarge, "Pius XII As Christ's Vicar Is Not a Political Pope, *America*, March 18, 1939, 556–557.

214 **The church creates "an unswerving devotion . . ."** Ibid.

215 **"If you wish, you may now profit . . ."** Maher letter to LaFarge, Easter Monday 1939, Stanton Papers, BLBC.

215 **"Slim chance of that,"** Gundlach letter to LaFarge, Stanton Papers, BLBC.

215 **"We are hoping . . ."** Ibid.

216 **"I have insistently asked the Holy Father . . ."** Peter Godman, *Hitler and the Vatican* (New York: Free Press, 2004), 163.

217 **Hurley took his first open step** Gallagher, *Vatican Secret Diplomacy*, 99; and *The* (London) *Times*, July 5, 1939, 3.

217 **The *Times* of London reported** *The* (London) *Times*, July 5, 1939.

219 **He did not criticize** Bishop Hurley address, Columbia Broadcasting System, July 6, 1942, ACDSA.

Epilogue

221 **"He had read my book . . ."** LaFarge, *Manner Is Ordinary*, 273.

222 **"A priest's life," he wrote** John LaFarge, *An American Amen: A Statement of Hope* (New York, Farrar, Straus and Cudahy, 1958), ix.

222 **Ledóchowski had died at the age** Father Lavalle letter to Father Nota, July 30, 1973; Passelecq Suchecky, *Hidden Encyclical*, 15.

223 **"I asked him . . ."** Undated note to Stanton, Stanton Papers, BLBC.

223 **LaFarge said yes** Ibid.

223 **"I made a mistake . . ."** Undated note, Walter Abbott, Stanton Papers, BLBC.

223 **"He told us the whole story . . ."** Ibid.

223 **President John F. Kennedy invited LaFarge** Western Union telegram, June 12, 1963, Lafarge Papers, GUL, 1-10.

223 **He was too frail to walk** Laura Sessions Stepp, "King's Words Still Resound as Thousands March Today," *Washington Post*, August 27, 1988, 1.

224 **Interviewed by a *New York Times* reporter . . .** "March on Washington," *NYT*, August 25, 1963.

224 **"After all, the mechanism . . ."** Hecht, *Unordinary Man*, the description of LaFarge's death, 251–253.

225 **"I can't escape the feeling . . ."** Ibid.

225 **"Let us cherish . . ."** Ibid., 254, and cf. 278.

226 **"The encyclical, had it been published . . ."** Castelli, "Unpublished Encyclical," 1.

226 **An official, the Reverend Burkhart Schneider** Passelecq and Suchecky, *Hidden Encyclical*, 5, and cf. 13, 279.

229 **"For a long time I waited . . ."** Thomas Merton and Patrick Hart, *The Literary Essays of Thomas Merton* (New York: New Directions Publishing, 1985), 266.

229 **Pius XII once hinted** Tad Szulc, *Pope John Paul II* (New York: Simon & Schuster, 1995), 109.

NOTES

230 **The archbishop of Krakow** Ibid., 107.

230 **Pacelli "was by neutral temperament . . ."** Ibid., 109.

231 **After Kristallnacht, Hitler felt "he could go . . ."** Conor Cruise O'Brien, "Could Pius XI Have Averted the Holocaust?" *The* (London) *Times*, February 10, 1989, Custom Newspapers, Web., April 12, 2011.

231 **One strong piece of evidence** Frank J. Coppa, "Pope Pius XI's Crusade for Human Rights and His Hidden 'Encyclical,' Humanis Generis Unitas, Against Racism and anti-Semitism," *World Religion Watch*, February 19, 2011, http://www.world-religionwatch .org.

232 **"Only a boldly . . ."** Ibid.

323 **"Considering that Hitler had only begun . . ."** Castelli, "Unpublished Encyclical."

BIBLIOGRAPHY

Aarons, Mark, and John Loftus. *Unholy Trinity: The Vatican, the Nazis, and Soviet Intelligence.* New York: St. Martin's Press, 1991.

Alvarez, David. *Spies in the Vatican.* Lawrence: University Press of Kansas, 2002.

Alvarez, David, and Robert A. Graham. *Nothing Sacred: Nazi Espionage Against the Vatican.* London: Routledge Press, 1998.

Anderson, Robin. *Between Two Wars: The Story of Pope Pius XI.* Achille Ratti, 1922–1939/1977.

Aradi, Zsolt. *Pius XI: The Pope and the Man.* Garden City: Hanover House, 1958.

Baxa, Paul. *Roads and Ruins, The Symbolic Landscape of Fascist Rome.* Toronto: University of Toronto Press, 2010.

Bosworth, R.J.B. *Mussolini.* New York: Arnold Publishers and Oxford University Press, 2002.

Bottum, J., and David G. Dalin. *The Pius War: Responses to the Critics of Pius XII.* Lanham, MD: Lexington Books, 2010.

Brustein, William I. *Roots of Hate: Anti-Semitism in Europe before the Holocaust.* London: Cambridge University Press, 2003.

Chadwick, Owen. *Britain and the Vatican During the Second World War.* Cambridge: Cambridge University Press, 1986.

Chenaux, Phillipe. *Pie XII, diplomate et pasteur.* Paris: Editions du Cerf, 2003.

Ciano, Galeazzo. *Diary, 1937–1943.* New York: Enigma Books, 2002.

Confalonieri, Carlo. *Pius XI, A Close-Up.* Altadena, CA: The Benzinger Sisters Publishers, 1975.

Coppa, Frank J. *The Modern Papacy Since 1789.* New York: Longman, 1998.

———. *The Papacy, the Jews, and the Holocaust.* Washington, DC: Catholic University of America Press, 2008.

Cornwell, John. *Hitler's Pope: The Secret History of Pius XII.* New York: Penguin, 2008.

Deutsch, Harold C. *The Conspiracy Against Hitler.* Minneapolis: University of Minnesota Press, 1968.

Falconi, Carlo. *The Silence of Pius XII.* London: Faber & Faber, 1970.

Fattorini, Emma. *Hitler, Mussolini and the Vatican.* Malden, MA: Polity Press, 2011.

Friedlander, Saul. *Pius XII and the Third Reich.* New York: Octagon, 1986.

Gallagher, Charles R. *Vatican Secret Diplomacy: Joseph P. Hurley and Pope Pius XII.* New Haven: Yale University Press, 2008.

Gannon, Michael. *Secret Missions.* New York: HarperCollins, 1994.

Gilbert, Martin. *Kristallnacht: Prelude to Destruction.* New York: Harper Perennial, 2007.

Godman, Peter. *Hitler and the Vatican.* New York: Free Press, 2004.

Hecht, Robert A. *An Unordinary Man: A Life of Father John LaFarge, SJ.* Lanham, MD: Scarecrow Press, 1996.

Herczl, Moshe. *Christianity and the Holocaust of Hungarian Jewry.* New York: New York University Press, 1995.

Hughes, Philip. *Pope Pius XI.* London: Sheed and Ward, 1937.

Kent, Peter C. "A Tale of Two Popes." *(London) Journal of Contemporary History* 23 (1988): 589–608.

Kertzer, David I. *The Popes Against the Jews.* New York: Alfred A. Knopf, 2001.

Knightley, Phillip. *The First Casualty.* London: Prion Books, 1975.

LaFarge, John. *The Manner Is Ordinary.* New York: Harcourt Brace, 1954.

———. *Interracial Justice.* New York: America Press, 1937.

Larson, Erik. *In the Garden of the Beasts.* New York: Crown Books, 2011.

Lewy, Guenter. *The Catholic Church and Nazi Germany.* Cambridge: DaCapo Press, 2000.

Martin, Malachi. *The Jesuits: The Society of Jesus and the Betrayal of the Roman Catholic Church.* New York: The Linden Press, 1987.

Mazzenga, Maria, ed. *American Religious Responses to Kristallnacht.* New York: Palgrave Macmillan, 2009.

McCormick, Anne O'Hare. *The World at Home.* New York: Alfred A. Knopf, 1956.

MacDonogh, Giles. *1938: Hitler's Gamble.* New York: Basic Books, 2009.

McDonough, Peter. *Men Astutely Trained: A History of the Jesuits in the American Century.* New York: Free Press, 1992.

Michael, Robert. *A History of Catholic Anti-Semitism: The Dark Side of the Church.* New York: Palgrave Macmillan, 2008.

Morgan, Thomas B. *A Reporter at the Papal Court.* New York: Longman, 1937.

Padallaro, Nazareno. *Portrait of Pius XII.* London: J. M. Dent, 1956.

Painter, Borden W. *Mussolini's Rome: Rebuilding the Eternal City.* New York: Palgrave Macmillan, 2007.

Passelecq, Georges, and Bernard Suchecky. *The Hidden Encyclical of Pius XI.* New York: Harcourt Brace, 1997.

Phayer, Michael. "Pope Pius XII, the Holocaust, and the Cold War." *Holocaust and Genocide Studies* 12, no. 2 (Fall 1998): 233–257.

———. *The Catholic Church and the Holocaust, 1930–1965.* Bloomington: Indiana University Press, 2000.

Phillips, William. *Vatican Diplomacy,* private printing.

Pollard, John. *The Vatican and Italian Fascism.* London: Cambridge University Press, 1988.

———. *Money and the Rise of the Modern Papacy.* London: Cambridge University Press, 2008.

Preston, Paul. *The Spanish Civil War.* New York: W. W. Norton, 2007.

Ramati, Alexander. *While the Pope Kept Silent.* London: Allen & Unwin, 1978.

Rhoden, Anthony. *The Vatican in the Age of the Dictators 1922–1945.* New York: Holt, Rinehart and Winston, 1973.

Ridley, Jasper. *Mussolini, A Biography.* New York: St. Martin's Press, 1997.

Sale, Giovanni. *Le Leggi Razzziali In Italia E Il Vaticano.* Milan: Editoriale Jaca, 2009.

Sanchez, Jose M. *Pius XII and the Holocaust. Understanding the Controversy.* Washington, DC: The Catholic University of America Press, 2002.

Shirer, William L. *The Rise and Fall of the Third Reich.* New York: Simon & Schuster, 1960.

Shoumatoff, Nicholas, and Nina Shoumatoff. *The Alps: Europe's Mountain Heart.* Ann Arbor: University of Michigan Press, 2001.

Smith, Jean Edward. *FDR.* New York: Random House, 2008.

Southern, David W. *John LaFarge and the Limits of Catholic Interracialism, 1911–1963.* Baton Rouge: Louisiana State University Press, 1996.

Stille, Alexander. *Benevolence and Betrayal.* New York: Penguin Books, 1991.

Szulc, Tad. *Pope John Paul II.* New York: Simon & Schuster, 1995.

Tisserant, Cardinal Eugène. "Pius XI as Librarian." *Library Quarterly* 9 (Oct. 1939): 389–403.

Walpole, Hugh. *The Roman Fountain.* New York: Doubleday, Doran and Co., 1940.

Warren, Donald. *Radio Priest.* New York: Free Press, 1996.

Wick, Steve. *The Long Night: William L. Shirer and the Rise and Fall of the Third Reich*. New York: Palgrave Macmillan, 2011.

Wills, Gary. *Papal Sin*. New York: Doubleday, 2000.

Wolf, Hubert. *Pope and Devil. The Vatican Archives and the Third Reich*. Cambridge, MA: Belknap Press of Harvard University, 2010.

Zimmerman, Joshua, ed. *The Jews in Italy Under Fascist and Nazi Rule 1922–1945*. London: Cambridge University Press, 2005.

Zuccotti, Susan. *Under His Very Windows*. New Haven: Yale Nota Bene, 2002.

INDEX